I Have Heard Your Prayer

I Have Heard Your Prayer

The Old Testament and Prayer

Michael E. W. Thompson

EPWORTH PRESS

All rights reserved. No part of this publication may be reproduced, stored in a retrieval system, or transmitted, in any form or by any means, electronic, mechanical, photocopying, recording or otherwise, without the prior permission of the publisher, Epworth Press.

Copyright © Michael E. W. Thompson 1996

0 7162 0509 2

First published 1996
by Epworth Press
20 Ivatt Way
Peterborough PE3 7PG

Typeset by Regent Typesetting
and printed in Great Britain by
Biddles Ltd, Guildford and King's Lynn

For Hazel

Prayer is to the spiritual life what the beating of the pulse and the drawing of the breath are to the life of the body.

>John Henry Newman
>*Parochial and Plain Sermons*

I have heard your prayer.

>*Isaiah 38.5*

Contents

Preface	ix
Introduction – 'Made in the image of God'	1
1. 'And Cain said to the Lord . . . ' People Praying, God Hearing	12
2. 'O Lord, hear my prayer' Prayers in the Psalms	39
3. 'O Lord, hear; O Lord, forgive' Prayers in Ezra, Nehemiah and Daniel	64
4. 'Moses besought the Lord' The Ministry of Intercession	89
5. 'Man . . . is full of trouble' Prayers from the Depths	119
6. 'For him shall endless prayer be made' Praying for the Nation's Leader	147
7. 'My house shall be called a house of prayer' The Place of Prayer	172
8. 'I have heard your prayer' Old Testament Prayer	197
Abbreviations	222
Notes	223
Further Reading	249
Index of Biblical References	251
Index of Authors	257
Index of Names and Subjects	260

Preface

The genesis of this book lies in my becoming aware a decade or so ago of a paucity of works on the specific subject of Old Testament prayer, and the general area of Old Testament spirituality. If what is presented in the following pages is of some interest and help as regards the former, I trust that it will also thereby make some small contribution to a study of the latter.

It is my hope that this work may be of service to at least two groups of people. I have in mind, in the first place, those in the Christian church who have a desire to understand more of the Old Testament, and in particular how its prayers may enrich theirs and the church's prayers. But I am also thinking of those who study the Old Testament in a more academic way, and hope that here there may be something about its theological approaches to prayer that will be of help. May they find, as I have found, that to study the subject of prayer is to go to the heart of how the relationship of God and his people is understood.

I have incurred many debts along the way. Various people, both in the church and the academy, have encouraged me to continue with a subject that at times threatened to overwhelm me. Over the years numerous groups in the church have listened patiently to my talking on this subject, and by their queries have sent me back to ask further questions about the texts. In more academic contributions I have benefited greatly by comments and questions on the part of my hearers.

I am grateful to the Editorial Committee of the Epworth Press for accepting this work for publication, and in particular to Cyril Rodd, the Editorial Secretary, for help in making this the book that it is, rather than the book that earlier I had in mind.

My greatest debt is to my wife Hazel, who over the years has encouraged me to work at the subject, more sure than I was at times that a book would emerge from my reading, writing and rewriting. Not only has she helped me in sundry places to express what I was trying to say, but she has also done all the word-processing: surely, a labour of love!

The translations of most of the prayers discussed in this book are my own. Apart from these, biblical quotations are in the rendering of the New Revised Standard Version. Where there is a difference between the Hebrew and the English, the English chapter and verse enumeration is cited.

I trust that I shall not be too presumptuous if I end with the words that Origen (c.AD 185–254) used to conclude his treatise *On Prayer*:

> All this I have struggled through as I have been able . . . And I do not doubt that if you reach forth unto those things which are before, and forget those things which are behind (Phil. 3.13), and meanwhile pray for me, I shall be able to receive from God the giver greater things and more divine in addition to all these, and when I have received them, to discourse again on the same subject with greater excellence, depth, and clarity; but for the present please read this with indulgence.

Bishop Auckland   Michael E. W. Thompson
St Barnabas Day 1996

Introduction

'Made in the image of God'

I

The troubles for Jonah the son of Amittai were only just beginning when, seeking to get away from God and the demanding call to go and preach in Nineveh, he took ship from Joppa to Tarshish (Jonah 1.1–3). All too soon there was a great storm at sea, and we read of the sailors crying out to their gods for help, and of the captain in somewhat accusatory tone suggesting that Jonah should arise from his deep sleep and call upon *his* (Jonah's) God (1.6). Jonah should be praying, not sleeping! We are reminded of the story with which Dorothee Soelle begins a study of prayer. It is about another great storm at sea, but the conversation now is between the ship's captain and a pastor. The storm is indeed bad, and the captain says, 'Now we can only pray', to which the pastor responds, 'Is it that bad?'[1] At least in Jonah's ship there was some human action taken: the sailors began heaving things overboard to lighten the ship, eventually also sending Jonah as well, for he had perceived that he himself was the cause of the problem (1.5, 12, 15). The suggestion in the story of the pastor's ship is that the situation is so very desperate that the only course of action left is to pray. I will say more later about prayer with, or without, human action.

In the Old Testament it is not that prophets have the monopoly of troubles. Many a king prays in a moment of crisis. When King Hezekiah became mortally ill, the prophet Isaiah visited him, and with what we may feel was commendable honesty – but perhaps a somewhat rudimentary bedside manner – told him to give his last instructions to his household, for he was dying. Hezekiah, we read, turned his face to the wall, and wept and prayed:

> Remember now, O Lord, I implore you, how I have walked before you in faithfulness with a whole heart, and have done what is good in your sight. (II Kings 20.3; Isa. 38.3)

But there was more done than only praying on this occasion, for the prophet gave instruction about the application of a poultice of figs to an inflammation that was troubling him. Just how much the poultice, and how much the prayer contributed to the king's recovery we cannot now know. And the editor of the story seems none too sure about the contribution of the poultice, for when we read of the king's healing we find no mention of the figs. The response of the Lord, given through Isaiah, speaks only of the prayer and the tears: 'I have heard your prayer, I have seen your tears; indeed I will heal you' (II Kings 20.5).

Prayer is our subject; in particular the prayers, and references to prayers, that we find in the Old Testament. But if we ask – so we may be clear in our minds as we set out in this study – what *is* prayer?, we may not find it easy to come up with a neat definition.[2] We have sympathy with that imaginary religious believer spoken about by D. Z. Phillips:

> One can imagine a religious believer asking, 'What is prayer?' Who can readily and briefly explain this? Who can even in thought comprehend it, so as to utter a word about it? But what do I utter in discourse more familiarly and knowingly than prayer? And, I understand when I pray; I understand also when I hear another praying. What then is prayer? If no one asks me I know; if I wish to explain it to one that asketh, I know not.[3]

But if we find it difficult to define prayer, we can say much about it, and about its widespread prevalence in religions. 'Prayer', says John Macquarrie, 'is a universal phenomenon in the life of faith, and it would be hard to imagine any faith or religion without prayer, or something like prayer'.[4] Friedrich Heiler began his famous study of prayer: 'Religious people, students of religion, theologians of all creeds and tendencies, agree in thinking that prayer is the central phenomenon of religion, the very hearthstone of all piety.'[5]

But what about prayer in the Old Testament scriptures? The Old Testament witnesses to the God who is totally other than the creatures of earth, one whose power and wisdom are beyond all human bounds:

> By awesome deeds you answer us with deliverance,
>   O God of our salvation;
> You are the hope of all the ends of the earth
>   and of the farthest seas.
> By your strength you established the mountains;
>   you are girded with might.
> You silence the roaring of the seas,
>   the roaring of their waves,
>   the tumult of the peoples.
> Those who live at earth's farthest bounds are awed
>   by your signs;
>   you make the gateways of the morning
>   and the evening shout for joy. (Ps. 65.5–8)

Yet this same psalm speaks of God as being attentive and responsive to the prayers of the people of earth:

> O you who answer prayer!
> To you all flesh shall come. (Ps. 65.2)

This is the God to whom another can say in prayer:

> Hear my voice, O God, in my complaint;
>   preserve my life from the dread enemy.
> Hide me from the secret plots of the wicked,
>   from the scheming of evildoers . . . (Ps. 64.1–2)

There is a relationship between people and God, springing, made possible, intended no doubt, according to at least one strand of thought in the Old Testament, by the very will of God:

> Then God said, 'Let us make humankind in our own
>   image, according to our likeness . . .' –
> So God created humankind in his image,

> in the image of God he created them;
> male and female he created them. (Gen. 1.26–27)

This relationship between people and God is a central aspect of the uniqueness of human beings, one of the most significant features that mark them off as being different from the rest of the animal creation. Within that relationship, and from the human side to the divine, is prayer, the speech of one or more, who thus bring before God their fundamental or current situation.[6] Such prayers are in the main believed to be heard, even answered, by God.

And all sorts and conditions of people may make their prayers to God. Abraham can pray,

> And Abraham said to God, 'O that Ishmael might live in your sight!' (Gen. 17.18)

So too can Abraham's servant,

> 'O Lord, God of my master Abraham, please grant me success today and show steadfast love to my master Abraham.' (Gen. 23.12)

Not only does the national leader Moses, pray:

> 'O Lord, why have you mistreated this people? Why did you ever send me? Since I first came to Pharaoh to speak in your name, he has mistreated this people, and you have done nothing at all to deliver your people.' (Ex. 5.22–23)

But so also can a woman. Thus Hannah says to the priest Eli,

> 'No, my lord, I am a woman deeply troubled; I have drunk neither wine nor strong drink, but I have been pouring out my soul before the Lord.' (I Sam. 1.15)

Naomi, the mother-in-law of Ruth, prays,

> 'May the Lord deal kindly with you, as you have dealt with the dead and with me. The Lord grant that you may find security, each of you in the house of your husband.' (Ruth 1.8–9)

And so do the non-Israelite sailors on the Tarshish-bound ship upon which Jonah has paid his fare:

> Then they cried out to the Lord, 'Please, O Lord, we pray, do not let us perish on account of this man's life. Do not make us guilty of innocent blood; for you, O Lord, have done as it pleased you.' (Jonah 1.14)

And Jonah himself will pray:

> Then Jonah prayed to the Lord his God from the belly of the fish . . . (Jonah 2.1)

A number of themes are to be observed in the prayers of the Old Testament, most of which are familiar to us from the Christian tradition of prayer, in prayers uttered either by individuals or in the liturgy of the church. In the Old Testament there are prayers of confession, intercession and petition, and examples of such prayers will be considered in the following chapters. By 'petition' I mean to indicate a prayer that a person makes for himself or herself, while I use the word 'intercession' when prayer is being offered by one on behalf of another or a group. Also to be found in the Old Testament are prayers of praise, and prayers of thanksgiving, and I shall be discussing examples of these. Then there is a type of prayer less well-known in the church today – the prayer of complaint, the cry of anguish to God, more technically known as the 'lament', and found chiefly (but by no means exclusively) in the book of Psalms. This prayer will receive consideration first of all in Chapter 2, and will be returned to later in the work. These 'laments' are prayers 'from the depths'; utterances that come from people who are engaged in a 'wrestling' with God.

In Hab. 3.1 we have an introductory word to what is to follow:

> A prayer of the prophet Habakkuk . . .

The word translated 'prayer' is a frequently occurring one in the Old Testament, employed in a number of instances to introduce formal prayers such as those in Hab. 3.2–15, and Jonah 2.2–9. But the Hebrew word translated 'prayer' in Hab. 3.1, and the verbal form translated 'prayed' in Jonah 2.1, is not the only word for 'prayer' or 'pray' in the Old Testament. This is not unexpected, of course. In English we have a number of words that are employed to speak of our prayers. In general, these different English words are used to express different aspects, or even nuances, of prayers. Thus, we speak of our 'intercessions', our 'entreaties', our 'supplications', and so forth, and use such words to 'shade' our meaning. Similarly, in the Old Testament we find a number of words employed to refer to prayers and praying, used to emphasize certain aspects of prayers, and in some cases to indicate something of the level of 'intensity' of the address to God. In fact, there is a rich vocabulary of Hebrew words employed to speak of prayer, and to convey something of the particular depth and the nature of feeling on the part of the one who prays. Some brief attention will be given to this in Chapter 2 below, so that those who wish to pursue this topic further will have an introduction to the subject, and indications as to where more detailed treatments may be found. Those who have no Hebrew will be able to read on without delay, skipping such detail.

II

Something must now be said about three aspects of this book – its *method*, its *approach*, and its *arrangement*.

By the first of these I mean this: what *method* am I adopting as I study a particular prayer? For there are a number of 'methods' available to the Old Testament reader or student today. Shall I be concerned with such matters as the possible date when the prayer was composed; who wrote it; and in what social, religious and historical setting it was uttered or written? For whom was the written prayer intended? All these are concerns of what in general terms we might reasonably label the 'historical critical' method. Shall we be concerned about whether the prayer was written, or recorded for us by, say, the 'Yahwistic', or the 'Priestly' writer? – a concern of the 'source critical' method. Or might we, rather, be concerned with the way in which one of the longer prayers came over the years to be built up, expanded, elaborated upon, adapted perhaps for different situations and needs? – the concerns of the 'redaction critical' method, where there is a particular interest in the role and the purposes of the editor (redactor) of the material. Or will the concern here be with the 'final form', with the text as we now have it, whatever the processes and vicissitudes through which it has passed all along the way – the method of 'canonical criticism'? And, as something of an extension of that method, will our concern be with the more literary aspect, where we look for style and nuance in the writing, seeking through the study of the writer's and storyteller's art to understand what it is that the ancient author wished to say to those for whom he wrote? This is the 'literary critical' method, one that is less concerned than other methods with who wrote, and when, and whether or not all the text comes from the same source. Many contemporary Old Testament scholars would stress that just as important as what a text said to people when it was written, is what it *now* says to us who read it today. While the history of the text and its supposed authorship (the world 'behind' the text) are important considerations for us as we come to an ancient text, so too are those of the contemporary reader who brings to it so much of his or her own situation, concerns, needs, presuppositions and so forth (the world 'before' the text). What *method* for the study of the Old Testament will be adopted in this book?[7]

The *method* adopted here is quite deliberately mixed, and will vary from passage to passage, from prayer to prayer. At times I believe it will be appropriate to enquire into the purposes of an author, or authors. In such a work as, for example, the book of Jonah I believe it is possible to discern the work of at least two authors. Further, with that book I believe one can make some reasonable assumptions as regards those authors' concerns, the general historical background to their work and the reasons that led them to write as they did. In the case of the book of Jonah the methods of 'historical', 'source', even 'redaction' criticism will yield us some harvest. And with Jonah, so too will the 'literary critical' method, as we shall see. But with other parts of the Old Testament, the historical setting in which the author wrote is less clear than it is with Jonah. While the book of Jonah was intended, I believe, to set forth a quite specific message for a particular era in the life of the Jewish people, the concern of the book of Ruth, by contrast, is more general, intended to be applicable to a wider range of historical and social settings. Historical, source, redaction critical methods will not yield such results here as they do with Jonah, and therefore our approach will need to be different. All this is to say that the *methods* of Old Testament study employed in this book will be varied, depending upon the material being considered at any given time.

Then let me say something about the *approach* of this book. I write from a Christian perspective, and the principal reader I have in my mind is in all likelihood a Christian – if not a believer, then perhaps a searcher. At least, I think that in all probability my reader and I will have two canons of scripture, two testaments, Old and New, and that both of them will have for us words of grace and judgment. I think we shall be content to go along with B.S. Childs when he says about the Bible, 'Both testaments make a discrete witness to Jesus Christ which must be heard, both separately and in concert.'[8] While the focus of this book is on the prayers of the Old Testament, I shall also make reference to the prayers and teaching about prayer that we find in the New Testament, and not infrequently I shall be referring to the comments on Old Testament prayers by Christian biblical interpreters.

Further, what follows comes from the setting of the Christian church, wherein over these past years my work and main activities have lain. My imaginary reader, coming as he or she probably does from this church, will surely be able to perceive within the words of this book my own involvement in 'Christ's body on earth', for it has been no small part of my work to lead the prayers of a few of the people of God. Moreover, some of the prayers I discuss here, I have preached sermons about – and many of them have been my subjects when I have talked to and led discussions with preachers and others. No doubt those who come from other communities of religious faith, or from none, will prefer to adopt other terminology, and that will be entirely appropriate. But for us it seems both appropriate and felicitous to speak of the *Old* Testament,[9] whose personalities lived and the events it recounts, took place 'BC' (Before Christ), and the *New* Testament, whose personalities and events are dated 'AD' (Anno Domini, 'in the year of the Lord').

Thirdly, what is the *arrangement* of this book? I shall begin at the beginning – the beginning of the Old Testament as we have it. That is, I go to the book of Genesis, focussing at the start on the first prayer we come to if we read through the Old Testament from the beginning. Whether this is the 'first' prayer from a historical point of view is a very different matter! In fact, it is hardly possible, with the information that we have, to know what is historically the 'first' prayer of the Bible. (Rather clearer, however, is what are historically the 'last' prayers of the Old Testament.) Thus, Chapter 1 will focus on some of the prayers we have in the book of Genesis, and we shall read of such personalities as Cain in a moment of crisis; of the servant of Abraham sent on his matrimonial mission; and of Jacob in a series of events, all of them in their different situations and needs praying to the Lord. We shall also consider Hannah's prayer in I Sam. 2, and prayers of the prophets Elijah and Elisha. In this chapter, I shall also be considering a central aspect of prayer – namely, the belief that God hears the prayers of his people. Not infrequently, we read how God heard a particular prayer, and responded to the wishes and desires expressed in it. But in other situations we read that God did not grant the petitioner's request. At other times there would appear to be even a deafness, and perhaps also a silence, on the part of God. We must ask why this might be.

In Chapter 2, the emphasis will be directed towards prayers in the book of Psalms – perhaps the part of the Old Testament in which Christians feel most at home, and of the Old Testament books the most obvious place where one might look for prayers. But I shall place considerable emphasis upon prayers that we do not commonly use in the church today – perhaps to our loss. I refer to the many prayers of 'complaint', sometimes even 'protest', to God, prayers that have come to be known technically as 'laments'. It will also be in this chapter that I shall give some attention to the Hebrew vocabulary of prayer.

In Chapter 3 I shall be considering some prayers that we can fairly safely say come from a late time in the history of the people of Israel. For such a time, we may expect to be better informed as to historical details about political, social and religious thought, than we are about earlier periods. The focus here will be upon prayers in the books of Ezra, Nehemiah and Daniel, a good number of which are rather formal, even elaborate and in some case very extensive, prayers and prayer compositions. As such, they may be said to represent the full development, as far as the Old Testament is concerned, of this type of formal and elaborate composition of prayer.

In Chapter 4, the theme will be intercession and those who engage in a ministry of intercession. There will be much here about Samuel and Moses. Chapter 5 will direct attention to people who for a variety of reasons find themselves in extreme and parlous situations. What is the place and significance of prayer for such people in their particular circumstances? Frequently they cry out to God in a sense of deep agony, and often their prayers to God are far from polite! But the likes of Job will keep praying!

Chapter 6 will focus upon the Israelite king: he is the subject of particular concern in certain Old Testament prayers. This chapter will be the natural place to go into some detail over the differing approaches to prayer as we find them in various parts of the Old Testament. We shall also be asking here, 'If in those days they prayed for a king thus, for whom and in what ways might we perhaps be praying today?' In Chapter 7 the emphasis will be upon the place of prayer, whether that be in temple, synagogue or elsewhere. In this chapter attention will also be directed to Solomon's long prayer in I Kings 8.14–61 and II Chron. 6.13–42.

In the final chapter, I shall attempt to draw together the various threads of this book, to speak about theology and prayer, and to ask what contribution the Old Testament has to make to the understanding and practice of prayer by those whose scriptures are Old and New Testaments, and whose prayers are generally offered in the name of the Lord Jesus Christ. What has the Old Testament to say to the present day successors of those disciples of old who said to their master, 'Lord, teach us to pray'?

1

'And Cain said to the Lord...'
People Praying, God Hearing

I

The high ceiling of the Sistine Chapel in Rome is decorated with a vast series of frescoes, the incomparable work fashioned by the artist Michelangelo between 1508 and 1512. It depicts the history of the human race as set forth in the book of Genesis. At the west end of the ceiling the story begins with God separating light from darkness, and as we move eastwards, and towards the centre, we trace the story as we are familiar with it from those early chapters of Genesis: the creation of sun, moon and plant life; God separating the water and the earth, and creating life in the sea; the creation of Adam; the creation of Eve. Then just past the centre of the ceiling is the portrayal of the sin of eating the forbidden fruit, and the expulsion of Adam and Eve from the garden. The cherubim with what looks like a sword is driving the sinners – who now indeed look a more closely-knit couple, but who also seem to have aged so much! – out of the paradise garden.

This is the story we read in Gen. 3, and in the following chapter we are told about the sons born to Adam and Eve:

> Now the man knew his wife Eve, and she conceived and bore Cain, saying, 'I have produced a man with the help of the Lord.' Next she bore his brother Abel. Now Abel was a keeper of sheep, and Cain a tiller of the ground. (Gen. 4.1–2)

The story goes on to tell how in the course of time these brothers brought offerings to the Lord, Cain an offering of the fruit of the ground and Abel a firstling of his flock. For some reason not made clear to us, Cain and his offering were not acceptable to God, while Abel and his gift were. Thus was Cain angry (Gen. 4.3–5). What took place next seems to have happened in the field,[1] and the upshot was that Cain killed his brother. After the murder, the Lord speaks to Cain:

> 'What have you done? Listen; your brother's blood is crying out to me from the ground! And now are you cursed from the ground, which has opened its mouth to receive your brother's blood from your hand. When you till the ground, it will no longer yield to you its strength; you will be a fugitive and a wanderer on the earth.' (Gen. 4.10–12)

Now occurs the Bible's first prayer, not necessarily the most ancient prayer that we have in the Old Testament, but rather the first that we come to if we read from the beginning.[2] It is Cain who prays to the Lord:

> And Cain said to the Lord, 'My punishment is greater than I can bear. See, you have driven me this day away from the ground, and from your face I shall be hidden; and I shall be a fugitive and a wanderer upon the earth. And whoever finds me will slay me.' (Gen. 4.13–14)

Those who are portrayed as being the ancestors of the human race – Adam and Eve – have sinned, and have been expelled from their original world. Now the first murder has taken place, and in the nature of the matter it is a fratricide. Sin is beginning to take on frightening proportions, and yet what is portrayed here is remarkable – the man who has murdered his brother is able to cry out to God in prayer! What is more, there is mercy available for this sinner. Cain's prayer is represented as being heard by God, for Cain was assured of divine protection and support. More, as tangible evidence of this protection and support, he was given a mark, so that no one would kill him (Gen. 4.15). Yet it is not that his punishment is removed – Cain must ever be a wanderer and a fugitive. His new country was to be not only 'away from the presence of the Lord', but in the land of Nod, a Hebrew word meaning 'fugitive, wandering'. There is a certain irony expressed in a verse which speaks of

Cain's future as *settling* in the land of *Nod*, that is, he must 'settle' in 'restlessness' (v.16)! It is important that we understand that although Cain's prayer is represented as having been heard by God – and even responded to by God – yet there is also the cry of Abel, in particular the cry of Abel's blood, that comes to the Lord. The prayer of Cain does indeed elicit the divine mercy for the sinner, but in no way is the Lord portrayed as having been 'won over' to the side of Cain, as against that of Abel. God's mercy is represented as being available for *both* of these brothers.

Now we would surely wish to say that in these early stories of Genesis the characters are portrayals of types of people, in particular of ourselves. Cain, like Adam and Eve, is a type, a representation of human beings, who sin, who murder – even their own brothers. But if this story of Cain and Abel is to remind us of our propensity to sin, of the danger we each experience when we are jealous of those who appear to be more successful in life, of the peril that we ourselves might commit murder, yet it carries within it the assurance that such sinners may continue to pray to God. The Bible's 'first' prayer is not from the lips of some paragon of virtue, but from a man consumed with jealousy, one who has murdered his brother. He prays, and his prayer is heard by God. We are reminded of the plea of the penitent criminal to the crucified Jesus, 'Jesus, remember me when you come into your kingdom.' To which the Lord gave the assurance, 'Truly I tell you, today you will be with me in Paradise' (Luke 23.43).

II

Let us now consider some prayers in a later chapter of the book of Genesis. We move beyond chapters 1–11 which, in their portrayal of how things were at the beginning seek to address us about fundamental and all-important aspects of our individual and corporate lives under God in the world today. In Gen. 12–36 we have stories of individuals we are accustomed to call the 'Patriarchs', Abraham, Isaac and Jacob.[3] Genesis 24 is a long chapter, made up of some sixty-seven verses, being in fact the longest narrative among the stories of the patriarchs. It is a story with a number of scenes; there is a plot with a series of sub-plots. The theme of the story concerns the matter of a wife for Isaac, the son of Abraham, and the underlying issue is how the line of Abraham is to continue. For the Lord has declared that his purposes are to be fulfilled through Abraham and his descendants (Gen. 12.1–3), but how will those divine purposes be fulfilled unless there *are* descendants – sons, daughters, husbands, wives, children? In particular, how will the purposes of God continue if there is not found a wife for Abraham's son Isaac? And in view of the significance of the matter, how important it is that the proper, the appropriate, wife is found!

The scenes, the sub-plots, in this 'short story'[4] take us from the time when Abraham gives the instructions to his servant (vv.1–9), through the journey to the city of Nahor and the encounter with Rebekah at the well (vv.10–27), on to the invitation to and conversation at the home of Laban, Rebekah's brother (vv.28–54a). This leads on to the debate over the matter of the possible marriage of Isaac and Rebekah (vv.54b–61), and so to the final resolution of the story when Rebekah accompanies the servant to Isaac's house, and to the account of how Isaac took her as his wife and loved her (vv.62–67). Now was the line of Abraham secure; now the purposes of God would go on!

But our particular interest in this story is centred on the second of these scenes, that is on Gen. 24.10–27 which tells of the journey of the servant to the well, and the meeting there with Rebekah. Within the account of this scene are two prayers, both uttered by Abraham's servant. The first of these is in vv.11–14, and here the servant prays for the good success of his important mission:

> And he said, 'O Lord, God of my master Abraham, grant me, I pray, success today, and show steadfast love to my master Abraham. Behold, I am standing by the well of water, and the daughters of the men of the city are coming out to draw

> water. Let the maiden to whom I will say, "Pray let down your jar that I may drink", and who will say, "Drink, and I will water your camels", let her be the one for your servant Isaac. And by this I shall know that you have shown steadfast love to my master.' (Gen. 24.12–14)

The servant having made his address to God ('O Lord, God of my master Abraham'), then makes his prayer ('grant me, I pray, success today . . .'). If we understand that he is praying for himself in the context of the particular task that he has been given to fulfil, then it is a prayer of petition. Alternatively, we may interpret the prayer as an intercession, in the sense that his prayer is for his master Abraham, that the proper wife may be found for his son Isaac, and that the family line may thus be secured. To be more specific, the servant prays for a sign ('Let the maiden to whom I will say . . .'). This is not a request for the type of miraculous sign that Gideon asked for (Judg. 6.36–40), and yet it was a sign that had a definite resonance with the purpose of the mission: the servant was seeking the proper wife for his master's son, and so he prayed for a sign that would reveal the attitudes of kindness and helpfulness. We should take note of the fact that apart from asking for this sign, the servant does no more than pray. As we shall see later, there are many prayers in the Old Testament that are accompanied by actions: in such instances what we might call 'prayer and action' go together. But here, apart from the asking for the sign, there is no 'action' that accompanies the prayer.

In the following verses we hear how the prayer was answered. And, the necessary matrimonial arrangements having been made, Abraham's servant gave praise and thanks to God in prayer:

> And the man bowed his head and worshipped the Lord, saying, 'Blessed be the Lord, the God of my master Abraham, who has not forsaken his steadfast love and his faithfulness toward my master. As for me, the Lord has led me in the way to the house of my master's kinsmen.' (Gen. 24.26–27)

We may notice that the servant gave specific praise and thanksgiving to God that the Lord had demonstrated the continuance of his steadfast love to Abraham. We also read of the servant's own particular thanksgiving for having been led providentially to the proper locality for the fulfilment of his task. The servant thanks God for the good success of his mission, the joy of his master, and what we might call the tangible and earthly continuation of the purposes of God.

But it is as if the whole of this particular scene (vv.10–27) in the short story (Gen. 24) is permeated with prayer. Prayer is portrayed here as being the natural accompaniment to this rather worldly task that the servant has been given and in the execution of which, we observe, he deploys a commendable measure of worldly wisdom. Yet at the same time it is a task that is concerned with the purposes of God, and we may not be totally wide of the mark if we see the prayers here as providing the means of associating these 'worldly' and 'heavenly' concerns. In the setting of life lived both in the world and in God, prayer is portrayed as being an entirely natural activity on the part of this person. Through prayer, this little part of worldly life is made into a part of the on-going and providential purposes of God. What is more, the Lord is portrayed in these texts as undoubtedly ready to hear these prayers: certainly there is not the slightest hint that he will *not* be available and ready to hear these prayers! But will he answer this prayer of petition/intercession? The story does not state what God did as a result of the prayer being made to him. Equally, we do not know what God might otherwise have done, or not done, if no prayer had been made to him. Certainly, although he may have been prayed to, yet he remains the sovereign Lord, and it is his will that is done. But we are perhaps intended to understand by the writer of this story, that the fact that things worked out in the way they did was owing in some measure at least to the prayer that this worldly-wise, faithful, but also pious and God-fearing servant made to God.

III

So Rebekah became Isaac's wife, and they had two sons, the twins Esau and Jacob, whose conception, we may note in passing, is portrayed as having been aided by prayer (Gen. 25.19–26). Esau as the eldest son should by rights have received his father's blessing, but by a ruse, a trick, Jacob secured it for himself. Thus Jacob had to flee his father's house, in particular from Esau's wrath.

We move on through the stories about Jacob. He has had his dream at Bethel (Gen. 28), he has met Rachel, and though he himself has been deceived, yet through a further deception on his own part he has been able to marry Rachel and has amassed something of a fortune (Gen. 29–30). But he must flee again, this time from his father-in-law Laban, and although he may be able to come to terms with Laban, all too soon another situation of grave potential danger confronts him – he has to meet with his brother Esau! In the face of a confrontation fraught with such possible danger, we are not surprised that he prays to God.

> And Jacob said, 'God of my father Abraham, and God of my father Isaac, O Lord who said to me, "Return to your country and your kindred and I will do you good". [10] I am not worthy of all the steadfast love and all the faithfulness which you have done to your servant, for only with my staff I crossed this Jordan, and now I have become two companies. [11] Deliver me, I pray, from the hand of my brother, from the hand of Esau, for I fear him, lest he come and strike me, and mothers and children. [12] But you said, "I will do you good, and make your descendants as the sand of the sea which cannot be counted because of its number."' (Gen. 32.9–12)

What are we to say about the character of the man Jacob who prays this prayer? We know something about the Jacob of old, the one who through deception stole his brother's birthright (Gen. 27). But is this a different Jacob, a reformed character? I

People Praying, God Hearing

want to suggest that at least to some extent he is a reformed character, that he is now a more humble man than before, aware of his 'smallness' (v.10). I am well aware of the fact that some will consider this to be a rather naive approach: they will argue that just because Jacob uses pious words does not mean that he is inwardly changed. They will perhaps feel that it is the same scheming Jacob who is speaking, but now saying the 'correct' things, merely using words of humility and piety.[5] On the other hand, I think that von Rad is going too far (that *he* is being naive) when he says, 'One will not be wrong if one interprets this prayer also as the expression of a purification taking place in Jacob.'[6]

Whatever we make of the character of Jacob who now prays, what we can say with more certainty is this: Jacob is here praying for himself; his prayer is one of petition. Let us give some attention to this prayer, especially to its form and arrangement, for it does exhibit a logical progression of thought.

v.9 This is the Address to God. Sometimes it is called the Invocation, the calling on God. What it signifies is that the one praying is establishing contact with the invisible God who clearly is believed to be ready and open to hear the prayers of his people. Here Jacob addresses God, and seeks to lay at least some of the responsibility for the crisis of the moment upon God: it is God who has called him to return to his people.

v.10 Now is struck the note of humility, perhaps even abasement. Jacob professes himself unworthy of all God's gracious acts, and acknowledges that his own strength is little. He speaks of his 'smallness', the same word that we shall later find used by Amos about Israel when he makes intercessions for them in a time of crisis (Amos 7.2, 5; see Ch. 4 below). Jacob is here stressing his dependence upon God, and what God, and perhaps God alone, can do on his behalf.

v.11 Thus he comes to make his petition: that God will deliver him from the hand of his brother Esau, that God will save him. And perhaps we may say that his concern is for greater matters than just his own, for he brings before God his problem about the future and the whole matter of the ongoing purposes of God, which the Lord has promised will be effected through his family. Thus he speaks in his prayer about the 'mothers and children'.

v.12 This is what we may call the 'ground' of Jacob's prayer, the reason that he has that emboldens him to pray, what encourages him to appeal to the mercy and the constancy of God. It is on account both of the existing relationship with God that Jacob has, and because of God's ancient promises to him and his family, that he can now make his prayer in this time of potential crisis.

Perhaps we may think of Jacob as a Cain-like figure: like Cain, he is a sinner, yet a person who can still pray to God in a spirit of hope. At the same time as acknowledging his own weakness, he professes God's power, and trusts in God's attentiveness to his life and divine openness to his prayers. Whatever Jacob may have done – and he has done much that is unsavoury – our narrator intends us to see that he still has a real relationship with God, and that in spite of all his sins the divine purposes can still go on through him. Even for this rogue, the grace of God is still available!

It is to be noted, however, that this prayer having been offered, Jacob seeks to approach Esau with generous presents (vv.13–21). Westermann says, 'Presents are now sent ahead. This act is portrayed in such detail that it must be of particular importance to the narrator.'[7] Is it to emphasize the fact that the concept of prayer here is one which sees an association between work and prayer, that merely to pray about something is perhaps not sufficient, but that some appropriate human work is also needed? This is perhaps an example of that principle stated for Christians by Origen in his *Treatise on Prayer*:

> ... the man who links together his prayer with deeds of duty and fits seemly actions with his prayer is the man who prays without ceasing, for his virtuous deeds or the commandments he has fulfilled are taken up as a part of his prayer. For only

in this way can we take the saying 'Pray without ceasing' as being possible, if we can say that the whole life of the saint is one mighty integrated prayer.[8]

Before we leave Jacob, we should consider three further prayers we read of him making. These prayers, though they come from the lips of Jacob are in a long story that above all concerns one of his sons: Gen. 37–50 is generally called the 'Joseph Story'.[9] This story begins with Joseph as a young man (ch. 37) and ends with his death (ch. 50); it tells of a large family, of which Jacob is the head, but within which there is jealousy and rivalry. It also tells of famine in the land of Canaan, but of plenty in the land of Egypt. Above all, it tells of a member of the family, highly placed in the counsels of Egypt, with authority to give to his brothers and his family adequate supplies of food – but only there in that far-away land because his brothers had sold him into slavery! And about what would appear to be his providential presence in that land at that time (through the evil intentions of his brothers), the story reflects and ponders. When the moment of revelation comes, Joseph will say to his brothers,

'So it was not you who sent me here, but God . . .' (Gen. 45.8a)

'Even though you intended to do harm to me, God intended it for good, in order to preserve a numerous people, as he is doing today.' (Gen. 50.20)

This story about Joseph begins at Gen. 37.1, but until 43.14 there is no prayer. We have to wait until the brothers' second journey to Egypt to have a recorded prayer. And what we have in Gen. 43.14 is in the nature of a 'prayerful blessing'. It is accompanied by prayerful resignation on the part of the father Jacob, resignation that he may be bereaved of one, or even more than one, son:

'And may God Almighty grant you mercy before the man, and may he send back your other brother and Benjamin. And I, if I am bereaved – I am bereaved.'

A second prayer, again a prayer of blessing, and again from Jacob, comes in Gen. 48.15–16. This may in fact be a conflation of two blessings: this is suggested by the fact that we read of a blessing upon Joseph and another upon his children.[10] In this prayer, Jacob speaks of definite and specific blessings that he has himself experienced.[11] Now Jacob, addressing God in the third person (not addressing him as 'you') prays such blessings for Joseph and his sons:

> And he blessed Joseph, saying,
> 'The God before whom my fathers Abraham and Isaac walked,
> The God who was my shepherd, all my life until this day,
> The angel who redeemed me from all my distress, bless the boys,
> And in them may my name live on,
> and the name of my fathers Abraham and Isaac;
> May they become a multitude in the midst of the land.'
>   (Gen. 48.15–16)

And the third and final prayer in the the 'Joseph Story' – again from the lips of Jacob, once more a prayer of blessing, also stressing the matter of the increase of offspring – is in Gen. 48.20:

> And he [Jacob] blessed them [Joseph's sons, Ephraim and Manasseh] that day, saying,
> 'By you Israel is to bless, saying,
> "God make you as Ephraim and Manasseh." '

Now what is remarkable about these three prayers in the 'Joseph Story' is simply that there are so few of them. It is further remarkable that the few prayers that are to be found in the 'Joseph Story' concern the theme of 'blessing'. There are no petitions, and there are no intercessions in the 'Joseph Story'. Yet this is an intensely 'religious' story. Although the setting of the tale is very much the earthly world, with its famines and its plenty, with its families beset with rivalries, jealousies, hatreds and violences, yet also the whole story is indisputably about God and his ongoing purposes for and with people in the world.

People Praying, God Hearing

The story exhibits a confident hope in God, an assurance that whatever men and women may do, the purposes of God will go on. More, the purposes of God may even be fulfilled through human machinations and evil deeds. This story carries the assurance that all along the way God will be there with his providential care for his people. And yet it must be said that in this story, there is no suggestion that prayer may be a means of effecting change in the world. We have seen, and we shall see, that in many parts of the Old Testament there is displayed the belief that prayer, when it is offered in the right spirit to God, may indeed effect some perceptible changes in the world. But this is not the case in all parts of the Old Testament, and it is important to understand that the Old Testament has within it a number of attitudes towards prayer. That is, these scriptures display a number of different understandings of the relationship of God, the world, and people, and in particular of the meaning, the purpose and the function of prayer, within that nexus of relationships. Certainly, the 'Joseph Story' seems to ask questions and to probe the issue of the relationships between God, his purposes in the world, and the place of his people, but we have to say that while it does have a series of prayers in which Jacob asks God's blessings on his son Joseph and upon Joseph's sons, other people are not prayed for in blessings, nor do we hear of any prayers of confession, or even of anyone who prays for himself. We have to say that the 'Joseph Story' gives only a very limited place to prayer.

IV

But then, by way of contrast, how different is the understanding of prayer in those texts that tell of the birth of the boy Samuel. Here it is as if the circumstances and events surrounding the birth of this child, and the very birth itself, are permeated with prayer. It all begins in I Sam. 1.10, 12–18, a passage that is of considerable interest to us in that we are given a word picture of a person at prayer. The setting of this passage is that of an annual pilgrimage of the man Elkanah with his two wives, Peninnah (who had children) and Hannah (who did not), to Shiloh where in those days there was a temple, whose priest was Eli. We read:

> And she [Hannah] was deeply distressed and she prayed to the Lord and wept bitterly ... [12] And it was as she continued to pray before the Lord, that Eli observed her mouth. [13] And Hannah was speaking in her heart; only her lips moved, and her voice was not heard; and Eli reckoned that she was drunk. [14] And Eli said to her, 'How long will you be drunk? Put away your wine from you'. [15] But Hannah answered, 'No, my lord, I am a woman much troubled; I have drunk neither wine nor strong drink, but I have been pouring out my soul before the Lord. [16] Do not regard your servant as a worthless woman, for I have been speaking all this time out of great anxiety and vexation. [17] And Eli answered, 'Go in peace, and the God of Israel grant your petition which you have asked of him'. [18] And she said, 'Let your servant find favour in your eyes.' And the woman went her way and ate, and her face was no longer sad. (I Sam. 1.10, 12–18)

Hannah is praying out of a distress occasioned by her childlessness. Her distress would be acute for the reason that in those times married women would be expected to bear children. Hannah's situation was made the more distressing in that her husband's other wife Peninnah did have children. Thus, her prayer is accompanied by weeping, a combination we also read about in Joel 2.17.

When the priest Eli observed Hannah's mouth moving, but heard no voice, he assumed that she was drunk – and in view of what we are told about the general situation in those days, we may well feel that that was not a completely unreasonable conclusion for him to draw (vv.9–10, 12–13, 18; cf. 2.12–17, 22–25). We may also bear in mind that Eli's eyesight was not as good as perhaps it once was (cf. 3.2; 4.15)! Or was it maybe his hearing that was going? But Hannah's response was that she was praying silently, 'pouring out her soul' before the Lord (v.15). It is sometimes suggested that this might be an indication to us that in ancient Israel prayer was normally spoken aloud, and that the silent prayer is the exception to the general rule, but about this we have to say that we cannot be sure. The other question posed for us by the account of this little incident concerns what we might call private devotions: was it the practice of at least some people in those days to have times of private devotions, which might have included prayers, maybe on a regular basis? Again, we hardly have the evidence to decide about this.

What is clearer is that the prayer Hannah utters is portrayed as a natural response to her situation of distress (v.10), great anxiety and vexation (v.16). Prayer is portrayed as being a natural activity in which such a person would engage.[12] Certainly, when the situation is explained to Eli he bids her go in peace, and himself prays that her petition to the Lord may be granted (v.17). Moreover, there is portrayed a marked contrast between Hannah before praying and afterwards: no longer is her face sad and she is not eating, 'but the woman went her way and ate, and her face was no longer sad' (v.18). Thus, praying to God is portrayed here not only as being the natural activity for a distressed and anxious person to engage in, but also as that which may result in a sense of peace and the absence of that sense of distress and anxiety. Moreover, subsequent verses will suggest that the prayer was in fact answered. Later, we hear of the birth of the child Samuel, and how his mother brought him to the house of the Lord at Shiloh. And the same priest, Eli, is there at the temple:

> And she [Hannah] said, 'O my lord! As you live, my lord, I am the woman who was standing here in your presence praying to the Lord. [27] For this child I prayed, and the Lord granted me my petition which I asked of him. [28] And now I have lent him to the Lord; as long as he lives he is lent to the Lord.' And they worshipped the Lord there.
> (I Sam. 1.26–28)

Then, the usual offerings – bull, flour and wine (v.25) – are accompanied by the statement to Eli in which Hannah reminds him that she was the woman who some time ago was standing before him praying. Moreover she makes the statement, 'For this child I prayed, and the Lord granted me my petition which I asked of him' (v.27). What is being said here is that it was the *woman*, Hannah, who did the praying – rather than the priest Eli. Of course, it may well be that the narrator is intending to make a particular point here, namely that Eli and his priestly line are as good as finished. They have been found wanting, and a new person is needed (and will be given by God) for the new age that is dawning. And this person who will be called upon to lead his people through the birth pangs of the new age is none other than this Samuel. We may take note of the fact that the beginnings of the life and work of Samuel are suffused in prayer. It may well have been an entirely natural thing that a woman in Hannah's situation should pray to the Lord, but we should also see a deeper significance in Hannah's prayers, namely that they surround and suffuse the events of the birth of this new leader of Israel. We may say that I Sam. 1 is intended to tell us about a new beginning in Israel's history that is taking place. It has been effected to at least some extent through the prayers of a mother and the intervention of God in the birth of Samuel, the one who was to bring life out of the national barrenness.

With the birth of Samuel there comes another prayer, Hannah's prayer of thanksgiving (I Sam. 2.1–10). It stands at the beginning of the story of Samuel, a story that will end with the prayer of Samuel in II Sam. 22.[13] In I Sam. 2.1–10 there is a joyful and thankful celebration of what will happen in the time of Samuel, especially as regards kingship and people.

I Sam. 2.1 And Hannah prayed, saying,
'My heart rejoices in the Lord;
   my strength is exalted in the Lord.
My mouth derides my enemies,
   because I rejoice in your salvation.
v.2 There is none holy like the Lord,
   there is none besides you,
   there is no rock like our God.

v.3 Do not any longer talk proudly;
   do not let arrogance come from your mouth;
 For the Lord is a God of knowledge,
   and by him actions are tested.
v.4 The bows of the mighty are stopped,
   but the feeble put on strength.
v.5 Those of plenty have hired themselves out for bread,
   but the hungry have grown fat on booty.
v.6 The barren has borne seven,
   and she who has many children is forlorn.
v.7 The Lord kills and brings to life;
   he brings down to Sheol and raises up.
 The Lord makes poor, and makes rich;
   he brings low, but also raises up.
v.8 He raises up the poor from the dust;
   he lifts up the needy from the rubbish-dump,
 To make them sit with nobles,
   and inherit a seat of honour.
 For the pillars of the earth are the Lord's,
   and on them he has set the world.
v.9 He will guard the feet of his faithful,
   but the wicked will be cut off in darkness;
   for not by might shall a man prevail.
v.10 The adversaries of the Lord shall be broken in pieces;
   against them he will thunder in heaven.
 The Lord will judge the ends of the earth;
   he will give strength to his king,
   and exalt the power of his anointed.'

This is an address to the God who is Lord of all (v.8b). Further, this God is active in the world, in particular bringing about radical change in people's lives – he kills, he brings to life; he makes poor, he makes rich; he brings low, he exalts. We should see this as a prayer of adoration and acknowledgment of the presence of God in the world, of the sheer reality of his being. It is also a prayer of thanksgiving that this great God does good things for his people, especially when they suffer, and are weak and powerless. And at the same time, he has the strength to bring down those who use their power and might arrogantly or wickedly. There are no special requests to God in this prayer, a fact that may serve to remind us that not all prayer (and certainly not all prayer in the Old Testament) is taken up with asking things of God. Here in thanksgiving and praise it is acknowledged that God is Lord, that people depend upon him, and that he is the one who is believed to be in ultimate control of the lives of the people of earth.[14]

Yet the change that is spoken about here, which God works in the world, is not portrayed as happening in a 'miraculous' way, in the sense that laws of nature are disturbed, varied, or suspended. Rather, this is change effected by God through the hand and the action of the human person Samuel, he who was given in answer to a woman's prayer. It is a commonplace to observe that Samuel fulfilled a crucial role in the movement of Israel into a new age, an age ushered in by the increasing encroachment of the Philistine peoples into Israelite lands. The need of the Israelite people to have a king to rule over them, to protect and lead them, became clamant. As the story of Samuel is presented to us, prayer to God had no insignificant place in the eventual transformation of the fortunes of those people.

V

Samuel, then, was a national leader at a time of great change for his people; he is portrayed in the Old Testament as occupying a key role in the life of his people as they moved into a further phase of nationhood. The prophet Elijah is another such person who is presented to us in the scriptures as having been sent to his people at a moment of crisis. Perhaps we may say that with Elijah it was not so much that he helped his people to move through a time of change, but rather that he stood firm and helped his people not to become involved in change for the worse. For it would seem that in northern Israel in the years between c.870–c.850 BC, in the days of Ahab's kingship, there was the grave danger of the nation apostasizing to the gods of Ahab's Phoenecian wife Jezebel (I Kings 16.31–34 and 18.1–19). There were those in Israel in danger of forgetting the ways of justice, especially for the weak of society (I Kings 21). But the prayers associated with Elijah are very different from those we find in the stories about Samuel. Moreover, there are far fewer; only three in fact. We have no prayers in connection with the birth of Elijah, or even with his call to serve the Lord. Rather, by the time we come to the first prayer from Elijah he is already deeply involved in aspects of his ministry in the Lord's name, in this case in the ministry of healing. The setting of this first prayer is that of a time of severe drought – caused, we learn, by the word of the prophet and as a judgment upon the sins of King Ahab (I Kings 17.1). Elijah himself is commanded by the Lord to go to the land east of the River Jordan where he will find water in the Wadi Cherith and where the ravens will feed him (vv.2–4). When that source of water failed him, he was commanded to go to Zarephath where he would receive food and drink from a certain widow in that place (vv.7–9). This he did, and there he received food and drink (vv.10–16). But then the widow's son became ill, and, 'his illness was so severe', we are told, 'that there was no breath left in him' (v.17). And in the face of the accusations on the part of the widow that it was Elijah who had caused this to happen ('You have come to me to bring my sin to remembrance, and to cause the death of my son!' [v.18]), Elijah prayed for healing for the child:

> And he cried out to the Lord, saying, 'O Lord my God, have you brought calamity upon the widow with whom I am staying, by killing her son?' Then he stretched himself upon the child three times, and cried out to the Lord, saying, 'O Lord my God, let the life of this child return, I pray, to him.' (I Kings 17.20f.)

In the following verse we are told that the Lord 'listened to the voice of Elijah' (there is no mention of any effect that may have resulted from the prophet's action in stretching himself out upon the child) and that 'the life of the child came into him again, and he revived' (v.22).

What we have here is Elijah making a prayer of intercession (a subject to which we shall return in Ch. 4), that is a prayer in which he prays not for himself, but for the widow's son. In the Old Testament illness is sometimes portrayed as being the consequence of sin (Lev. 26.14–16; Pss. 38.1–8; 41.3–4; 107.17–20), but this is not always the case (as we shall see in the next chapter, when we consider some of the psalms). But what are we to say about the role of a human being in the healing process, in particular when that role is fulfilled through prayer?[15] We should bear in mind that in ancient Israel medical knowledge seems to have been fairly rudimentary. We read of physicians embalming Jacob (Gen. 50.2), and the reference in Jer. 8.22 suggests that Gilead was the home of some healers. King Asa, according to the author of the books of Chronicles, was able to consult a physician (II Chron. 16.12), but perhaps that was something of a king's privilege. Even in as late a text as Ecclesiasticus 38.14 (dating perhaps from about 180 BC) the physicians must rely on prayer to God for their diagnostic success! Indeed, the physician for the people of ancient Israel was the Lord himself, a point of view reflected in Ex. 15.26, with its, 'I am the Lord your healer.' In the Old Testament people generally turn to God for healing, for to whom else can most of them go? Thus we are not surprised at the occurrence of prayers of intercession in settings where people seek healing. And it is to be observed that in the prayer that Elijah prays on behalf of the child, it is acknowleged that all comes from the Lord: that is, he is invoked as the Lord who gives all things, whether it be the healing that is being sought (v.21), or on the other hand whether it is the calamity that is at present afflicting the child (v.20)! It is an acknowledgment here that God is the author and cause of *all* things in the world, and, in the particular instance under consideration, that the future, the fate of this child lies with God. The prayer is that the child may receive from the giver of all things, his gift of life.

There remain two prayers in the stories about Elijah, each having some significance in this introduction to the subject of prayer in the Old Testament, each exhibiting features we shall find recurring.

The prayer of Elijah in I Kings 18.36f. comes towards the climax of the great contest on Mount Carmel between the one prophet Elijah and his God, the Lord God of Israel, and the many prophets of Baal. The sacrifice has been prepared and, although it is a time of dreadful drought, the altar and the offerings have been liberally soaked in water (vv.20–34), 'so that', we are told, 'the water ran all around the altar, and filled the trench also with water' (v.35). Now was the moment for prayer:

> And at the time of the offering of the oblation, Elijah the prophet drew near and said, 'O Lord, the God of Abraham, Isaac and Israel, let it be known this day that you are God in Israel and that I am your servant, and that at your word I have done all these things. Answer me, O Lord, answer me, that this people may know that you, O Lord, are God, and that you have turned around their hearts.' (I Kings 18.36f.)

I would not call this a prayer of intercession. Rather, it is a plea on the part of Elijah that God will demonstrate his lordship over all things and all beings. In the context of the hard task in the Lord's service that Elijah is portrayed as having to undertake, we may say that here Elijah is praying for himself, and that thus we are dealing with a prayer of petition. But once again, it need occasion no surprise that at this particular moment there is a prayer from the lips of Elijah: humanly speaking he is in a desperate situation, one prophet on his own against so much. There is the looming contest, and against him there seem to be so many – the people, the prophets of Baal, the king and queen. To whom else in his extremity can he turn but to his Lord God? The fact that at this climactic moment in this story there is recorded a prayer is itself an eloquent testimony to the fact that those who passed this story on to us believed that prayer could be made to God, and that there was benefit in praying. Here, we read that the effect of the prayer was the vindication of the power and authority of the Lord God of Israel and his prophet Elijah.

But we may wish to note the fact that this prayer does seem to exhibit some repetition. The 'let it be known this day that you are God in Israel' in v.36 is followed by the very similar expression, 'that you, O Lord, are God' in v.37. It has been suggested that maybe two stories have been combined, one dealing with the drought and the other with a different situation, one in which there was water a-plenty.[16] Further, it is not without interest that the Greek text of the Old Testament prepared by Lucian (AD 240–311/2), a presbyter of Antioch, does in fact have a text that omits the first part of v.37 ('Answer me, O Lord, answer me, that this people may know that you, O Lord, are God.'). Does that perhaps indicate Lucian's thought that the text was rather cumbersome and repetitive? But, we may respond, we are dealing here with a prayer, and as one commentator on the Books of Kings, maybe correctly, observed, 'liturgical language is diffuse'.[17] We know that it can be so in our own age, and we can well believe that it was so in times past! What is portrayed as a prayer of a servant of the Lord in a very critical and demanding situation will not necessarily be expressed in the most succinct and compressed style. Thus we are not surprised that we have a certain element of repetition in the prayer of Elijah.

The third prayer associated with Elijah comes from the setting of his long journey to Mount Horeb. Having killed all her prophets, he is fleeing from Queen Jezebel. The message that the Queen sent to Elijah was both grim and threatening: 'So may the gods do to me, and more also, if I do not make your life like the life of one of them by this time tomorrow' (I Kings 19.2). Thus, in understandable fear, Elijah went to Beersheba. Leaving his servant there, he went on alone (v.3).

> And he himself went into the wilderness a day's journey, and he came and sat down under a certain broom-bush and he asked that he might die, saying, 'It is enough; now, O Lord, take my life, for I am no better than my fathers.' (I Kings 19.4)

This is a prayer of distress and anguish, a prayer 'from the depths', a prayer from a person who is 'at the end of his

People Praying, God Hearing

tether'. In both Chapters 2 and 5 below we shall return to give further consideration to such prayers of anguish on the parts of individuals. In some of these prayers, the one praying protests that they are innocent, and there is perhaps the implied criticism of God that it is he who is causing unjustified suffering. We shall come across examples of such prayers in certain of the psalms. But there are other prayers of anguished personal concern coming from those who are experiencing deep suffering, apparently as a result of their seeking to be faithful to the will of God! The most obvious example of this, as we shall come to see in Ch. 5 below, is the prophet Jeremiah. The depths of suffering and anguish he experienced as he obediently fulfilled what he believed to be the will of the Lord caused him to utter exceedingly harsh words in prayer to God. Jeremiah certainly questioned the will of God in giving Jeremiah the gift of life (Jer. 20.14–18), and in the prayer of Elijah before us now this earlier prophet suggested in prayer to God that really he would be better off dead than alive. Moses, in a very demanding and stressful situation in the long desert march, had uttered much the same thought, again in a prayer to the Lord:

'If this is the way you are going to treat me, put me to death at once – if I have found favour in your sight – and do not let me see my misery.' (Num. 11.15)

But it is not that Elijah protests a total innocence of sin; he says that he is no better than his fathers, and the intended meaning may be that he feels himself to be no better than the earlier prophets.[18] Perhaps he is saying that he does not have it within him to be a true prophet of the Lord. He has done his best, but even that seems not to have been sufficient! As Skinner expressed it: 'he has reached the limit of human endurance: life has become a useless burden, because he feels he can never again rise to the height of the effort that has failed.'[19] If this is correct, then here is a prayer that will find an echo in the heart of many a disciple and servant of the Lord! But we shall return to this theme – and the associated prayers.

I Kings 19.19–21 makes up something of an appendix to the story that with v.18 culminates in the appearance of the Lord to Elijah on Mount Horeb, and tells how Elijah called Elisha to be his servant. But the stories about Elisha portray him as being more than Elijah's servant; he became his prophetic successor. In the series of stories connected with Elisha there are only two occurrences of prayers. The first of these is in II Kings 4.33 and concerns Elisha praying to the Lord for a dead child. As we have already seen, the story of this healing, effected at least in part through prayer, is remarkably similar to the story of the healing of the widow of Zarephath's son by Elijah, recorded in I Kings 17.20f., and that the Elisha story may perhaps constitute the original upon which the Elijah story came to be based. At any rate the II Kings 4 story need not detain us.

What is of more interest to us is the prayer – more correctly the series of prayers – made by Elisha to the Lord in a very different situation to any we have encountered thus far, namely, in the setting of a battle. The text we are dealing with is II Kings 6.17–20, where we read:

> And Elisha prayed, saying, 'O Lord, I pray, open his [the servant of the man of God] eyes that he may see.' And the Lord opened the eyes of the servant and he saw; and the mountain was full of horses and chariots of fire round about Elisha. [18] And when the Syrians came down against him Elisha prayed to the Lord, saying, 'Strike, I pray, this people with blindness.' So he struck them with blindness according to the prayer of Elisha. [19] And Elisha said to them, 'This is not the way, and this is not the city; follow me and I will bring you to the man you seek. And he led them to Samaria. [20] And as they came to Samaria Elisha said, 'O Lord, open the eyes of these men that they may see.' And the Lord opened their eyes, and they saw that they were in Samaria.
> (II Kings 6.17–20)

The setting of all this is of war between Syria and Israel, and a theme running through the account has to do with vision and blindness. Not only is Elisha a man with what we might call 'second sight' who is able to deploy that gift so that the Syrians' plans are frustrated, but also Elisha enables his servant to see what is actually taking place. Further, the soldiers of the Syrian army are blinded and captured, and they remain blind until they are brought to the city of Samaria. Then they are allowed to see that they are captives! But clearly there is a sense of commonality of theme in the main subject areas of the prayers in the Elisha story: they are to do with aspects of what we may generally refer to as healing. But in II Kings 6.17–20, the prayers are quite specific requests that at one time God will do one thing and at another time he will act in another way. Thus, Elisha first prays that his servant may see – see, that is, all the hosts of heaven who are with them in their conflict against the Syrians (v.17). He then prays that those Syrians may be struck with blindness, that is so that they may not be able to fight (v.18). Finally, he prays that these same Syrians may be granted sight, that is so that they may be able to see they have been defeated (v.20)! In the case of these prayers there is specific reference to the fact that the Lord responded to each prayer as it was prayed, granting what Elisha asked.

It may be felt, and with some justification, that this is a somewhat crude way of regarding prayer; crude in the sense that little choice is left to the Lord who is believed to hear such prayers. Perhaps a more mature style of prayer would be content to place a situation, a problem before the Lord, and in an appeal to the mercy of God ask that help may be given. Such prayer would not run such a risk of appearing to manipulate, rather than appeal to, God.

VI

While it may be true that there are examples of prayers in the Old Testament in which prayer is portrayed in somewhat manipulative terms, so that all a person had to do was to pray to the Lord and that specific wish was granted, that is not what may be called its mainstream view about prayer. In the Elisha example, it should be remembered, we have a story concerning a prominent personality who in the circles of those who recorded his activity clearly came to be known and revered as having an ability to perform miraculous acts. The majority of the prayers in the Old Testament are uttered in the belief that God hears prayers, but there is also that sense that what will happen as a result of prayer is something that must be left to the mercy of God. He is not the God who is to be rather easily *manipulated* in prayer.[20] But he may be *appealed to* in prayer – and much of the Old Testament displays a lively faith that God does hear such prayers of his people.

Eliphaz (one of the friends, the so-called 'comforters' in the book of Job) is confident that God hears prayers that are made to him:

'You will pray to him, and he will hear you.' (Job 22.27)

Indeed, Eliphaz suggests that Job, while he insists on being argumentative with God, is neglecting aspects of the spiritual life:

'But you are doing away with the fear of God, and hindering meditation before God.' (Job 15.4)

But the experience of Job is that the practice of prayer is not quite so easy and straightforward as Eliphaz seems to be suggesting. Though we shall return to this topic in Ch. 5, it may be noted here that in the Book of Job it is Job alone who is portrayed as continuing to pray to God: whereas we do not hear of his friends Eliphaz, Bildad, Zophar – or even Elihu – praying! It is Job who protests that his 'prayer is pure' (Job 16.17), but who eventually cries out:

'What is the Almighty, that we should serve him? And what profit do we get if we pray to him?' (Job 21.15)

We shall see in the next chapter that the Old Testament gives us examples of people who feel that their prayers are neither heard nor answered by God. But there is also in the Old Testament a more confident approach to prayer, namely, that it is heard by God, and that often it is answered. In parts of the Book of Proverbs is the assertion that the prayers of the righteous person are not only heard by the Lord, but heard with delight:

The sacrifice of the wicked is an abomination to the Lord, but the prayer of the upright is his delight. (Prov. 15.8)

The Lord is far from the wicked, but he hears the prayer of the righteous. (Prov. 15.29)

Yet, there must be the desire, the attempt, to live a righteous, a good, a godly, life on the part of one who would pray:

When one will not listen to the law, even one's prayers are an abomination. (Prov. 28.9)

Prayer must proceed from a life guided by the instruction ('law') and the ways of the Lord. The unacceptability to God of prayer being offered by those who practise unrighteousness is expressed starkly by Isaiah: he hears the Lord addressing those who act as the people of old in Sodom and Gomorrah were believed to have acted (Isa. 1.10). To such people comes the divine word:

When you stretch out your hands,
 I will hide my eyes from you;
even though you make many prayers,
 I will not listen;
 your hands are full of blood. (Isa. 1.15)

The reference to stretching out of the hands is clearly to one of the acts associated with prayer that we read about elsewhere in the Old Testament (see Ps. 28.2; I Kings 8.22, 54; Ezra 9.5). To hold out one's hands to God in prayer, was to open oneself to God, to make oneself ready to receive all that he in his greatness and his mercy might offer. The irony here is that by doing so, those praying are only making it all the more clear to God that they are sinners with bloodstained hands![21]

But, to return to where we were at the beginning of this chapter, Cain's hands were surely bloodstained, and whether or not he stretched them out to God, God must have known that they were bloodstained. Yet Cain's prayer was heard, and he received divine mercy. But perhaps it was because Cain's prayer was such an agonized cry for help, a help that he perceived could only be given by God. Clearly, the people about whom Isaiah complains, gave the appearance of being religiously active (Isa. 1.11–14), but what caused the divine displeasure was the corruption and exploitation that was taking place, the sense of arrogance on the part of those who were praying (Isa. 1.16f.). But Cain was no longer arrogant. Now he was a person whose burden and punishment were greater than he could bear, and, in desperation he cried out to the Lord. It was this perception of his own situation before God that made him so different from those spoken about in Isa. 1, and that made his prayer so different from theirs.

And Cain said to the Lord, 'My punishment is greater than I can bear. See, you have driven me this day away from the ground, and from your face I shall be hidden; and I shall be a fugitive and a wanderer upon the earth. And whoever finds me will slay me.' (Gen. 4.13f.)

2

'O Lord, hear my prayer'
Prayers in the Psalms

I

R. E. Prothero in his extensive work, *The Psalms in Human Life,* gives us some details of the death of George Herbert:

> In 1632, he died at Bemerton, dwelling, like Jewel, with his latest breath, on the text, 'Forsake me not when my strength faileth' (Ps. lxxi, verse 8), and committing his soul to God in the familiar words, 'Into Thy hands I commend my spirit' (Ps. xxxi, verse 6).[1]

This holds a twofold interest for us. First, Prothero maintained that the last words of the saintly poet, and parish priest, George Herbert (born 1593) were prayers from the book of Psalms. Then secondly, the whole of Prothero's purpose with his book was 'to collect together some of the countless instances in which the Psalms have . . . guided, controlled and sustained the lives of men and women in all ages of human history, and at all crises of their fate . . .'[2] And it is indeed a remarkable catalogue that Prothero gave to us.

These two considerations helpfully serve to remind us of the abiding influence of the Old Testament Psalms in the Christian church and in the lives of individual Christians. We can also say that the book of Psalms continues to play an important role in the church today and in Christian living, being used extensively in liturgy and devotion.

While a small number of the Psalms – an obvious example being Ps. 137 – clearly come from a comparatively late stage in the history of Israel, in general we believe that most of them are to be dated in the pre-exilic period, that is before the fall of Judah and Jerusalem to the Babylonian army in 587/586 BC. Further, the Psalms are poems, they are compositions in poetic form, and in so far as some of them may be termed 'prayers', they represent a style of prayer rather different from those we have already considered. Here in the book of Psalms is a further strand in the total make-up of the prayers in the Old Testament. It is a more formal style of prayer than that we have looked at already. We are dealing here with prayers that have been consciously 'composed', rather than those that have been uttered spontaneously by a believer in some particular situation, joyful, distressing, or with consciousness of sin. In all probability the Psalms were composed and prepared for use in the formal, organized setting of worship, in what we might call the ancient Israelite cult.

One of the great scholarly works of this century on the biblical Psalms was that of the German scholar H. Gunkel. In a commentary on the Psalms, and also in a work of Introduction completed after his death by his student J. Begrich, Gunkel defined Psalms according to their types (*Gattungen*), and he sought to relate each type to an original life-setting (*Sitz im Leben*).[3] Five main types of Psalms that Gunkel analysed were: Hymns, Communal Laments, Individual Laments, Individual Thanksgivings, and Royal Psalms (the last was not strictly a group distinguished by 'form', but by common content). There are also some less common types of Psalms: Communal Thanksgiving Psalms; Pilgrimage Psalms; Liturgies; Wisdom Psalms. Our present purpose is a study of prayer in the Old Testament so we shall not be considering the Hymns; nor will the Pilgrimage Psalms, the Liturgies, or the Wisdom Psalms be treated here. In Ch. 6 below some attention will be focussed on the Royal Psalms, while in this chapter our concern is with some representative Psalms of lament, confession and thanksgiving. At appropriate points, we shall look at the occurrences of certain Hebrew words for prayer and aspects of prayer.

II

Psalm 17 is what Gunkel called an Individual Lament Psalm. By 'lament' we mean a crying out in a sense of agony and distress to God. The term 'lament' is not completely satisfactory. When we talk about 'laments' in the book of Psalms, this is not the same as laments in, say, the book of Lamentations. In the latter we have a series of expressions of great distress occasioned by the terrible fate that has befallen Jerusalem, apparently in the sack of the city by the Babylonians in 586/587 BC. That 'lament' is an aspect of 'mourning'. By 'lament' in the Psalms we mean an agonized cry of an individual or a group about their distressed situation *in life*, here and now, and in particular when that distress is felt to be unjustified. R. Murray suggests that for these psalmic 'laments' we should use the word 'supplications',[4] but I do not feel that this is a strong enough word. In the laments in the Psalms we encounter some extremely forthright talking, praying, to God. They are nothing less than complaints.

This lament, complaint type of Psalm is the commonest in the Psalter, accounting for nearly one-third of the total. In Psalm 17 an individual cries out in prayer to God: the psalmist cries to God for protection. Further, behind this lamenting cry to God is the sense that the great pressures and burdens now being experienced are felt to be undeserved. It has been suggested that the Psalm has been carefully constructed in three parts – in fact in three prayers – with each part exhibiting a skilful interweaving of the double themes of the innocent and the opponent.[5] Thus:

1. A prayer based on the psalmist's innocence (17.1–5)
   (*a*) A prayer (vv. 1–2)
   (*b*) Description of the psalmist's innocence and testing (vv. 3–5)
2. A prayer based on the enemy's attack (17.6–12)
   (*a*) A prayer (vv. 6–8)
   (*b*) Description of the enemy attack (vv. 9–12)
3. A prayer for the enemy's destruction and the psalmist's deliverance (17.13–15)

We may translate the first part of this Psalm as follows (with words for prayer in v.1, which will be discussed, indicated in *italics*):

> Ps.17.1 Lord, hear a just cause
> be attentive to my *cry*;
> give ear to my *prayer* –
> not from deceitful lips.
> v.2 May my judgment come from you;
> let your eyes see the right things.
> v.3 You have tested my heart,
> you have visited by night;
> you have refined me, but you will find nothing:
> my mouth does not transgress.
> v.4 As for the deeds of humankind –
> by the word of your lips,
> I have kept myself
> from the ways of robbers.
> v.5 My steps were firmly in your tracks,
> my feet have not slipped.

In v.1 the psalmist calls upon God: this is the 'invocation', the means, as we have already seen, of the one who prays seeking to make their 'contact' with God. Such an invocation is the common beginning of a Psalm of lament.[6] This is the address to God, who is asked to 'hear' what the psalmist is sure is a just cause. The psalmist, though suffering grievously, believes himself to be innocent, and therefore makes his address about his situation to none other than God. We are not given specific details of the problem experienced by the psalmist; in general it is clear that some people regard him as guilty of some word or deeds. He seeks the assurance that God will regard him as innocent, and thus he makes his prayer. The psalm begins, 'Lord, hear a just cause', rather in the sense, 'Lord, hear my plea for vindication.'

Verse 1 has two words for prayer: first, the word translated above 'cry'.[7] RSV, NRSV, REB, and NIV all translate it 'cry'; GNB has 'cry for help' and JB 'appeal'. The word indicates a cry that may be an expression either of joy or distress, but its use indicates a particular emphasis in the tone of voice being used. It is a word that expresses a sense of the *intensity* of the approach to God. The psalmist is crying out to God in a loud voice, clearly determined that at the highest level he is going to be heard. He urgently needs to receive a hearing!

In the third line of verse 1 is the word that almost all versions translate 'prayer'.[8] It is an entirely general Old Testament word for prayer, without particular emphasis on the type or the subject of prayer, or on the tone of voice being used by the one praying. It is an extremely common word in the Psalms, and many of the longer and more formal prayers in the Old Testament, such as those in Jonah 2, Hab. 3, Neh. 1, are introduced by this word, or its verbal form.

Then the psalmist having expressed his 'loud cries' and his 'prayer' – for the combination of these two words does perhaps suggest an element of intensity in his calling upon God – brings his problem before God. In the face of accusations on the part of unnamed people, the psalmist protests his innocence to God. He asserts that when God has tested his heart, when he has seen into this man's heart in the night hours [9], even when he has refined him, there will be nothing found that warrants these accusations made against him (v.3). Whereas v.3 concerns the psalmist's inner life, vv.4 and 5 are about his deeds: he has not robbed; his feet have not slipped. On the contrary, he has walked in God's ways.

A reaction of some readers of this Psalm may be one of a certain unease because of what seems to be rather much self-righteousness on the part of the psalmist. While there are Psalms that clearly and eloquently express a deep sense of contrition on the part of the worshipper before his or her God (e.g., Ps. 51.3, 5), here we are dealing with an example of a lament Psalm. In these Psalms there is expressed a distinctive approach to suffering. In the lament tradition we hear cries from the very depths being articulated before God. Whatever may have been the decorous or correct words that might perhaps have been uttered in prayer, in a Psalm of Lament we hear what the speaker really is feeling and experiencing. Shakespeare has Edgar say at the end of the tragedy of *King Lear*,

The weight of this sad time we must obey;
Speak what we feel, not what we ought to say.[10]

But this form of lament is not only to be found in the book of Psalms. It is in the Pentateuch, in the cry of distress uttered by the Israelites in their oppression in Egypt; 'Then we cried to the Lord' (Deut. 26.7). It is present in the book of Judges : '. . . they were in sore straights', and, 'the Lord was moved to pity by their groanings' (Judg. 2.15; 15.18). We see it in the personal lament in Ps. 130, 'Out of the depths I cry to you, O Lord', while Westermann speaks of the book of Job being 'a mighty fugue based on the cry of lamentation'.[11]

In this tradition of thought and belief it is acknowledged that there are in life dark, antagonistic forces that appear to operate against a person's happiness and prosperity. There is also the acknowledgment that those who experience such difficulties are but mortal, and unable to turn such antagonistic forces aside. Life is difficult and attended by many perils. But the cry in the lament is to God. In this tradition of prayer it is affirmed that a part of full human life is to be able to make such lamentation to God, who for his part is concerned about his people's sufferings and who does hear their cries of distress (Ps. 116.1). In the book of Genesis we are told about the distress of Hagar's child Ishmael, cast out into the wilderness: 'And as she sat over against him, the child lifted up his voice and wept. And God heard the voice of the lad . . .' (Gen. 21.16f.). In the New Testament we read of Christ at the time of his greatest agony and suffering uttering some words of a psalm of individual lamentation, 'My God, my God, why have you forsaken me?' (Mark 15.34, quoting Ps. 22.1).

Yet it has to be said that this prayer of lament does not have any great prominence either in the New Testament or in the Christian tradition. It is as if in the New Testament, the lament tradition gives way to the belief that sufferings should be borne with patience and resignation (see, for example, I Peter 4.12-19). Thus Christians who suffer participate in the divine glory (I Peter 1.7; 4.14), and so Stephen, when he was put to death was, 'full of the Holy Spirit', and 'saw the glory of God', while his face was 'like an angel's face' (Acts 7.55). Thus there came about the sense in the early church of glory in the face and experience of martyrdom. But perhaps we may suggest that this development has not been all gain; the associated cost was the loss of this lament tradition which involved a hanging-on in faith to God in the face of suffering, and which insists on asking of God why life should go in this way. In this tradition, God is neither left free of the great questions that arise in the experiences of life of individuals or communities, and nor is faith in him abandoned. While the latter approach may have been unthinkable in ancient Israel, it is sadly all too common in contemporary Western life.[12] We shall return to this theme in Ch. 5.

III

The second part of the Psalm is a prayer based on the enemy's attack (vv.6–12), which we may translate as follows (as before, the word for prayer is *italicized*, and will be discussed):

Ps. 17.6   I *call* upon you, for you will answer me, O God;
            incline your ear to me, hear my words.
  v.7   Reveal your steadfast love,
            you who deliver by your right hand
            those who take refuge in you from their foes.
  v.8   Guard me as the apple of the eye,
            hide me in the shadow of your wings,
  v.9   from the wicked who attack me,
            my deadly enemies who surround me.
  v.10 They close their hearts to pity,
            their mouths speak with arrogance.
  v.11 They track me down – they surround me;
            they set their eyes to throw me to the ground.
  v.12 They are like a lion longing to tear,
            like a young lion lurking in a hiding-place.

Our psalmist continues in prayer; now he *calls* on God. In the first line of v.6 is the word generally translated 'call' (so NRSV, NIV, REB; JB has 'invoke', GNB 'pray'); it is the translation of a word [13] in no way used exclusively of praying to God. Its meaning is 'call, proclaim, read', perhaps with a certain sense of loudness, and it is used of calling upon another person or persons, as well as 'calling upon', 'crying to' God. Frequently it is used when addressing God (the vocative) 'O Lord', as in Ps. 28.1 (see below). What is also expressed in v.6 – along with the expressions of God in very human terms ('incline your ear') – is the assurance that God will indeed hear this person who calls upon him. Prayer is a reality because the God to whom one prays is the God who *hears* and *answers*. The particular request the psalmist makes is that God will deliver him from his oppressors, and that he will show his steadfast love, his lovingkindness (v.7). And not only is this the God who hears and answers prayers, but the one who *delivers*, whose 'right hand' is thus employed (v.7). The psalmist prays that God will guard him ('as the apple of the eye'), and hide him ('in the shadow of your wings') (v.8) from his enemy.

In vv.9–12 the psalmist goes into details about the machinations of the enemy. It is a general feature of these lament psalms that there are usually three dimensions: the lament comes from the lamenter himself; the lament is directed toward God in accusation or complaint against him; and the lament is also directed against another person or persons. That is, in the third place there is the complaint against an 'enemy'. Westermann has pointed us to the real significance of this, namely, that for the lamenter himself or herself there are some vital relationships both with those in human society round about, but also with God to whom the lamenter is praying and asking these questions about life. What this means is that there is no question here of seeking to abandon the relationship either with fellow human beings or with God.[14] And certainly in the case of this particular Psalm there is given in considerable detail the attacks that the 'enemy' (whoever, whatever he, she or it is) makes upon the psalmist. This leads to the psalmist's wish, expressed in the third part of the Psalm, and which may be translated as follows:

Ps. 17.13   Arise, O Lord; confront them, bring them down;
              rescue me from the wicked by your sword,
   v.14   from mortals, by your hand, O Lord,
              from mortals, whose portion of life is from this
                world.
              But your treasured ones – you will fill their belly;
                sons will have plenty,
              and they will leave abundance to their children.[15]
   v.15   And I, in righteousness, will see your face;
              when I awake, I shall be satisfied, seeing your
                likeness.

It cannot be denied that the prayer in vv.13 and 14a[16] has a violent expression of vengeance upon the enemy. Some commentators try to soften the sense of violence. Weiser speaks of a 'force of accumulated emotions, [which] finds its relief in a prayer for vengeance', while Craigie suggests that the words should be interpreted metaphorically rather than literally.[17] But neither of these suggestions is of satisfactory help to those who have been called to display a very different attitude to enemies, indeed, even to love them, and pray for those who persecute them (Matt. 5.44). At least we may say that the psalmist is being honest – both with himself and with God! But honesty, perhaps we feel, should be tempered with love.

Yet in the closing verse of the Psalm (v.15) all talk of the enemy has gone, and so too has any lamentation addressed to God. On the contrary: the notes struck in v.15 are those of abundant hope and overwhelming confidence in God. This is another of the characteristic features of the Psalms of Lament: in so many cases there is this change of mood towards the end, so that the psalmist is able to complete the prayer in the confidence that it has been heard.

The phenomenon of this, at times, very abrupt change in mood in a Psalm has been explained in a number of ways. It has been suggested, for instance, that sometimes the Psalms of Lament are really thanksgiving Psalms. But that is hardly very convincing, for the reason that in such Psalms so much is taken up with the aspect of lament, with only a comparatively small unit at the end exhibiting the note of thanksgiving. Another suggestion (and this has gained more acceptance) is that a priest delivered a word of hope and salvation between the end of the lament and the beginning of the 'hopeful' words. The latter, in this view, represents the response of the individual or the group to the priestly oracle. The 'Achilles heel' of this theory is that in no Lament Psalm is there present an example of such a 'salvation oracle'. We do know of such a divine oracle in other parts of the Psalter (see Ps. 60.6–8) – but never in a Psalm of Lament!

But perhaps this characteristic feature of the change from lament to hope towards the end of a Lament Psalm can be explained along quite different lines. The psalmist has in prayer brought and entrusted the problem to God, and, quite simply, things now have a different appearance for him. Calvin said of the last verse of this Psalm:

> After he has, in anguish of his heart, laid before God the troubles which galled and wrung him . . . he flies up into clear calmness on the wings of faith, where he may behold things set in due order.[18]

But Heiler also speaks of this phenomenon in his book on prayer:

> The chief content of prophetic prayer is the utterance of need . . . It begins with the expression of need, but it rises to a height where want and desire are forgotten and trust, joy and surrender prevail. A wonderful metamorphosis takes place in the prayer itself, unconsciously, involuntarily, often quite suddenly. The harassing, painful emotion, the ardent desire, pass; with a sudden bound the spirit finds itself in a mild, pleasurable mood of confidence and peace, of hope and trust; the feeling of uncertainty and instability is replaced by the blissful consciousness of being cared for, hidden in the hand of a protecting higher power.[19]

Thus the psalmist has made this lament to God. In prayer, uttered in that intensity of 'loud cries', the psalmist has approached and spoken to God out of anguish of heart. Like

Edgar at the end of *King Lear*, so has the psalmist spoken: 'Speak what we feel, not what we ought to say.' The somewhat vindictive complaint and imprecation over the enemy has been uttered to God, but at the end of the Psalm the lamenter has come to new realms of hope and confidence. He has experienced what Heiler called the 'wonderful metamorphosis', and is confident that he will be satisfied (v.15).

IV

Let us now turn to another Psalm, Ps. 28, also an Individual Lament. Here again is to be observed the marked transition from the lament prayer, in which God is implored to deliver the psalmist and punish the enemy (vv.1–5), to the expression of thanksgiving, confession and intercession (vv.6–9). We may translate this Psalm as follows (and once again the translations of Hebrew words relating to prayer are indicated in *italics*):

Ps. 28.1 To you, O Lord, I *call*;
    my rock, do not be deaf before me,
Lest, if you be silent before me,
    I shall become like those who go down to the pit.

v.2 Hear the voice of my *supplications*,
    when I *cry* to you,
When I lift up my hands
    to your most holy place.

v.3 Do not drag me away with the wicked,
    and with those who do evil,
who speak peace with their neighbours,
    but have evil in their hearts.

v.4 Repay them for their deeds,
    and for their evil work;
repay them what their hands have done
    and give to them what they deserve.

v.5 Because they do not understand the works of the Lord,
    or what his hands have done,
he will tear them down and not rebuild them.

v.6   Blessed be the Lord,
         for he has heard the voice of my *supplications*.
v.7   The Lord is my strength and my shield;
         in him my heart trusts;
         So I was helped, and my heart exults,
         and with my song I give thanks to him.
v.8   The Lord is the strength of his people;
         and a refuge of deliverance for his anointed.
v.9   O save your people, and bless your heritage;
         be their shepherd, and carry them for ever.

In v.1 the psalmist *calls* (a word for prayer already considered under Ps. 17.6) to God, addressing him as 'rock', an expression that speaks of permanence, strength and security. Yet at the same time, the imagery must not be overdrawn: in another sense this 'rock' is not inanimate, for he may be called upon. The psalmist's request is that God will not be *deaf* to what his servant has to say to him. It may be that the psalmist is asking for more than the divine listening ear; also that God will not be *silent* before him. The same Hebrew word which means both 'be deaf' and 'be silent' is used *twice* in this verse, and it is quite likely that the psalmist intended this double meaning to come out, as I have tried to represent in the above translation. May it not be suggested that behind this verse is a concept of prayer in which, ideally, God both *hears from* and *speaks to* the one who is praying? And the particular fear of the psalmist here is that if God were silent before him (or deaf?), then he, the psalmist, would 'become like those who go down to the pit'. The 'pit' is the silent area of the burial chamber, perhaps here symbolizing the general realm of death. Without God's response to his prayer, the psalmist feels that he would be, as we might express it, 'as good as dead'.

In v.2 the psalmist asks that God will hear 'the voice of my *supplications*', something of a roundabout way of saying 'my supplication'. The same expression is there in v.6. 'Supplication' is the translation employed by RSV and NRSV for another Hebrew word for prayer:[20] NIV has 'cry for mercy', GNB 'cry for help', REB 'plead for mercy' and JB 'raised in petition'. This word in Hebrew, and the words associated with it linguistically, are not used only of prayer. The verb, for instance, can be used in a situation where a person is asking something of another, as in Jer. 37.20 where Jeremiah 'pleads' with King Zedekiah not to send him back to the prison in the house of the secretary Jonathan. But it is a word that is used in situations when the asking is 'polite', where, maybe, there are expressions of respect, bowing to the ground and so forth. It is used to indicate requesting, asking, even pleading.

But if the word for prayer in the first line of v.2 is a 'polite' word, expressing the sense of 'pleading, requesting', the word in the following line expresses something, once again, of a 'cry for help'. In the translation above this word is rendered 'cry'.[21] In a number of translations the rendering is 'cry for help' (so RSV, NRSV, JB), in some 'call for help' (NIV, REB).[22] This word is usually employed in speaking of crying out to God. It is found most commonly in the books of Psalms and Job. This is the word used when Habakkuk asks how long he is to *cry out* to God (Hab. 1.2), and is also employed when Jonah *cries out* to God from the belly of the fish (Jonah 2.2).[23]

Thus, in the opening two verses of this Psalm we are given a graphic word-picture of the psalmist approaching God. A number of words for prayer are used, which together inform us of different nuances and aspects in the psalmist's coming to God. The resulting picture is one of a deep sense of need and urgency on the part of this person to speak to and be heard by God, conveyed in no small way by the use of words that emphasize, 'calling to', and 'crying out', to God, as well as 'pleading' with him.

Moreover, in addition to the talk about this calling to God (v.1), about this supplicating, pleading, and about the crying out to the Lord (v.2), there are also details about the posture of this person: the psalmist speaks of lifting up his hands to the Lord's holy place. In some of the references to prayer in the Old Testament we hear of people standing for prayer (I Kings 8.22), and at other times kneeling (I Kings 8.54; Ezra 9.5). Sometimes hands are lifted up to heaven (I Kings 8.22; Lam. 2.19; 3.14) or toward the temple (I Kings 8.35, 38, 42; Ps. 5.7; 134.2). Yet 'toward heaven' and 'toward the temple' amount to much the same thing, as the temple was clearly regarded in some way as the earthly representation of the Lord's heavenly abode. Here the temple is referred to as God's 'most holy place' – a clear reference to the Holy of Holies, that most holy part of the temple that contained the ark of the covenant and the cherubim. When the psalmist speaks of his lifting up his hands to the Lord's most holy place, we are given, through 'body language' a further picture of his deeply-felt need of God, and of his reaching out to him.

In vv.3–5 we come to the content of the prayer. The psalmist is troubled lest he be delivered up with the wicked; perhaps as we might express it, he is concerned that he might be 'dragged down' with them (v.3). A prayer is then uttered that these wicked people may have a drastic end, another of those prayers with which we find difficulty in associating (vv.4–5).[24]

Then, with v.6, comes the great turning point in the Psalm: vv.6–9 are made up of thanksgiving and intercession. Clearly, the psalmist believed that God had *heard* his prayer (v.6). Did he perhaps feel that in some way or other God had not been *silent* before him, but that by some means or other he had spoken to this one who had been praying (v.1)? At any rate, things were now indeed transformed: whether or not the danger was past, the *sense* of danger seemed no longer to be such a threat. Calvin observed of this psalmist:

> For hitherto we have seen in what manner he has occupied himself with praying while he was in danger; and now in his thanksgiving he shews that his prayers were not in vain; and so by his own example he confirms that God is ready to help His servants as often as He is sought truly and heartily.[25]

Thus the psalmist utters his 'Blessed be the Lord' (v.6), acknowledging that God is his strength and shield. In God his heart trusts, and he has truly been helped (v.7). Now the psalmist goes on to affirm that God is the strength of his people, in a particular way, perhaps, the strength of their leader, the king, the 'anointed' (v.8.).[26] So his prayer, which has begun in lament and deep distress, has continued in thanksgiving, ends now in intercession (v.9): will God save his people and bless his heritage. That is, may the Lord grant happiness to the special people of his possession. More, will he be their shepherd, and carry them for ever. Clearly, the psalmist believed that God was not deaf to his prayers, supplications and cries! Here, at the end of his Psalm, he makes his witness about the help he has been given, so that others too may experience blessings like this for themselves.

V

In the preceding pages some attention has been given to words used in the Old Testament in reference to prayer. These words, as we have seen, far from having similar meanings, express quite distinctive nuances in the approach to God, and indicate certain aspects of particular prayers. It may be appropriate now to set out briefly a number of other words that are employed in the Old Testament to indicate prayers and particular features of prayers.

1. There is yet another word – in fact occurring in two forms[27] – which is generally translated 'cry'. The words occur frequently throughout the Old Testament, and the main emphasis in the meaning 'falls on the loud and agonized "crying" of someone in acute distress, calling for help and seeking deliverance with this emotion-laden utterance'.[28] Again, these words are not used exclusively of prayer: examples of their use when the cry is addressed to a fellow human being can be found in II Sam. 19.4; Job 31.38; I Kings 8.3; II Kings 2.12, etc. But perhaps the more frequent usage is where the cry is addressed to God: Judg. 3.9,15; I Sam.7.8; 12.10; I Chron. 5.20; II Chron. 32.20; Ps. 22.5; 107.13; Micah 3.4 etc. This is the verb used of the cry to God uttered by the Israelites in their Egyptian captivity (Ex. 2.23f.; 3.7,9; Deut. 26.7). The Lord heard this cry and intervened to deliver his people, so that Hasel observes, 'Theologically, it was always extraordinarily significant for Israel that its beginnings as a people were grounded in a cry for help.'[29] At an early stage was the prayer!

2. Now we turn to a word [30] that occurs only three times in an address to God in the Old Testament, and that conveys a sense of urgency in the approach to God. The three occurrences are Jer. 7.16; 27.18 and Job 21.15. The renderings in recent English translations are as follows, and indicate something of the range of meaning of this word:

	Jer. 7.16	Jer. 27.18	Job 21.15
REB	intercede	intercede	entreat his favour
RSV	intercede	intercede	pray
NRSV	intercede	intercede	pray
GNB	plead	ask	pray
NIV	plead	plead	pray
JB	plead	pray	pray

3. Then there is a word [31] with the meaning 'entreat', perhaps even 'appeal to'. It does not occur in the Psalms; it is never used in address to fellow human beings; it is only used in address to God. Its occurrences are: Gen. 25.21; Ex. 8.8, 9, 28, 29, 30; 9.28; 10.17, 18; Judg. 13.8; II Sam. 21.14; 24.25; I Chron. 5.20; II Chron. 33.13, 19; Ezra 8.23; Job 22.27; 33.26; Isa. 19.22. Here are the renderings of our translations in the case of three sample occurrences of the word:

	Ex. 10.18	Gen. 25.21	Isa. 19.22
REB	intercede	appealed	prayers
RSV	entreat	pray	supplications
NRSV	pray	pray	supplications
GNB	pray	pray	prayers
NIV	pray	pray	pleas
JB	intercede	pray	turn to

4. Another word – perhaps rather better described in the Hebrew as an expression [32] – that signifies a 'polite' and reverential approach to God in prayer is found some fourteen times in the Old Testament: Ex. 32.11; I Sam. 13.12; I Kings 13.6 (twice); II Kings 13.4; II Chron. 33.12; Job 11.19; Ps. 119.58; Jer. 26.19; Dan. 9.13; Zech. 7.2; 8.21,22; Mal. 1.9. NRSV translates it 'entreat the favour, seek the favour, implore

the favour, implore, entreat'. It is an expression used, it seems, to indicate a quiet, calm, gentle – certainly reverential – approach to the Lord.

5. But then, in so many cases, none of these words for 'prayer' or 'to pray' are used in the Old Testament when clearly the activity *is* prayer. Many prayers are introduced quite simply by such language as so-and-so *said* such-and-such to God, or to the Lord. In those cases the prayer is introduced with the normal and extremely common Hebrew verb 'say, speak'. Among many possible examples see, for instance, Gen. 18.23–32; 24.12, 27; Ex. 5.22; Josh. 7.7 etc.

6. Finally, we should take note of a very small word, a particle,[33] that although occurring in many prayers, is, in fact, not a word for prayer. There are a great number of occurrences, for example Gen. 12.11,13; 18.4,30; Ex. 33.18; Num. 12.12; Judg. 9.38. It is what we call a 'particle of entreaty', and may be rendered 'pray', as in, for example, Gen. 18.4, which somewhat literally reads, 'Let, *I pray*, a little water be brought . . .'. The particle may be rendered 'please', but is often left untranslated.[34]

Thus, it is to be observed that the Old Testament has quite a range of words that are employed to speak of prayer. While some of them are general words for prayers, others express something more particular about the prayer concerned, while others may perhaps be employed to indicate the tone in which the prayer is uttered, maybe something of the sense of need and urgency on the part of the one who is praying. Certainly, the Hebrew Old Testament has a wide and varied range of words to express aspects of its prayers.

The preceding study of two prayers of Individual Lament has made clear for us the reality of prayer on the part of those who 'composed' such works. The fact that such Psalms came to be 'composed' and handed on to others perhaps indicates a belief that they would be of help and benefit to others in their prayers as they in their turn passed through difficult times, feeling themselves to be troubled by an 'enemy' of some sort. And perhaps others may have come to feel at the end of *their* prayer that though the 'enemy' was still physically present with them, yet at the same time they experienced a new hope and confidence for life. Maybe through the medium of such an existing prayer (perhaps deliberately composed in 'general' terms so as to be applicable to a wide range of contemporary and subsequent situations), many were able to experience what Heiler called a 'wonderful metamorphosis'. Certainly for so many generations of Jews and Christians the Psalms have been treasured for their spiritual worth and have become a staple of liturgy and devotion.[35] Perhaps that is so because in no small measure the Psalms are prayers, and as such have enabled many others over the years and the centuries to make their own prayers to God, especially in their times of trouble.

The book of Psalms contains many more Individual Laments, but there are also the Communal Laments. In the latter, it is the nation as a whole, rather than an individual, that is lamenting before God its present plight, and is praying for deliverance. The setting of such Psalms tends to be political or military disasters, and outside the psalter we have examples of such Communal Laments in Isa. 63.7–64.12; Jer. 14.2–9, 19–22 and Lam. 5. In Joel 1–2 we have a Communal Lament occasioned by drought and locusts. Perhaps the setting of at least some of these prayers was that of certain days of national lamentation in the temple (see I Sam. 7.6; II Chron. 20.3ff.; Jer. 14; Joel 1–2; Zech. 7.3,5; 8.19). If this is so, then the Communal Laments come from larger and more formal settings than those of the more numerous Individual Laments. Here in the Communal Laments is the nation at prayer: 'When the nation finds itself hard pressed, it brings its needs before Yahweh.'[36]

VI

We have noted in these Individual Laments, that one of the distinctive features of the lament tradition lies in the feeling on the part of the one praying that he or she is innocent of sin, and therefore undeserving of the present crisis. Thus God is asked why life should be like this, at this particular time. But in other Psalms, the psalmists have a very different perception of them-

Prayers in the Psalms

selves and their lives: their Psalms of prayer may come out of a painful awareness of sin and failure on their part. Thus there are Psalms of Confession, an example of which is Ps. 130. From the point of view of its 'type', this psalm shares some of the characteristics of the Individual Laments, for there is the crying out to God, but present also is an overwhelming emphasis that the one who utters these words has a conviction of sin against God, and comes in penitence to him. Ps. 130 was one of Luther's favourite Psalms; he called it a 'Pauline' psalm because of its emphasis upon the one praying throwing himself upon the grace of God. Other psalms that Luther referred to as 'Pauline' were 33, 51 and 143.

We hear the psalmist's agonized cry to God, springing from his consciousness of sin, in Ps. 130.1–4, which we may translate as follows:

Ps. 130.1 Out of the depths I cry to you, Lord.
    v.2 Lord, hear my voice.
        May your ears be attentive
          to the voice of my supplications.
    v.3 If you, Lord, were to mark iniquities,
        Lord, who would stand?
    v.4 But with you there is forgiveness,
        so that you may be revered.

Once again, a psalmist cries out to God – from the 'depths'. The same word ('depths') is used of the depths of the sea (Ps. 69.2; Isa. 51.10; Ezek. 27.34): it is as if the psalmist is in something of a 'sea of troubles'. He *cries* and *calls out* (vv.1 and 2a), *imploring* that the Lord will be attentive to his entreaties for himself. Clearly, there is a feeling of hopelessness on the part of the psalmist, and he expresses those feelings to God. In vv.3 and 4 it emerges that these feelings of hopelessness spring from a consciousness of sin – whether directly from a sense of conviction of sin or because of misfortunes experienced which have been attributed to sin, we have to say we do not know. But the psalmist finds comfort in the belief that God does forgive his people their sins (v.4), and that therefore a person may stand before him (v.3). The thought of v.4 would seem to be that the Lord, far from being merely judgmental about the sins of men and women, is forgiving: this fact leads to even greater reverence and glorification. Weiser says, 'In forgiving sin, God proves himself to be more powerful than sin itself, and, because he alone has the power of overcoming sin by his forgiveness, he is to be feared just because he is also God who forgives.'[37]

Thus hope is engendered in this sinner (so conscious of sin within) whose prayer continues:

Ps. 130.5   I wait for the Lord, my soul waits,
              and in his word I hope;
v.6   My soul waits for the Lord,
              more than watchmen for the morning,
              more than watchmen for the morning.

While there is great hope, there must also be the patience to wait; and this waiting is like that of the watchmen for the new day to dawn. Luther finely said, '. . . but those who wait for God, they pray for grace, but they freely leave it to God's goodwill when, how, where, and by what means he will help them.'[38]

Yet the psalmist is possessed of a certainty that such forgiveness of sin is granted by God, and about that he rejoices. This he does in the closing two verses of the Psalm, at the same time exhorting others boldly to place their trust in God with whom is steadfast love, great power to redeem – indeed sufficient to redeem a whole nation of people from *all* its iniquities!

Ps. 130.7   Israel, hope in the Lord!
              For with the Lord there is steadfast love,
              and with him is great power to redeem.
v.8   And he will redeem Israel
              from all its iniquities.

In v.8, grammatically the 'he' is emphasized: thus NRSV translates, 'It is he who . . .'. It is God, and God alone, who grants this great gift of forgiveness. The whole of this Psalm is a perfect example of a prayer of confession with a thanksgiving to God for the assurance of the granting of forgiveness. But it is also eloquent testimony to the fact that at least in some circles in ancient Israel there was held the firm belief that a person burdened by sin could make their prayer of confession and know the sense of sin forgiven. Thus the psalmist who began 'in the depths' ends with heart-felt thanksgiving, now free of burdens. And, no doubt, a concern on the part of those who passed on this Psalm was that others might in a similar way experience this sense of divine forgiveness through prayer.

VII

The final theme from the prayers in the book of Psalms is, appropriately enough, thanksgiving. Among the Psalms are Individual Thanksgivings, and a lesser number of Communal ones. In these Psalms the Lord is thanked for the specific acts of deliverance he has wrought, either for an individual or a community. Psalm 40.1–10 is an example of an Individual Thanksgiving.[39] In vv.1–2, which may be translated as follows, the psalmist looks back on a time, now happily in the past, of distress and difficulty:

Ps. 40.1   I waited patiently for the Lord,
    and he turned to me, and heard my cry.
 v.2   He drew me up from the desolate pit,
    from the muddy bog,
  and set my feet on a rock
    making my steps secure.

Once again the prayer has been made to the Lord: the psalmist has 'cried' to him, and the Lord has 'heard'. Yet once again, on the part of the psalmist there had to be the faith to 'wait'; in this instance we are told that he 'waited patiently' (v.1). Habakkuk in his crying out to God, seeking an answer to some agonizing problems, also had to wait patiently – in his case on his 'watchtower' (Hab. 1.2; 2.1).

The references in v.2 appear to be to illness. With 'desolate pit' and 'muddy bog' the psalmist is, of course, speaking in metaphor, but these are expressions for the concept of the underworld of the dead. Probably the psalmist is saying he was near to death, 'as good as dead'; he was ill, was 'at death's door', as we might express it. Yet he has been restored to health – and for that the praise and thanksgiving are to the Lord! Continuing the metaphor, his feet are now on rock, his steps are secure. That is, now he experiences all that is firm and unshakable. Thus there is the psalmist's thanksgiving:

Ps. 40.3 And he put a new song in my mouth,
   a song of praise to our God.
Many will see and revere,
   and they will trust in the Lord.
v.4 Blessed is the one who puts
   his trust in the Lord,
and does not turn to the proud,
   going after false gods.
v.5 Many are your wonders, Lord my God,
   that you have done,
and your plans for us.
   None can compare with you!
Were I to proclaim and speak of them –
   They are too many to count!

All is of God: not only are his wonders and his plans too many to count, proclaim or speak of (v.5), but the very song of thanksgiving has itself been given as a gift from God (v.3)! Further, it is a *new* song, for there are *new* mercies about which to sing. The greatest cause of thanksgiving is the great benefits that come to those who put their trust in the Lord: there is no such help and benefit for those who search elsewhere, either among people or gods (v.4).

Ps. 40.6 Sacrifice and offering you do not desire,
   But you have given me ears.
Burnt offerings and sin offerings you did not ask for.
v.7 Then I said, 'Here I am:
   in the scroll of the book it is written about me.
v.8 I desire to do your will, my God;
   your teaching is within me.'

It is possible to read v.6 as a condemnation of sacrifice as such, and some do read it in that way.[40] But it is more likely that what is being spoken about here is a concern that sacrifices and offerings be made in the correct spirit. They must never become merely mechanical acts. This is probably the burden of other passages in the Old Testament that speak of sacrifices in similar ways (e.g., I Sam. 15.22; Ps. 50.8–14; 51.16f.; 69.30f.; Isa. 1.11ff.; Jer. 7.21f.; Hos. 6.6; Amos 5.21f.; Micah 6.6ff.). The emphasis in Ps. 40.6–8 is on the fact that God has given to his people the means of a close relationship with him. That is, God has given to his people ears (v.6): presumably God has things he wishes to say to them. More, a person may come to the Lord (v.7), delight to do his will, and have the Lord's teaching right there *within* themself (v.8). It is as if alongside the institution of sacrifice, which at times ran the danger of being carried out with a certain lack of deep thought as to just what a worshipper was doing and what was happening, there are also these more spiritual ways whereby a person could come into a deep relationship with God. And although various aspects of this divine-human relationship are emphasized here – on the one hand, God's will that he speaks to, and is heard by, his people (vv.6, 8), and on the other, the psalmist's coming to the Lord (vv.7, 8) – yet prayer is not mentioned explicitly. But then that is surely presupposed, for here is the approach of an individual to the Lord in prayer; the full expression of the relationship between God and an individual is made in a prayer to the Lord by that person.

In vv.9–10 the psalmist returns to the theme of his testimony before his people. We may translate these verses as follows:

Ps. 40.9   I have proclaimed deliverance
                in the great congregation;
              see, I have not restrained my lips,
                Lord, as you know.
   v.10   Your deliverance I did not hide
                in the depths of my heart.
              I have spoken of your faithfulness and your help.
              I have not hidden your steadfast love and your faithfulness
                from the great congregation.

What had begun as an individual expression of thanksgiving has become something of a public declaration, a powerful testimony on the part of this individual who has experienced the grace of God, that others might know the same in their lives. Is it in this person's prayer, as it has been prayed aloud, that the proclamation of God's deliverance has taken place? Thus, not only is an individual making his act of thanksgiving to God, but that thanksgiving has also become the means whereby others may be helped in their times of consciousness of weakness or sin. Further, in so far as this Psalm is a formalized composition it is available for the future generations who through its words may be enabled both to make confession of their sins to God, and also to gain hope and comfort through another's testimony.

While so many people over the generations have found in the biblical Psalms a rich resource for their spiritual lives, and, in particular, models and examples for their own prayers, others will feel that true prayer must spring from within them rather than from page or scroll. Yet not all can muster the confidence to pray without the words being given to them, and for that reason at least the legacy of the Psalms must be reckoned to be great. Indeed, the spirit that must enliven the written word is present in the Psalms. The author of Ps. 40.1–11 was well aware of the grave dangers of formality in worship (Ps. 40.6–8), and the last two Psalms we have considered have both stressed the importance of the listening attitude of both partners in the divine-human relationship: both those partners wish to speak to one another and both wish to be heard. Certainly, through these prayer Psalms many have been enabled to make their pleas to God, whether those have been in the form of laments, or confessions, or thanksgivings. Yet all such prayers, 'set' and formal as they are, must arise from the hearts of those who are humble and who desire purity – as St Benedict (*c*.480–*c*.550) reminded his monks:

> If we wish to prefer a petition to men of high station, we do not presume to do it without humility and respect; how much more ought we to supplicate the Lord God of all things with

humility and pure devotion. And let us be sure that we shall not be heard for our much speaking, but for purity of heart and tears of compunction. Our prayer, therefore, ought to be prolonged by the impulse and inspiration of divine grace.[41]

3

'O Lord, hear; O Lord, forgive'
Prayers in Ezra, Nehemiah and Daniel

I

In *Alice in Wonderland*, when the White Rabbit asked the King where he should begin, he was told, 'Begin at the beginning and go on till you come to the end . . .'. The King added – no doubt wisely – 'then stop.' To a certain extent we have been following that advice: we began in Ch. 1 considering some of the 'early' prayers in the Old Testament, 'early' in the sense that they occur early in our reading of the book from the beginning. But whether such prayers come from an early date is often hard to determine: the material we are dealing with has frequently gone through a complicated process of growth, with parts added from here and there. It is not always easy to decide from what setting or date some particular part of the literature comes. Also, when we deal with historically 'early' prayers, the social, political and religious background can be very difficult to determine – just because it is of a time so long ago. Easier in some ways is to be at the other end of things – at the latest stage. Because there is a much smaller time span between that age and the present time, we may well be on somewhat surer ground as regards the background details, while the written material has gone through fewer vicissitudes – ups and downs – in its process of being handed down to us. So it is that we now turn to prayers in Ezra, Nehemiah and Daniel, what we might call the Old Testament's 'late' prayers.

We may call these 'late' prayers because the books of Ezra, Nehemiah and Daniel are some of the latest writings in the Old Testament. Though these books are not the most commonly read of the Old Testament in the Christian church they are of considerable interest in our study of prayer. They contain a goodly number of prayers, but prayers that have distinctive styles and characteristics, rather different from those we have looked at so far. While some of these prayers are set out as if they are spontaneous utterances of an individual to God, the most noteworthy feature of the majority is their *formality*. Certainly there are some very lengthy prayers in these books, and we may reasonably regard these as representing (at least as far as the Old Testament is concerned) the final stage in a process of the development of a formally composed prayer. Moreover, the prayers in these books embrace a wide range of subjects: here are prayers of praise, thanksgiving, confession, intercession and petition.

The book of Daniel, in its completed form, in all probability dates from the time of the Greek ruler Antiochus IV (Epiphanes), who reigned from 175 BC. The book speaks of the disruption of the daily service in the temple caused by Antiochus in 167 BC (11.31), but is silent on the matter of his death in 164 BC.[1] The books of Ezra and Nehemiah are more difficult to date. Ezra 1–6 may well be the latest part of these two books and might be dated around 300 BC, at about the time when there was a concern to justify the claim that the Second Temple was the legitimate successor to Solomon's Temple as Israel's real and only sanctuary – and certainly not the Samaritan Temple on Mount Gerizim. The rest of the material in the books of Ezra and Nehemiah may have gone through a major stage of composition around 400 BC.[2]

The books of Chronicles may or may not come from the same author as the books of Ezra and Nehemiah. My own view is that they probably do not, and that they are to be dated from a time before the rise of the Greek kingdoms. It has been suggested that the main parts of the books of Chronicles are to be dated around the time of Haggai and Zechariah 1–8.[3] While there are many prayers in the books of Chronicles – and clearly the author of these books had some quite definite ideas about prayer – I am not considering those prayers at present. I shall, however, return to them in Ch. 6.

II

In Daniel ch. 6 we are given an example of how prayer might have been practised, at least by some members of the Jewish community, in the centuries before Christ. Dan. 6 concerns the plot against Daniel, the story of his being thrown into the den of lions, and of his deliverance from them. It is the story of conflict at a royal court, of the fall and rehabilitation of a person holding high office. Above all, it is the story of a man who in the moment of conflict, pressure and stress, continued to believe in God, and who insisted on maintaining the practice of his religion. And this in spite of human and wordly authorities who were commanding him to do otherwise! The real threat for Daniel was that –

> The presidents and satraps conspired and came to the king and said to him, 'O King Darius, live forever! All the presidents of the kingdom, the prefects and the satraps, the counsellors and the governors are agreed that the king should enforce an interdict, that whoever prays to anyone, divine or human, for thirty days, except to you, O king, shall be thrown into a den of lions.' (Dan. 6.6f.)

We go on to read:

> Although Daniel knew that the document had been signed, he continued to go to his house, which had windows in its upper room open toward Jerusalem, and to get down on his knees three times a day to pray to his God and praise him, just as he had done previously. (Dan. 6.10)

And indeed the conspirators did find Daniel 'praying and seeking mercy before his God' (v.11). Of course, we should bear in mind that Daniel is no doubt intended to be portrayed in very favourable light. There is something of the ideal about him: this is how a person in his situation should conduct himself. Nevertheless the picture we are given here suggests to us once again that to pray was a natural religious activity in which a person such as Daniel the Jew might engage. But the Daniel who prays is presented to us as an example of a person who under pressure from others maintains the practice of their faith in God. Daniel 'simply perseveres in the exercise of his faith in the Living God. Daniel's resistance lies in his constancy and faithfulness.'[4] Yet at the same time, prayer is here portrayed as the means whereby a human being put under such pressure can find a source of strength for the hour. What is more, Daniel is portrayed as finding that strength, and in adequate proportions!

The Old Testament does not inform us anywhere else about prayer being offered three times a day. The 'evening and morning and at noon' in Ps. 55.17 is most likely to be understood in the sense of 'continually'; and similarly the seven times of Ps. 119.164.[5] Yet we do read in I Chron. 23.30 of morning and evening as times of prayer. Prayer in the evening is spoken about in Dan. 9.21; Ezra 9.5. (see also Judith 9.1; Acts 3.1; 10.3,30.).[6]

The Mishnah, a great body of Jewish teaching that was intended to expand upon and explain the sacred Torah ('Instruction'), speaks of prayer (Tefillah) being said three times a day – in the morning, the afternoon, and the evening.[7] Now whether the practices of the early Christian church developed from these Jewish ways or whether from specifically Christian concerns (for example the events of the crucifixion),[8] it is not easy for us to determine, and differing views are held. What is clearer is that in the early church various of the church Fathers were speaking and giving teaching about set hours for prayers. Hippolytus (c.170–c.236), for instance, in his *Apostolic Tradition* mentions no less than seven times a day for prayer! Neither Clement of Alexandria (c.150–c.215) nor Tertullian (c.160–c.220) are quite so rigorous: they are content with six times a day.[9] Origen (c.185–c.254) taught that regular times of prayer throughout the day were important: when they were associated with Christian acts and deeds, then life was indeed made 'one mighty integrated prayer'. But Origen thought that for prayer to be considered regular it should be made at least three times a day, and he drew attention to the example of Daniel in his time of crisis. It is worthwhile quoting him in full:

The man who links together his prayer with deeds of duty and fits seemly actions with his prayer is the man who prays without ceasing, for his virtuous deeds or the commandments he has fulfilled are taken up as a part of his prayer. For only in this way can we take the saying 'Pray without ceasing' as being possible, if we can say that the whole life of the saint is one mighty integrated prayer. Of such prayer, part of what is usually called 'prayer', and ought not to be performed less than three times each day. This is clear from the practice of Daniel, who, when great danger threatened him, prayed three times a day (Dan. 6.10).[10]

We are told that Daniel knelt for his thrice-daily prayer. The usual posture for prayer appears to be standing (I Kings 8.22; I Chron. 23.30; Neh. 9; see also Matt. 6.5; Mark 11.25; Luke 18.11,13). But there are references to kneeling for prayer (I Kings 8.54; Ezra 9.5; see also Luke 22.41; Acts 7.60; 9.40; 20.36; 21.5). Further, Daniel's prayers were 'toward Jerusalem'. In the long prayer of Solomon at the dedication of the temple in Jerusalem (I Kings 8.14-61; II Chron. 6.3–42), the whole emphasis is on that temple as a place of prayer – the meeting place of people and God. Moreover, there is an emphasis on prayer being made towards the temple, an emphasis reflected in the teaching of the Jewish Rabbis, though with due allowance being made for one's particular circumstances at the time of prayer. Thus:

> If he was riding on an ass he should dismount [to say the Tefillah, prayer]. If he cannot dismount he should turn his face toward Jerusalem; and if he cannot turn his face, he should direct his heart toward the Holy of Holies.
>
> If he was journeying on a ship or a raft, he should direct his heart toward the Holy of Holies.[11]

III

We shall now consider one of the prayers that Daniel is portrayed as making. It is in Dan. 2.20–23, and is a prayer of praise (vv.20–22) and thanksgiving (v.23):

Dan. 2.20 Daniel said:
> 'Blessed be the name of God from age to age,
> for wisdom and power are his.

v.21 He changes times and seasons,
> deposes kings and sets up kings;
> he gives wisdom to the wise
> and knowledge to those who have understanding.

v.22 He reveals deep and hidden things;
> he knows what is in darkness,
> and light dwells within him.

v.23 To you, O God of my ancestors,
> I give thanks and praise,
> for you have given me wisdom and power,
> and have revealed to me
> what we asked of you,
> for you have revealed to us what the king ordered.'

This combination of praise and thanksgiving in a prayer is comparatively rare in the Old Testament. However, one example that we have already considered occurs in the prayer of Abraham's servant which he prayed at the well outside the city of Nahor, asking that he might find the divinely appointed wife for Isaac, his master's son (Gen. 24.12–14; see above, Ch. 1, pp.14ff).

Daniel's prayer begins with the note of praise, and in particular is couched in the style of blessing of God, a style that was to become dominant and important in Jewish prayers.[12] Many Jewish prayers do begin with the form, 'Blessed are you, Lord our God . . .', as for example in the grace before meals:

> Blessed are you, Lord our God, King of the universe, who brings forth bread from the earth.

A characteristic of these 'blessing' prayers is that they address the God who is no less than the King of the universe, but who also is believed to be 'our God', and who may be addressed personally as 'you'. God may be a majestic Lord whose authority knows no bounds, but his worshippers are in a personal relationship with him.

Thus we observe at the beginning of Daniel's prayer the deep sense of reverence, here receiving added emphasis by the substitution of 'The name of God' for the more usual 'Lord'. This is a style of reverential address to God that became more common after the exile (see I Chron. 5.25; 12.17; II Chron. 33.12). The Lord is praised because 'wisdom' (that is, what we might call 'divine insight') and power are his. Moreover, it is in his hands to depose and to set-up kings. As background information we should bear in mind that Daniel in his dream saw the 'little horn' (which clearly represents Antiochus Epiphanes) as the one who, 'shall think to change the times and the law' (Dan. 7.25). Daniel, in his prayer of praise, seeks to ascribe the *real* power and authority in the world to the Lord, and certainly not to these trumped-up and rather insignificant human rulers!

Other expressions of the praise and adoration of the Lord then follow: not only is he the giver of wisdom and knowledge to certain people (v.21), but all realms of hiddenness and mystery are penetrated by his knowledge (v.22). We are reminded of Psalm 139.12 with its,

> even the darkness is not dark to you;
> the night is as bright as the day,
> for darkness is as light to you.

With v.23 Daniel's prayer moves into thanksgiving. Daniel acknowledges that God has provided for him just what was needful in his hour of crisis and opportunity. We notice in this verse how the language becomes more personal. Daniel addresses the Lord as 'God of my fathers' and acknowledges that the prayers, both of himself and of those who are with him, have been answered. This is that part of the prayer of blessing where the one praying addresses the great Lord of all as the one who also has the personal relationship with his worshippers and people. In this particular prayer, the note of the personal relationship between God and this person praying is brought out in the thanksgiving for Daniel's having been given divine insight and strength, sufficient indeed for his needs in the time of crisis! All in all, we may say that this prayer holds together in a satisfying way praise to the mighty God, and thanksgiving that the same God is with us, and more, acting for our good. We might compare this with Rom. 8.31b, with its: 'If God is for us, who is against us?'

IV

We now turn to a series of prayers in the books of Ezra, Nehemiah and Daniel that have as their theme confession of sin to God. Prayers of confession are present in a range of the Old Testament literature. An example is the prayer King David uttered when it became clear to him that he had sinned. The cause of the sin was the taking of a census of his people: presumably taking a census was sinful because it signified a reliance upon human resources rather than a full dependence upon God. The result of this sin on the part of David was a dreadful plague, which caused great distress among his people. So we read:

> But afterward, David was stricken to the heart because he had numbered the people. David said to the Lord, 'I have sinned greatly in what I have done. But now, O Lord, I pray you, take away the guilt of your servant; for I have done very foolishly.' (II Sam. 24.10)

This is a brief confession of sin to God, and on the part of an individual. Elsewhere in the Old Testament we read of a confession of a group of people. For example, in Joel 1.14 we have an appeal from the prophet to all the people to confess their sin:

> Sanctify a fast,
> call a solemn assembly.

> Gather the elders
> and all the inhabitants of the land
> to the house of the Lord your God,
> and cry out to the Lord.

No details of the content of this particular corporate confession are given, but in the books of Ezra, Nehemiah and Daniel we have a series of lengthy prayers of confession (Ezra 9.5–15; [see also 10.1]; Neh. 1.4–11; 9.6–37; Dan. 9.3–19). These prayers share a number of common aspects, and all are highly elaborate compositions. They are lengthy, but by no means formless, or lacking in logical arrangement. Indeed, if prayers today must be lengthy, let these prayers of old be the models for logical progression within them! They are noteworthy in that they contain quotations from other parts of the Old Testament, in the main from the Pentateuch.[13] These prayers deal in detail with the theme of Israel's great guilt, but also lay stress upon both God's original and his continuing faithfulness, mercy, and justice. We may understand this marked emphasis on the theme of confession to God in these prayers in the books of Ezra, Nehemiah and Daniel as representing one way that the people of Israel reacted to the experience of the Babylonian exile: much in the Old Testament interprets the experience of the exile as having been due to Israel's sin. Here, in prayer, that sin is confessed to God.

The first of these prayers we consider is in Ezra 9.5–15. It is too long to be quoted in full, but we may observe the following thematic outline:

Ezra 9.5	Introduction
9.6–7	General confession, in which there is movement from singular ('O my God, I am too ashamed . . . to lift up my face to you . . .') to plural ('From the days of our fathers we have been in great guilt . . .') expressions of penitence.
9.8–9	In spite of this human failure, the Lord has continued his mercies to his people ('. . . yet in our slavery God has not abandoned us, but

	has extended to us favour before the kings of Persia . . .').
9.10–12	These verses move to more specific statements of confession, in particular that 'we have forsaken your commandments which you have commanded through your servants the prophets . . .' There are many quotations from the Pentateuch in these verses.
9.13–14	Here is an acceptance that any future sin would indeed put the community in jeopardy, for 'Would not you [God] be angry with us to the point where there would be no remnant at all?'
9.15	Conclusion to the prayer: there is the note of renewed and humble confession: 'Behold, we are before you in our guilt, and none can stand before you because of this.'

The book of Leviticus makes provision for the confession of both individual (5.1ff.; 26.40) and corporate sins (16.21). In the book of Psalms, as we have already seen, are a number of what have come to be known as Penitential Psalms (Pss. 6, 32, 38, 51, 102, 130, 143). Further, we shall also come upon the theme of confession in Solomon's prayer (I Kings 8.14–61, esp. vv. 46–47 and 49: see Ch. 7 below). But nowhere else are there to be found such elaborate expressions of the confession of sin to God as here in these penitential prayers in Ezra, Nehemiah and Daniel.

However, a contrast is to be noted here. In those prayers of lament we find in the biblical Psalms and elsewhere (see Ch. 2 above), an individual or a community protests that they are *innocent* of sin. But here in these penitential prayers there is a full acceptance of *guilt*. At the same time it is in a profound sense of hope in the everlasting mercy of the Lord that these expressions of confession are made to the holy and just God:

> Yet our God has not forsaken us in our slavery, but has extended to us his steadfast love . . . to give us new life . . . (Ezra 9.9)

Elsewhere, the faithfulness on the part of God with sinners is given emphasis,

> Ah, Lord, great and awesome God, keeping covenant and steadfast love with those who love you . . . (Dan. 9.4, cf. Neh. 1.5; 9.32)

At the heart of this long prayer is an acceptance on the part of the person praying that grave sins have been committed against God. Specific sins are confessed (9.10–12), and it is even acknowledged that these people are not worthy even to come before the Lord in confession (9.15). And even though there may be this mercy of God (9.8f.), Israel should in no way assume that in the future they might be spared the divine wrath, were they to sin again (9.13f.)! However, at the heart of the theological thought of this prayer is that statement of Israelite faith, found no less than nine times in the Old Testament:

> The Lord, the Lord,
> a God merciful and gracious,
> slow to anger,
> and abounding in steadfast love and faithfulness,
> keeping steadfast love for the thousandth generation,
> forgiving iniquity and transgression and sin,
> yet by no means clearing the guilty . . . (Ex. 34.6f.) [14]

Some today would claim that the element of confession in Thomas Cranmer's services, and those of his successors, is excessive:

> Almighty and most merciful Father; We have erred, and strayed from thy ways like lost sheep. We have followed too much the devices and desires of our own hearts. We have offended against thy holy laws. We have left undone those things which we ought to have done; And we have done those things which we ought not to have done . . . [15]

Yet there is here the appeal in penitence to the 'Almighty and most merciful Father'. Where maybe Cranmer invites our criticism is in having what we may feel is too great an emphasis on our sin, and not sufficient upon the grace of God.

But perhaps these twin themes of the sin of humanity and the mercy of the almighty God are held together, and so finely and beautifully, in George Herbert's third poem entitled 'Love' – though, to be sure, the matter is expressed in terms of much greater intimacy than anything we encounter in Ezra, or anywhere in the Old Testament.

> Love bade me welcome: yet my soul drew back,
>   Guilty of dust and sin.
> But quick-eyed Love, observing me grow slack
>   From my first entrance in,
> Drew nearer to me, sweetly questioning,
>   If I lacked anything.
>
> A guest, I answered, worthy to be here:
>   Love said, You shall be he.
> I the unkind, ungrateful? Ah my dear,
>   I cannot look on thee.
> Love took my hand, and smiling did reply,
>   Who made the eyes but I?
>
> Truth Lord, but I have marred them: let my shame
>   Go where it doth deserve.
> And know you not, says Love, who bore the blame?
>   My dear, then I will serve.
> You must sit down, says Love, and taste my meat:
>   So I did sit and eat.[16]

In Neh. 1.4–11 is a prayer from Nehemiah which is similar to the one in Ezra 9.5–15, but as well as being a confession it also has petition and intercession. It oscillates both between first person singular ('I') and plural ('we') speech, and also between concern for the people, and Nehemiah's concern with his own forthcoming encounter with the king. It has the following outline:

Neh. 1.4   Introduction
    1.5   The address to God ('Ah, Lord, God of heaven, the great and terrible God . . .')

1.6a	The appeal that God will hear the prayer ('let, I pray, your ears be attentive and your eyes open to hear the prayer of your servant . . .')
1.6b–7	The confession ('I and my father's house have sinned. We have acted very corruptly . . .')
1.8–9	Now an appeal is made to God's covenantal promises to his people ('Remember, pray, the word which you commanded Moses your servant, saying . . .')
1.10	Here we have intercessions for the people ('They are your servants and your people whom you have redeemed . . .'), and finally there is in
1.11	Petition for Nehemiah's own rather delicate situation in the service of the Persian King whose cupbearer he is ('and give success, I pray, to your servant today, and give him mercy in the sight of this man').

We begin here with the address to God (1.5), continuing with an appeal that God will hear the prayer (1.6a), before we come to the confession itself (1.6b–7). After an appeal to God's mercy, the prayer of confession moves into petition and intercession, somewhat breaking the bounds of the categories we employ to speak of matters of the inner life and those to do with the relationship between humankind and God. At any rate, the fact that once again a prayer can move from confession into petition and intercession betokens a vibrant hope in the forgiving nature of God – even in spite of continued sin and failure on the part of his people. We have also to say that this is indeed something of a 'portmanteau' prayer: there is much by way of content here, beginning with the address to God, and ending with intercession for the people, and petition for Nehemiah's own tasks in the near future. Yet there is a clear and logical shape to the whole of the composition.

Even longer is the prayer of Ezra in Neh. 9.6–37. It begins with praise to God (v.6), and goes on to a long narration about what God has done for his people (vv.7–15). To this goodness of God, his people have responded in rebellion (vv.16–18). Yet the Lord's mercy has continued to them, and we may surely see significance in the fact that the part of the prayer that deals with this aspect is, in relation to other parts of the prayer, so extensive. There is once again that twofold emphasis in these prayers of confession: not only that people are sinners, but also that God is ever merciful and forgiving (vv.19–31). So Ezra prayed for his people (v.32), though at the same time he continued to acknowledge that they had done nothing to deserve such goodness and mercy (vv.33–35). He ends on a note of communal lament, complaint:[17]

> Here we are, slaves to this day – slaves in the land that you gave to our ancestors to enjoy its fruit and its good gifts. Its rich yield goes to the kings whom you have set over us because of our sins; they have power also over our bodies and over our livestock at their pleasure, and we are in great distress. (Neh. 9.36f.)

Altogether it is a most powerful and deeply moving confession. There is not so much the sense here that a person may come before God and be heard, but rather, people who have lived lives like this *must* examine themselves and make such a confession of sin. Yet a confession like this can be made only in the light and assurance of God's ancient, present, and continuing mercies to his people. The whole story is again not that of the people's sin alone, for there are also the everlasting mercies. Nevertheless, this prayer does not end, as the previous one did, with any particular request for either the one who prayed or for those for whom he prayed. It is as if, with continued and continuing sin of this order, all that can be asked for is the continuing mercy of God.[18]

Now prayers of confession do not make up the most numerous class of prayers in the Old Testament. Nevertheless, they do constitute a significant group,[19] and it is probable that in the life of ancient Israel there was such a tradition of praying in a spirit of confession. To what extent such prayers were uttered within or apart from the formal cult we have to say we do not know. Bound up with this question is the matter of the language of the prayer in Neh. 9.6–37: in particular, is the text of this prayer in poetry or in prose? Scholars are divided in their views about this. Williamson suggests that it is in 'rhythmic liturgical language',[20] rather in the style, presumably, that we find and use today in formal liturgies and prayers.[21] The employment of this particular type of language, neither on the one hand mundane, day to day prose, nor on the other more formal poetry, suggests that there was a well-established tradition and practice of corporate praying which came to have its own style and characteristics, and which was regularly, perhaps even normally, used in worship in ancient times.

But of course, equally valid is the spontaneous prayer that comes from the lips of a person, for example in a time of crisis. Perhaps this may be illustrated in an example of such prayer from our own century. Dietrich Bonhoeffer tells us of a prisoner in a concentration camp who in a heavy bombing raid, when all were lying on the floor, kept saying, 'O God, O God.'[22] This sort of spontaneous prayer in the Old Testament has been the particular study of M. Greenberg. He makes the observation:

> Every human being is capable of formulating a petitionary prayer according to his need, not only such heroes as Moses and Jacob, but even such roughnecks as Samson, and even pagans.[23]

All this is to say that there are in the Old Testament, as in the church today, a series of styles of prayer. There is the spontaneous prayer we have thought about, then at a remove from that, the prayer having what we found described as 'rhythmic liturgical language', of which Neh. 9.6–37 is an example. But perhaps with the composition of the latter there has been a conscious attempt to make rather more formal that which might have begun as spontaneous. By this means the prayer is now available for use by others, perhaps in a more institutional setting. About these institutionalized forms of worship, Greenberg says,

> These are the properties of experts; their details are fixed and

prescribed. A unit of them – a given sacrifice, a given psalm – is infinitely reusable or repeatable since it is not determined by specific circumstances.[24]

Evelyn Underhill, in her book about worship, spoke about the difference between 'free' and 'ordered' worship, especially as regards prayer, arguing that both are needed, 'if the full span and possibilities of Christian worship are to be realized':

> There is here . . . a marked difference of ideal between the conceptions of 'free' and 'ordered' worship: the extempore prayer meeting where all make their personal contribution, and there is unreserved expression of individual aspirations and needs, and the grave movement of the Divine Service, with its note of impersonal objectivity, the subordination of individual fervour to the total adoring act. The first is the social expression of that naive prayer which is man's instinctive response to the besetting presence of God. The second is the social expression of cultus. These completing opposites, both present in the primitive Church, are both needed if the full span and possibilities of Christian worship are to be realized; and it is one of the many tragedies of Church history that they have often been regarded as hostile to one another.[25]

In this prayer of Ezra that we have been considering we may say that we have a 'social expression' of prayer, couched in more formal language than we have encountered earlier.

There is one final prayer of confession in these three books that remains to be considered. It is Dan. 9.3–19 in which Daniel prays for his people's exile to come to an end. With Dan. 7 there has begun a series of visions of the heavenly realm (which stands in marked contrast to the earlier series of stories in chs 1–6, each with an earthly setting) and within the account of these visions is this prayer. In Jer. 25.8–14 'seventy years' is mentioned as the term for the punishment of Judah's sin, and this provides the 'text' for this prayer of Daniel.[26] The concern of the prayer is with the matter of the exile of God's people: how long will it last, and when will God act again on their behalf?

There are marked similarities in phraseology between this prayer and those in Ezra 9; Neh. 1 and 9. It opens on an extended note of confession (vv.4–14), and then goes on to express a plea that God's mercy will yet prevail (vv.15–19). It exhibits a great awareness of the fact of sin on the part of the nation, and stresses that any hope for the future is grounded solely in the mercy of God. Part of the ending of the prayer,

> We do not present our supplication before you on the ground of our righteousness, but on your great mercies. O Lord, hear; O Lord, forgive; O Lord, listen and act and do not delay! For your own sake, O my God, because your city and your people bear your name! (Dan. 9.18b–19)

has been compared with the Christian 'Kyrie Eleison',

> Lord have mercy
> Christ have mercy
> Lord have mercy,

and has indeed been called the Old Testament's 'Kyrie Eleison'.[27]

Now some scholars have suggested that this prayer is out of place in its present setting among the visions of Daniel. The prayer is in good biblical Hebrew, while the material in ch. 9 before and after the prayer is in rather rougher style and language, like that found in chs 8 and 10–12. Also, the prayer can be taken out – and if anything the 'logic' of the chapter may be said to be improved! In this way, Daniel has read in Jeremiah that seventy years must pass before the 'end of the desolations of Jerusalem', and he prays for an interpretation. In vv.24ff. he is given that interpretation. But the prayer is one of repentance, one in which God is asked to *act*, and yet in the verses after the prayer there seems to be no *action*! And vv.20–21 do look rather clumsy, and it would not be difficult to conclude that their purpose is to join this prayer and the following verses.

But in spite of such considerations a convincing case can be made for regarding the prayer as an integral part of the whole chapter, along with the surrounding material. And indeed, in recent times there has been a greater scholarly willingness to see the whole of Dan. 9 as having a unity. It could be that the prayer does not come from the author of the rest of the chapter, but was a prayer that the author had 'available', and that he inserted it into the text at this point. And indeed the Dan. 9.5-19 prayer is in the style of other prayers that we know,[28] so suggesting the possibility of it being an existing composition that was added to the surrounding material. But there is still the matter of the conclusion of the chapter appearing to take no account of the petitions in the prayer. Or does it? 'Difference' in Daniel's situation may not have been effected, but perhaps he is 'changed', in a not dissimilar way to Job, who came to a sense of peace after the speeches of the Lord in Job 38-41 – speeches which did nothing to answer the questions raised in the earlier dialogues between Job and the friends![29]

We shall return to this subject (see Ch. 5), but for the present we may in general terms take note of the overall shape and outline of the book of Habakkuk. In this book, chs 1 and 2 concern the sufferings of the prophet's people, the cruelty of the nations to them, and also the seeming inactivity, and even injustice, of God. All these deeply trouble the prophet, and he is given no answer. And then in ch. 3 is an extensive prayer, which gives no 'answer' to Habakkuk's problem, but which does 'change' him to the extent that he becomes possessed of a new hope and confidence and is ready to face a whole new range of crises and problems (3.17-19). It is surely noteworthy that so much of the book of Habakkuk is expressed in the language of prayer, and that the resolution to the problem of which Habakkuk speaks is expressed in the language of prayer.[30] Perhaps in a similar way is the prayer in Dan. 9 intended to function in the book of Daniel. The prayer becomes the means of acknowledging, and making real and actual for the people involved, that the Lord reigns. It expresses the faith of those who were willing to put their lives into the hands of God, and who thus come to a sense of peace. So Porteous said, 'If this was indeed how men prayed in those days, then we are in a position to understand how the faithful among the Jews came through the storms and stresses of that terrible time.'³¹ As our study continues we shall come upon other examples of people who when they were in the 'depths' prayed to God, and who are portrayed as receiving through their prayers strength and hope for their times of need.

V

We turn now to consider a prayer of intercession – the one unambiguous example of a prayer of intercession in the books of Ezra, Nehemiah and Daniel. In the context of the whole of the Old Testament, intercessions make up a very large proportion of the totality of prayers. Yet there are some parts of the Old Testament that have no prayers of intercession. More, the books of Obadiah, Nahum, Haggai, Song of Songs, and maybe Ecclesiastes, have neither prayers nor references to prayer. We have seen how in the books we are considering at present there are the lengthy and elaborate prayers of confession. Even so prayers of intercession and petition are less in evidence in these books.

Nevertheless, in Ezra 6.10 we do have a reference to a prayer of intercession:

> And pray for the life of the king and his children.

These words occur in the decree of Darius authorizing the rebuilding of the temple in Jerusalem. In fact, this decree of Darius was an endorsement of an earlier decree of Cyrus, and confirmed the Persian undertaking to pay the costs of the enterprise (Ezra 6.1–8). Along with the royal permission goes the request that prayers shall be made for Darius and his family. We are reminded of how Jeremiah in his letter to the Judaean exiles in Babylon exhorted them to seek the welfare of the city where they were, and to pray on its behalf (Jer. 29.7). Further, the Cyrus Cylinder, in which Cyrus proclaims himself, 'Cyrus, king of the world, great king, mighty king . . .', appeals for prayers for himself and his family on the part of his subject peoples:

> May all the gods whom I have placed within their sanctuaries

address a daily prayer in my favour before Bel and Nabu, that my days be long, and may they say to Marduk my Lord, 'May Cyrus the king who reveres thee, and Cambyses his son . . .'[32]

Indeed, no small number of prayers in the Old Testament are taken up with the subject of the king. Clearly, the king's great responsibilities in the life of the nation were such that regular prayer was at least desirable, if not needful. It is a topic to which we shall return in Ch. 6, but for the present may content ourselves with a quotation from Ps. 72, (one of the so-called Royal Psalms), much of which is taken up with a prayer, or even prayers, for various aspects of the king's high responsibilities (vv.1–17).

> Give the king your justice, O God,
>   and your righteousness to a king's son.
> May he judge your people with righteousness,
>   and your people with justice.
> May the mountains yield prosperity for the people,
>   and the hills, in righteousness.
> May he defend the cause of the poor of the people,
>   give deliverance to the needy,
>   and crush the oppressor. (Ps. 72.1–4)

VI

Turning now to petition, we have a series of such prayers, all of which are to be found in the book of Nehemiah. Prayers of petition make up perhaps the largest single group of prayers in the Old Testament. In some books where there are prayers, they may be nearly exclusively petitions. The book of Judges, for example, has just one prayer of confession (10.10–16): apart from that, all the prayers and references to prayer are petitions, in which groups or individuals pray for themselves.

Nehemiah 2.4 serves as a useful setting-off point, a helpful example of a prayer of petition:

And the king said to me, 'For what do you seek?' So I prayed to the God of heaven.

The background to this is the rather sad Nehemiah, serving in the court in a foreign land, far away from Jerusalem, and about to make his big request for his people and their city to his master. Williamson says, 'Conscious of this turning point, Nehemiah gathers up in a flash his prayers of the past months . . .'[33] Whether or not that was really so, inevitably we shall never know. What, however, is clearer is the portrayal here of a prayer that is spontaneous, unpremeditated, and for that reason very different in style from the formal 'composed' prayers (especially of confession) which we have earlier considered in Ezra, Nehemiah and Daniel. But, as Evelyn Underhill has reminded us, we need to take seriously the different styles of prayer – 'free' and 'formal' – so that we are able to grasp more of the totality of prayer. A part of the background to this text is the belief that an individual person could make their request known to God who in his care and mercy would be attentive. As we now approach this text we may well feel that here in this spontaneous prayer is something authentic and, indeed, spiritual.[34] Here is fully evidenced a deep dependence of a believer upon God. We may, imaginatively, maybe somewhat fancifully, hear such a person making their confession of trust in and dependence upon God: 'Even though I walk through the darkest valley, I fear no evil; for you are with me . . .' (Ps. 23.4); 'Naked I came from my mother's womb, and naked shall I return there; the Lord gave, and the Lord has taken away; blessed be the name of the Lord.' (Job 1.21).[35]

Another prayer of petition on the part of Nehemiah occurs in Neh. 4.4f. Once again, Nehemiah is concerned with the particular tasks that he has to do in his life, and he prays about them. This prayer occurs in the so-called Nehemiah Memoir, and the setting is in Jerusalem where Nehemiah's task of rebuilding the city walls is being threatened by a renewal of opposition from Sanballat and his allies and the army of Samaria. So Nehemiah prays to God:

Hear, O our God, for we have become despised. Turn their

abuse upon their heads and give them up as plunder in the land of their captivity. Do not forgive their iniquity and do not let their sin be blotted out from your sight, for they have provoked you to anger in the presence of the builders. (Neh. 4.4f.)

What are we to say about the spirit of vengeance against enemies, expressed so strongly in this prayer? We have already considered some rather 'vengeful' prayers in the book of Psalms. We shall find others in some of the prayers of Jeremiah, (Ch. 5). Undoubtedly, as we have already acknowledged, there is a problem here for Christians in their use of the Old Testament, in particular for the appropriation by the Christian church of insights from prayers in the Old Testament. Some will seek to explain the problem by reference to the provocation that Nehemiah experienced, and by the fact that for Nehemiah the taunts and threats against himself were tantamount to taunts and threats against God himself. One may even perhaps defend Nehemiah in that at least he only prayed about these matters: he might have gone further, being moved to action, taking, as we would say, 'the law into his own hands'! Yet the problem remains for Christians who have been commanded in a new law, 'Love your enemies and pray for those who persecute you . . .' (Matt. 5.44). We are conscious that a new way and a new ideal has been given to us, seen and lived out in the triumph of love over evil in the cross of Christ.

> Few, if any, will feel that they have attained that ideal, and honesty will compel us to admit that we have breathed the atmosphere of Nehemiah's prayer more often than we should; but by that very confession we testify to our conviction that since the coming of Christ there has been opened before us the vision of a better way.[36]

There is a series of further brief prayers of petition of Nehemiah, again concerning his work. Some of these have the imprecatory, vengeful aspect we have considered, while some are without it (Neh. 5.19; 6.14; 13.14, 22b, 29,31b). An example is:

Remember for my good, O my God, all that I have done for this people. (Neh. 5.19)

Each of these prayers asks that God will 'remember' Nehemiah. Perhaps we feel that there is rather too much self-righteousness, self-importance, maybe self-aggrandisement, even 'hubris' (pride) here. Yet perhaps we may say at the same time that here there is the acknowledgment that it is only God who 'can be relied on to give credit where credit is due'.[37] And we may feel that we can associate ourselves with some words of Blenkinsopp about another of these short 'remembrance' prayers in the Nehemiah Memoir (Neh. 13.14). He says, 'There may be a higher level of religious sensitivity, but to look for assurance that one's life and work are of some worth in the sight of God is hardly an attribute to be despised.'[38]

We may perhaps allow ourselves to be reminded of a prayer of Dr Samuel Johnson (1709–84). Did it possibly arise out of his lexicographical labours? Be that as it may, here is surely a prayer whose spirit may be appropriated by Christians who seek to offer to God the work of their lives:

O God, who hast ordained that whatever is to be desired should be sought by labour, look with mercy on all our studies and endeavours. Grant us, O Lord, to design only what is lawful and right; afford us calmness of mind and steadiness of purpose; that we may so do thy will in this short life as to obtain happiness in the world to come; for the sake of Jesus Christ our Lord.[39]

VII

We may leave Nehemiah praying about his building work – and Samuel Johnson about his literary activities – and turn briefly to another aspect of prayer raised in the book of Ezra, namely, the matter of prayer and fasting. In both the Old and New Testaments we have a small number of references to a combination of these (I Sam. 7.6; Ezra 8.23; Dan. 9.3;

Jer. 14.12; Matt. 17.21; Luke 2.37; Acts 14.23). In Ezra we have this example:

> And we fasted and petitioned our God for this, and he heard our entreaty. (Ezra 8.23)

Now in the Old Testament there are a considerable number of references to the practice of fasting. Sometimes it is as a part of mourning the dead (I Sam. 31.13; II Sam. 1.12; 12.6, 21–23), or it may be in a situation of dire emergency (Judg. 20.26; Jer. 14.12; 36.6,9; Pss. 35.13; 69.11; 109.24). At a later stage fasting came to have ceremonial significance in the commemoration of the fall of Jerusalem and the destruction of the temple (Zech. 7.2–7; Isa. 58.3–9). Occasionally it is spoken of as an accompaniment to prayer, as in Dan. 9.3. We should also, perhaps, understand the prayer of confession in Neh. 9 to have been accompanied by fasting (see Neh. 9.1). Maybe the significance of this combination of prayer and fasting lay in the total opening up of a person to God. That is, one presented oneself before God as totally without one's own strength, wholly and totally in need of that strength and guidance that it was believed that God was able to give, and which he might give. It was also an expression of one's total dependence upon God. And so did Ezra and those around him believe and act as they prepared themselves, spiritually no less than practically, for their journey to Jerusalem, and the mission that awaited them there.[40]

Our final prayer in the books of Ezra, Nehemiah and Daniel takes us to a time a good deal later than that of Ezra's preparations for his departure to Jerusalem, back to the time after Nehemiah's arrival in Jerusalem.[41] Nehemiah is hard at work on the walls of Jerusalem, and yet troubled by his enemies, Sanballat, Tobiah and others. Clearly, this is a time that calls for both prayer and action:

> So we prayed to our God, and set a guard day and night because of them. (Neh. 4.9)

Now, as we are already beginning to see, there are what we might call a number of theologies of prayer in the Old

Testament. The Old Testament by no means has one monochromic way of regarding prayer: how and in what situations it is to be made; what, if anything, is to accompany it; how it 'works'. In some parts of the Old Testament we have seen that prayer is portrayed as that which will effect divine action, and at the same time little or even no human action is desirable. At other times we have noted a definite sense that some human involvement in the form of action as well as prayer is called for. Neh. 4.9 could with some justice be called the Old Testament's classic example of 'prayer and action'.[42] Indeed, the intertwining of prayer and action is something of a marked feature of those traditions in which we read about Nehemiah. The author of the books of Chronicles would surely have approved (as we shall come to see in a later chapter) that is, unless he himself was responsible for giving us the material that we have in the books of Ezra and Nehemiah! Many of the prayers in Chronicles are accompanied by actions. In II Chron. 20.5-12, for instance, the Chronicler gives us a long prayer from the lips of King Jehoshaphat of Judah on the eve of what looks to be a great, even decisive, battle with a numerically overwhelming foe. Understandably, prayer is made, and Jehoshaphat's prayer culminates in the appeal to God, 'We do not know what to do, but our eyes are on you' (II Chron. 20.12). Nevertheless, *something* has previously been done: the fortified cities have been equipped and manned (II Chron. 17.2, 12, 19) and an army in excess of *one million* warriors has been recruited and assembled (II Chron. 17.14-19)! Just so: and in a similar way Nehemiah turned both to prayer and to practical human action:

> So we prayed to our God, and set a guard day and night because of them.

In this chapter our main emphasis has been on prayers characterized by their formality, though we have also briefly considered the spontaneous prayer. In the following chapter we shall encounter prayers that exhibit a sense of *intensity*. Our subject will be prayers for other people, among which are those intercessory prayers of Samuel and Moses, made for Israel at crucial moments in its history.

4

'Moses besought the Lord'
The Ministry of Intercession

I

If you are going to speak about Old Testament intercession, and by that I mean prayer that is offered by one or more on behalf of another person or a group, then sooner or later you must speak about Moses. I choose to speak about him later, for the principal reason that the intercessory prayers of Moses are some of the most intensive and passionate in the whole of the Old Testament, prayers upon which so much for so many, in such desperate settings, is found to depend. So we shall come to Moses, but I prefer to begin at a more day-to-day level, and to look at examples of some prayers of intercession portrayed as having been uttered in rather more mundane settings. Thus I begin with the Book of Ruth, though to be sure, the wilderness obtrudes here too, albeit not to the extent that it does in the stories with Moses as the great intercessor.

The Book of Ruth begins with a scene of great difficulty: there is famine in the land of Judah (1.1).[1] So it was that a group of people took the road from Bethlehem to Moab in search of food. Moab had fertile areas, so we are not surprised that the story should tell of this migration of Naomi, her husband and her two sons to this country. In Moab the sons take Moabite wives, Orpah and Ruth, but all too soon the deaths occur of Naomi's husband and sons, leaving alone the Judaean woman and her two Moabite daughters-in-law. Ruth insists on staying with Naomi, so whether they stay in Moab or return to Judah, one of them will be an alien. As things turn out, it is Ruth who will be the stranger in a foreign land, for they receive news that there is food in Judah, and set out to go there. To those who seek to welcome her back, Naomi describes her plight:

> Do not call me Naomi [Pleasant], call me Mara [Bitter], for the Almighty has dealt very bitterly with me. I went away full, and the Lord has brought me back empty. Why call me Naomi, when the Lord has afflicted me and the Almighty has brought calamity upon me? (Ruth 1.20f.)

The book of Ruth has four major scenes, the first of which concerning 'The Road to Bethlehem' (1.6 18) we have considered briefly. The second scene takes place in 'The Field of Boaz' (2.1–17) and in this we read how Ruth gleans in Boaz's field, how she is given food and drink (2.9,14), how she eats until she is satisfied (2.14), and how she goes away with corn in plenty (2.15–18). The third scene is set at the Threshing Floor (3.6–15), and from this place of plenty (3.6) Ruth goes away well provided, in fact with more than the six measures of barley with which she trudges off in the early morning light (3.15, 17). For she has also found a kinsman (3.9), and a wealthy one at that (2.1). What is more, the language of this scene is heavy with sexual overtones, and the threshing floor becomes the metaphor not only for the place of plenty, but of potential offspring (3.3ff.). And all will be resolved in the final 'act', at the Gate of Bethlehem (4.1–12). Here we read how Boaz and Ruth married, how a son is born to Ruth (4.13) and thanks are given for this restorer of life, this nourisher of old age (4.15). But the child Obed is also, we are told, to be a son for Naomi (4.16). Perhaps we are intended to understand a grandmother's great delight in her grandchild. But even more, maybe our appreciation is sought for the fact that a *male* child has been born. Although the androcentric, patriarchal emphases may not be altogether to our contemporary taste, we may perhaps be able to accept that the grim necessities of life in those days made imperative the presence of men in the family. Thus we can understand the sense of relief and joy that now there is a male heir, who in the fulness of time will assume responsibility in the family and ensure its life both in day-to-day events, and in the long-term.

It is to be observed that I understand the book of Ruth as a story that begins with great desperation for the women in Moab, but ends with a future opening up with boundless possibilities. That is to say, the book portrays a movement from desperation in Moab to new life in the environs of Bethlehem, and the progress of this movement is drawn out in the different pictures of these four scenes.

But the book seeks to give some account of certain aspects of how this movement from desperation to plenty is effected. It has not always been appreciated how many are the prayers in the book of Ruth, and how centrally they feature in the movement of thought. Moreover, it is intercessory prayers that predominate.[2] While there are prayers of thanksgiving in 2.19–20 and 4.14, there are no less than four prayers of intercession; and what is more, one each of these occurs in the book's four scenes, outlined above. Thus in Scene 1 (The Road to Bethlehem, 1.6–18) there is the intercession by Naomi for a future of good things for Orpah and Ruth (1.8f.); in Scene 2 (The Field of Boaz, 2.1–17) is the intercession of Boaz for Ruth (2.12); Scene 3 (The Threshing Floor, 3.6–15) relates another intercession of Boaz for Ruth (3.10); and in Scene 4 (The Gate of Bethlehem, 4.1–2) we find the intercession of the people at the gate, and the elders, for the newlyweds (4.11f.).

Just to complete our survey of the prayers in this book, it is to be observed that there are prayers of thanksgiving at the close of Scenes 2 and 4 (2.19f. and 4.14). No such thanksgivings occur at the end of Scenes 1 and 3, but that is readily understandable – at those junctures in the story there is as yet nothing for which to give thanks. Nevertheless, Scene 1 closes on the note of hope expressed in 1.22b ('They came to Bethlehem at the beginning of the barley harvest'), while Scene 3 ends on a note of expectancy in 3.16–18.

What we are given in the book of Ruth is a series of scenes in which people are portrayed as finding themselves in, and reacting to, rather ordinary, everyday situations. The central figures in the story are characterized as being beset with problems and difficulties. But life must go on, and to that end they make their worldly decisions – whether it is to go to Moab, to return to Bethlehem, to go to the field, or to go to the threshing floor. In these situations, the central characters are full-blooded humans, and they make the adult decisions of life.

Yet we should not feel that there is not a central place given to the reality and the presence of the Lord through this fierce human drama. Who is it but the Lord who has visited his people and given them food (1.6), and it will be the same Lord, Naomi realizes, who will grant homes to her daughters-in-law (1.8–9). Indeed, the hand of the Lord is there in all those things that humanly speaking have gone wrong for these people (1.13, 20, 21). Then also, it will be the Lord who will make Ruth, about to be married to Boaz, like Rachel and Leah, who together built up the house of Israel (4.11). And it was the Lord who gave Ruth conception so that she bore a son (4.13).

What we have in the book of Ruth is a portrayal of a blending of human and divine action in the particular setting of these events which begin in the depths and end with such promise for the future. And it is in the prayers of intercession that these human and divine actions are portrayed as coming together. In no way are they like some magical incantations, for the human beings must continue to pursue their human activities, and make their worldly decisions. But perhaps the book, as it probes some of the mysteries of the providential care of the Lord for these people, suggests that there is a place for prayer, and in particular that there is a place for the prayer of intercession. As we have seen, each of the scenes in this book has such a prayer, and we are surely invited to consider what different outcome there might have been to the whole drama had these prayers *not* been uttered. But they *were* spoken, and God's involvement in the lives of these people was sought – and further, thanksgiving was made to him that he had given good gifts to his people.

In these prayers of intercession in the book of Ruth, those who intercede are quite simply characters in the story, what we might call ordinary members of the 'cast'. We have read of Naomi (1.8–9), of Boaz (2.12; 3.10), even of 'all the people who were at the gate, and the elders'[3] (4.11f.), making their intercessions to God. And there are a goodly number of further instances in the Old Testament where we read of an ordinary person who makes a prayer of intercession on behalf of another, or a group.[4]

II

But what we also have in the Old Testament is a series of stories that speak of the intercessions of particular personalities. It is as if there were some people who were believed to have something special that qualified them in a particular way to engage in a ministry of intercession. Perhaps it was because such individuals were believed to have a particular relationship, even authority with, the Lord. So from time to time – usually at moments of some crisis for a community or an individual – such a person was called upon. Psalm 99.6 bears witness to the fact that Samuel, along with Moses and Aaron, came to have something of a reputation in this regard:

> Moses and Aaron were among his priests,
>   and Samuel was among those who called upon his name:
> They called to the Lord, and he answered them. (Ps. 99.6)

Jeremiah is told by the Lord that so very great is the sin of his people that even if Moses and Samuel pleaded for them God would not receive them back to himself:

> Then the Lord said to me: 'Though Moses and Samuel stood before me, yet my heart would not turn towards this people. Send them out of my sight, and let them go!' (Jer. 15.1)

We should surely understand this as seeking to emphasize the very great sin of the people of Judah, rather than that either God's forgiveness or the efficacy of prayer are less than they used to be. At the same time, it points to the reputations that Moses and Samuel gained for themselves as those who were felt to have some particular qualification, or even gift, for a ministry of intercession.

In the first book of Samuel we read of a number of occasions when Samuel was called upon to intercede for his people. He whose birth, as we saw in Ch. 1, was surrounded, suffused in prayer, came to be acknowledged as an intercessor for his people in their time of crisis. That crisis in Samuel's day was caused by the encroachment of the Philistines upon Israelite land and their making of the Israelites a subject people. At this time the Israelites were governed by the Judges, a period that lasted from around 1250 to 1020 BC. But it was a time when the land of the Israelites was being invaded by others, not only by indigenous Canaanites but also by Philistines, a race called in Egyptian texts 'sea people', who at first seemed content to settle on the coastal strip, but who later, needing more land, expanded into the hinterland. So, for example, Samson was called to be a Judge, and to help his people in this crisis (Judg. 13–16).

I Samuel 7.2–4 tells of a desperate situation for the people of Israel. The sacred Ark[5] had been captured by the Philistines (I Sam. 4.11), and it did appear that the 'Glory has departed from Israel' (I Sam. 4.21f.). For a long time the Ark had been housed by the Philistines in Kiriath-jearim, and perhaps the time had now come when the people of Israel were ready to turn to the Lord (I Sam. 7.2–4):

> And Samuel said, 'Gather all Israel at Mizpah and I will pray to the Lord for you'. [6] So they gathered at Mizpah, and drew water and poured it out before the Lord, and fasted that day and said there, 'We have sinned against the Lord.' And Samuel judged the people of Israel at Mizpah. [7] Now when the Philistines heard that the people of Israel had gathered at Mizpah the lords of the Philistines went up against Israel. And when the people of Israel heard they were afraid of the Philistines. [8] And the people of Israel said to Samuel, 'Do not cease to cry to the Lord our God for us that he may save us from the hand of the Philistines'. [9] So Samuel took a suckling lamb and offered it to the Lord. And Samuel cried out to the Lord for Israel and the Lord answered him. (I Sam. 7.5–9)

As Israel makes a repentant move towards God, Samuel is

spoken of as the one who calls them together at Mizpah, offering himself as the one who is willing to pray for them (v.5). The prayer is accompanied not only by fasting, but also by a rite with water, the latter, though we cannot know for sure, perhaps indicating repentance. Maybe we are intended to understand that the people made a solemn act of self-denial.[6] Perhaps the thought here is that repentance must take place before prayer can be made to God, a thought given expression in Ps. 66.18:

> If I had cherished iniquity in my heart,
>   The Lord would not have listened.

So Samuel made his prayer, a prayer of confession, 'We have sinned against the Lord' (v.6). We are told that 'Samuel judged the people of Israel at Mizpah', and this word 'judged' means both 'to judge' (that is, decide, arbitrate, between people), and also 'to deliver'. And indeed here it is surely being indicated that as the people repent, turn to God, and as they submit themselves to the ministry of Samuel – both in prayer and in other ways – the seeds and hopes of their deliverance are already to be glimpsed. But it is as if the Philistines take advantage of the Israelites' occupation with repentance and prayer to make threatening advances upon them, which call forth from the Israelites the request to Samuel that he would continue without ceasing to pray to the Lord, that his people might be freed from the hand of the Philistines (v.8). And Samuel, as well as making a sacrificial offering, did indeed continue to cry to the Lord, and we are told that the Lord answered him (v.9). We do not generally hear of sacrifice and prayer going together. Prayer may have been made at the time a sacrifice was offered, but we do not hear about this. We have already seen that prayer may be offered with fasting (Ezra 8.23: see Ch. 3 above), but this is not common. In the particular matter of seeking forgiveness of sins, there is a strong tradition in the Old Testament that this is to be effected through the provisions of the sacrificial system, but there is also that strand of thought – given expression, for example, in Solomon's prayer (I Kings 8.14–61; see Ch. 7 below) where forgiveness is effected through prayer alone.

But, to return to this particular story, the fact that what ensues is a decisive victory for the people of Israel, and a gruesome and seemingly bloodthirsty rout for the Philistines, should not blind us to the central theological thrust of the passage, namely, that Israel has turned to the Lord in repentance and has sought his deliverance for its life. The people have called upon Samuel to pray for them, and the belief has been recorded that the Lord answered his prayers. With the Lord there is available for his people this deliverance, but it must be sought: in this story, that seeking takes place through the people's repentance and Samuel's prayers.

The days in which Samuel lived and ministered were days of political transition from the rather occasional and episodic direction of the Judges to the time when Israel, like the nations round about, had a king, first Saul and then David. Within the books of Samuel are stories that are favourably disposed to the institution of kingship, while there are others that regard it in an unfavourable light, seeing it as a denial of the sole kingship of the Lord God. And indeed, we are not surprised that at the time the possibility of such a major new departure for Israel should have caused much discussion and disagreement. It is no great surprise to us, further, that at later stages people could look back upon the founding of the monarchy, and in the light of its successes and failures could have reflected upon whether or not it could have been the will of God that his people should have a king to govern them. Certainly, the abiding impression we are given of Samuel is of a man who really is not happy about this new institution in the life of his people. Thus we read:

> But the matter displeased Samuel when they said, 'Give us a king to rule us', and Samuel prayed to the Lord. (I Sam. 8.6)

Samuel is old here, and this verse comes from a part of I Sam. that tells how Israel came to have the first king, Saul (I Sam. 8–15). From what follows in I Sam. 8.7f. it seems that Samuel's prayer must have reflected his own great unease about the request of the people, and perhaps about the way that he perceived things were inevitably going. We are told how Samuel repeated to the people the message he felt he

The Ministry of Intercession

had received from the Lord through his prayers (v.10). Yet he warned the people that were they to appoint a king to rule over them, the day would come when *they* would be crying out in distress to the Lord (v.18)! Yet, hearing further requests from the people, Samuel had more to take to the Lord in prayer (v.21). Perhaps strictly speaking we are not dealing here with intercession, and yet what is being told is about a national wish that is being expressed, and through the person of prayer is being offered to God. We are given a picture of Samuel in prayerful conversation with God over the matter of this possible new direction for the people of Israel.

This ministry of prayer on the part of Samuel for his people is also reflected in parts of I Sam. 12, a chapter that seems certain to come from a time a good deal later than the days of Samuel, and that seeks to give an interpretation of the events recorded in I Sam. 1–11.[7] The particular interpretation in I Sam. 12 is decidedly negative as regards the kingship, but as the author looks back and draws his conclusions, so also he looks into the future, seeking to give both promise and warning. The author of this chapter seems most likely to have been closely connected with that 'school' of theological thought we call 'Deuteronomistic' (because its principal theological concerns are to be found in the book of Deuteronomy) and which most likely eventually issued in the Deuteronomistic history, an immense work that is made up of the books of Joshua, Judges, I and II Samuel, and I and II Kings. This tells the story of Israel from the time of the entry into the promised land, right through to the release from imprisonment in Babylon of King Jehoiachin. It is because some of the central themes of the book of Deuteronomy permeate the whole of the larger work that it has come to be known as the Deuteronomistic history.[8] At certain key points in this extensive work, the overriding theological viewpoint – perhaps we might say, 'bias' – is expressed. One place where this occurs is in I Sam. 12, while another is in II Kings 17. In I Sam. 12, it is Samuel who is speaking:

'Is it not wheat harvest today? I will call upon the Lord and he will send thunder and rain, and you will know and see that your wickedness is great indeed which you have committed in the sight of the Lord in asking for a king for yourselves'. [18] So Samuel called upon the Lord, and the Lord gave thunder and rain that day, and all the people greatly feared the Lord and Samuel. [19] And all the people said to Samuel, 'Pray to the Lord your God for your servants, that we may not die; for we have added to all our sins an evil in asking for ourselves a king'. [20] And Samuel said to the people, 'Fear not; you have done all this evil, yet do not turn aside from following the Lord, but serve the Lord with all your heart; [21] and do not turn aside after vain things which do not profit or save, for they are vain. [22] For the Lord will not cast away his people, because of his great name, for it has pleased the Lord to make you a people for himself. [23] Moreover, as for me, far be it from me that I should sin against the Lord by ceasing to pray for you, and I will instruct you in the good and right way.' (I Sam. 12.17–23)

There is much in this passage about Samuel as the intercessor of Israel. In v.17 we are told about his calling upon the Lord, in that instance not so much for his people's immediate good, but to demonstrate to them, to remind them, of the Lord's power and authority. When the crisis of thunder and rain at the wheat harvest is upon them, the people request Samuel to pray for them (v.19), here acknowledging their sin. Thus Samuel admonishes them to live in ways that are in accordance with the Lord's will (vv.20–22), while he acknowledges that were he to cease to pray for them he himself would be sinning (v.23)! Thus, he pledges himself not only to instruct them 'in the good and right way', but also to pray for them (v.23).

A ministry both of guidance to and prayer for people is not found on the part of all those who lead in the Old Testament. In the wisdom tradition, for example, there is no shortage of guidance being offered, but there is precious little comment about prayer, much less about leaders praying for people. And although it has often been observed that the prophetic ministry also included praying,[9] yet in the Deuteronomistic picture of the prophet in Deut. 18.15–18 there is no mention of the responsibility of the prophet to pray. Nevertheless, we can understand the pain that Jeremiah experienced when he was told by the Lord that he was *not* to pray for his people (Jer. 11.14; 14.11; 15.1).

We are reminded of the fact that St Paul in his letter to the Philippians, as well as giving guidance and instruction to Philippian Christians, also says:

> And this is my prayer, that your love may overflow more and more with knowledge and full insight . . . (Phil. 1.9)

Richard Baxter, in his *The Reformed Pastor*, speaks not only about the fact that Christian pastors 'must teach them [the members of the pastor's flock], as much as we can, of the *word* and *works* of God', but also that, 'It is very convenient to pray for the repentance and restoration even of the excommunicated . . .'[10]

But, to revert briefly to Samuel's intercessions, we noticed earlier that the Israelites requested Samuel that he would not cease to pray for them and their deliverance (I Sam. 7.8): here he solemnly assures them that he will indeed continue to pray for them. Thus, in their time of rapid political change, a time in which new things were taking place, days in which a series of tribes were moving into nationhood, a time in which there were inevitably pitfalls, especially as much authority and influence were being put into the hands of a single human being, they were assured of the intercessory ministry of Samuel on their behalf.

III

We consider now another setting in which intercession is made: again this is intercession generally by a particular individual, but the setting is that of the broken relationship between God and his people. It is the setting of sin – the setting of at times a 'great sin' (Ex. 32.31f.) – like the sin of the people of Sodom.

The city of Sodom, in the plain of the Dead Sea, is for the

Old Testament a byword for sin and corruption. In Gen. 13.13 we read, 'Now the people of Sodom were wicked, great sinners against the Lord', while in Gen. 19 some of the crimes of the city's people (vv.1–11) and the Lord's judgment upon them (vv.24–28) are spoken of. While Abraham and Lot were spared this dreadful destruction, both Old and New Testaments keep looking back at this fearful example of the divine judgment upon human sin.[11]

Our particular interest lies in Gen. 18.23–33 in which is a dialogue between Abraham and the Lord concerning the people of Sodom and their sin, but also about the possibility that there may be some, possibly only a few, righteous people in the city. Abraham seems to accept that the Lord is more than justified in bringing his searing judgment upon the sinful, but questions whether the Lord would be acting with justice were he to slay the righteous with the wicked. Thus it is that with much boldness Abraham approaches the Lord:

> Will you indeed sweep away the righteous with the wicked? Suppose there are fifty righteous people within the city; will you then sweep away the place and not forgive it for the fifty righteous who are in it? Far be it from you to do such a thing, to slay the righteous with the wicked! Far be that from you! Shall not the Judge of all the earth do what is just? (Gen. 18.23–25)

And to this impassioned appeal, the Lord responded:

> If I find at Sodom fifty righteous in the city, I will forgive the whole place for their sake. (Gen. 18.26)

Thus encouraged, Abraham continues:

> Let me take it upon myself to speak to the Lord, I who am but dust and ashes. Suppose five of the righteous are lacking? Will you destroy the whole city for lack of five? (Gen. 18.27–28a)

Abraham, we may notice, does not set himself up in any exalted relationship with the Lord. This is not a conversation between anything like equals! Rather, this is an appeal to the great Lord of all by a mere mortal on behalf of fellow human beings. This is to say that there is a sense of humility in the approach of Abraham to the Lord. Yet the Lord responds favourably:

> I will not destroy it if I find forty-five there. (Gen. 18.28b)

Then Abraham speaks of the possibility of there being just forty righteous people in the city: will the Lord destroy it then? No, comes back the reply: if forty righteous people are to be found there, the city will be spared. And so for thirty, and for twenty, and even finally for ten, Abraham receives the assurance from the Lord that the city will not be destroyed (vv.29–32). So comes the final verse of the passage:

> And the Lord went his way, when he had finished speaking to Abraham; and Abraham returned to his place. (Gen. 18.33)

So far I have called this a dialogue, a conversation, between Abraham and the Lord. But is this the correct description of this remarkable passage, or would it be more accurately described as an 'intercession', an intercession on the part of Abraham on behalf of the righteous he believes there are in the city? Is Abraham simply having a conversation with God – a philosophical discussion with him – about the possible fate of righteous people in the city and reflecting upon the morality of a divine judgment that may sweep *all* away, or is he rather going further than that and pleading, interceding, either for the righteous or for all in the city? C. Westermann in his detailed commentary on Genesis is one of those scholars who argues that it is *not* an intercession, but rather a dialogue between Abraham and God.[12] He says that this is not designated a prayer and nor does it have the fixed structure that we would expect in a prayer. To that we may reply that Cain's crying out to the Lord in Gen. 4.10 is not designated a prayer, but yet is I think fairly clearly a prayer. And as to the expectation that a prayer will have a fixed structure, we may observe that there are a variety of structures, and forms, of prayer in the Old Testament.

Here, it may be argued, the 'form' is that of a dialogue, but, as Miller puts it, 'its character as intercession is unmistakable'.[13] Further, it should be observed that this hardly has the appearance of a general dialogue between a man and his God: on the contrary, here is an impassioned appeal by Abraham in the face of what is otherwise likely to be the moment of nemesis for the city and people of Sodom. Surely we should call that a prayer!

Moreover, there is in this prayer one particular feature that we find in some of the Old Testament's intercessions, namely the appeal to some aspect of the nature of God. We shall witness this with the intercessions of Moses in the wilderness, but in the case of the prayer of Abraham it is an appeal to the 'justice' of God. Abraham prays to the Lord on the grounds that surely the Lord would not wish to do other than what was just: 'shall not the Judge of all the earth do what is just?' And Abraham, with a remarkable blending of humility ('I who am but dust and ashes') and boldness, seems to be suggesting that were the Lord to destroy all the people of Sodom, even though there may be a few who were righteous, might indeed be acting with less than justice.

However, though it may be reasonable on our part to describe Abraham's activity before God as prayer, it should be appreciated that the story before us is not intended to *instruct* us about aspects or details of prayer. Essentially it stands between the announcements of God's plans on the one hand for Abraham (18.17–19) and on the other for Sodom and Gomorrah (18.20f.). As regards these two cities a great 'outcry'[14] about the very grave sin of the place has come to the Lord. As it was with the builders of the tower of Babel (Gen. 11.5), so here, the Lord must go down to see what has happened. In the material that follows the prayer, we read of the destruction of the city, yet also the deliverance of Lot: 'So it was that, when God destroyed the cities of the valley, God remembered Abraham, and sent Lot out of the midst of the overthrow, when he overthrew the cities in which Lot dwelt' (19.29). The material that we are dealing with here is in the first place about sin and judgment, above all about the overwhelming sin of the people of Sodom. But the final form in which the material has been handed down to us speaks of the intercession of Abraham. Sodom still experiences the divine judgment, but the saving of Lot is portrayed as being owed to the intercession of Abraham.

But Abraham ended his prayer to the Lord having secured the promise that were the Lord to discern ten righteous people in the city, then, for their sake, he would not destroy it. But Abraham, having succeeded in his pleas that far, went no further. Why? Might he not have argued that were just five righteous to be found, then the city might be spared? But perhaps that would have been to go too far for a prayer. When Abraham was praying for Sodom he was making a plea to God on the twin grounds of the presence of a few righteous people and the divine justice. To have argued further with the Lord might have been to seek to manipulate him, to seek from him an assurance that would take away his authority and his freedom.[15] And that, I suggest, would not have been prayer. Yet, here – as Habakkuk would pray – in wrath, mercy is remembered (Hab. 3.2).

IV

But, as it has already been observed, one cannot speak about intercession in the Old Testament without speaking of Moses and his intercessory ministry. Psalm 106.23 remembers Moses as the great intercessor of old, who in a moment of grave crisis for Israel, caused by the sin in the desert of the manufacture of the golden calf and the failure of the people to trust in the Lord (Ex. 32.11–14), was able to avert the divine wrath and save his people from destruction:

> And he said he would destroy them
>   had not Moses, his chosen one,
> stood in the breach before him
>   to turn away his anger from destroying them. (Ps. 106.23)

The expression 'stand in the breach' has a military flavour about it, suggesting the idea of an individual, or maybe a group, who stands in the break of a wall against many and much, and without whose action the defenders would be overrun. Perhaps we are also to understand that there is implied in the expression the element of danger involved for a person making such a stand. Thus Moses is depicted as by his intercession 'standing in the breach' and so averting the judgmental wrath of God upon his people.

This intercession of Moses was at a time when his people had sinned gravely, and is to be found in Ex. 32.1–14, verses that hold in focus two scenes: that on the mountain where matters are seen from a divine point of view, and that on the earth, where events take place that reveal deep human failure and sin. The only human who appears in both of these scenes is Moses. Moreover, Moses is active in both of these worlds, and will seek to interpret one party to the other, to mediate between the two when the gulf has become very great. Ex. 32.1–10 tells us of the people's becoming impatient with Moses' extended absence on the mountain, of their wondering what has happened to him, and of their call to Aaron to make 'gods' for them who would go before them (v.1). And so it was that under Aaron's leadership the golden calf was made. We are told of the Lord's reaction to this turn of events:

> Now let me alone, so that my wrath may burn hot against them; and of you [singular!] I will make a great nation. (Ex. 32.10)

Then, in vv.11–14, follows Moses' intercession to the Lord on behalf of his people, now in a dire situation:

> And Moses besought the Lord his God, saying, 'O Lord, why does your anger burn against your people whom you have brought out of the land of Egypt with great power and a mighty hand? [12] Why should the Egyptians say, "With evil design he brought them out to slay them in the mountains and to consume them from the face of the earth"? Turn from your fierce anger and turn from this disaster against your people. [13] Remember Abraham, Isaac and

Israel, your servants to whom you swore by your own self, saying to them, "I will multiply your descendants as the stars of heaven, and all this land which I have promised I will give to your descendants, and they shall inherit it forever".' [14] And the Lord repented of the disaster which he said he would do to his people. (Ex. 32.11–14)

As Abraham made his appeal to the Lord on the 'grounds' that surely the Judge of all the earth will do what is just, so here Moses makes his appeal to God on the basis of a number of 'grounds'. The first of these is that Israel is the Lord's people whom with great power and a mighty hand he has brought out of Egypt (v.11). Can the Lord really now be content with the destruction of those whom he has both chosen and delivered? The second 'ground' of Moses' appeal is that the Lord has already expended much power and might in bringing his people thus far (v.11). The third is that were the Lord to destroy his people, he would be inviting the mockery of the Egyptians for his apparent motive of bringing his people into the wilderness, only to slay them in the mountains (v.12). The fourth is to the morality of the Lord: not to bring them into the new land would be to fail to keep his ancient word to the ancestors of these people (v.13). All this is to say that Moses seeks to lay a range of considerations before the Lord. That his people are under judgment is not questioned by Moses; he does nothing to suggest that they are not guilty. It is as if he accepts that were the nature of God to be only wrath and judgment there would be no questions over the issue and its outcome. But it is as if Moses appealed to *other* aspects of the nature of God. He appeals to the mercy of the Lord, a mercy that had earlier been revealed in his choosing these particular people and in his working for their deliverance from the Egyptians. But Moses does not see things only from the human perspective – where he seeks rather jealously to protect the reputation of his Lord among the nations! – but also ranges himself on the divine side of things, seeking to remind the Lord of his ancient promises and his reputation. Moses does not seek to manipulate the Lord, merely to make an impassioned appeal to him. And we are told that in the face of this impassioned appeal, the Lord repented, and did not destroy his people (v.14).

We need to pause and give consideration to the three parties spoken about here. First, there are the people who have been loved, chosen, led and delivered. They have been called upon to be loyal to and trusting in God, and they have failed on both counts, manufacturing alternative deities whom they believe will lead them on their way. They now stand under the judgment of God.

Then, secondly, there is the Lord God who has been forsaken and not trusted, though it is he who has loved, chosen, led, and delivered his people. He has been utterly loyal to these people, and he demands loyalty from them. In the absence of this responding loyalty his judgmental wrath burns.

Yet the result of the intercession of Moses was that God 'repented', 'changed his mind', concerning the disaster which he had declared would take place. The prophet Jonah maintained that it was because of this aspect of the nature of God that he was chary of going to Nineveh to preach:

> For I knew that you are a gracious God and merciful, slow to anger, and abounding in steadfast love, and ready to relent from punishing. (Jonah 4.2; see also 3.9f.)

Of course, other parts of the Old Testament stress the immutability (the unchangeableness) of God:

> God is not a human being, that he should lie,
> or a mortal, that he should change his mind. (Num. 23.19)

> Moreover the Glory of Israel will not recant or change his mind; for he is not a mortal, that he should change his mind. (I Sam. 15.29)

> The Lord has sworn and will not change his mind. (Ps. 110.4)

Further, it is because of this immutability of God that his covenant people can truly put their trust in him:

> For I the Lord do not change; therefore you, O children of Jacob, have not perished. Ever since the days of your

ancestors you have turned aside from my statutes and have not kept them. (Mal. 3.6f.)

Yet this unchanging God may change his mind! And this because he is the God of mercy and compassion who ever thus gives hope to the sinners and purpose to those who make intercession for the sinners:

> For their sake he remembered his covenant,
>   and showed compassion according to the abundance of his steadfast love.
> He caused them to be pitied
>   by all who held them captive. (Ps. 106.45f.)

Thus Moses prayed for the people with the result that:

> . . . the Lord changed his mind about the disaster that he planned to bring on his people. (Ex. 32.14)[16]

P. D. Miller says,

> The Scriptures persistently testify that the heart of God is moved by the importuning prayers of chosen servants and that a dimension of the divine consistency is precisely the continuing inclination of God towards a merciful dealing with humankind, and especially those who are God's people. What is clear from the motivating appeals of Moses is that the prayer is not for the arbitrary or inconsistent action on God's part. It is a prayer for the divine will and purpose as it has been manifested over and over again – a faithful, redemptive, forgiving purpose grounded in perduring relationships and constantly being vindicated before the public audience of peoples and nations.[17]

This naturally leads us to talk about the last of the three parties, Moses, who appears to be at home with both his people and God, who in this story, as has been observed, is indeed portrayed as being both on earth (with his people) and also on the mountain (with God). And while undoubtedly it is God who repents and forgives, and does not destroy his people (v.14), yet the story accords a very significant place to Moses

and what he does by way of mediation between the people and
the Lord. It is Moses who both gives explanation as to the
Lord's anger over their conduct and lack of faith, and who also
on their behalf intercedes with God and seeks to avert the divine
judgment. That these sinful people have any future is portrayed
as owing at least in some measure to the fact that Moses prayed
for them.

The book of Deuteronomy has a parallel version of this intercession of Moses. It occurs in Deut. 9.25–29, a part of the
Second Address of Moses to Israel (Deut. 4.44 28.68):

> So I lay prostrate before the Lord for forty days and forty
> nights, for the Lord had said he would destroy you.
> [26] I prayed to the Lord, saying, 'Lord God, do not destroy
> your people and your heritage, whom you have redeemed
> through your greatness, whom you have brought out of
> Egypt with a mighty hand. [27] Remember your servants,
> Abraham, Isaac and Jacob, and do not regard the stubborn-
> ness of this people, or their wickedness or their sin, [28] lest
> the land from which you brought us say, "Because the Lord
> was not able to bring them into the land which he promised
> to them, and because he hated them, he has brought them
> out to slay them in the wilderness". [29] For they are your
> people and your heritage, whom you brought by your great
> power and your outstretched arm.' (Deut. 9.25–29)

If anything there is a heightened intensity now to the matter of
Moses' interceding for his people: here the intercession has to
take place over many days and nights ('forty days and forty
nights'). Moses is here portrayed as working even harder for the
forgiveness of the Lord in the face of this sin of his people!
Then, once again, there follows the impassioned plea on behalf
of a people who have gone disastrously astray. It is as if
Moses is searching around for grounds upon which he can make
his appeal to the mercy of God! So he reminds God that these
people are 'his' (God's) people, his 'heritage' (v.26); they are
descendants of the Lord's servants of old, Abraham, Isaac and
Jacob: surely the Lord will remember them rather than the
sins of the present generation (v.27); if the Lord now lets his

The Ministry of Intercession

people perish, then it will appear that he did not have the full measure, or reserves, of power to fulfil his purposes (v.28). And – as if to make sure that the matter has been stated with sufficient clarity, and the Lord really does understand! – the prayer ends with a repetition of the appeal to God that these people are his, the Lord's.

Once again, we see here the emphasis that any decision over life and death for these sinful people depends in the first place upon the Lord's mercy to them: without that mercy in full measure there can be no hope for them. And yet at the same time the human action and involvement of Moses play a vital part in securing a continued life for those who have sinned. Their future is portrayed as also dependent upon Moses' prayers for them. We are not told what might have happened had not Moses prayed for these people, or alternatively had there been no other intercessor to pray for them: what these stories do point up is the role of the human being, a person of prayer, whose words and acts contribute to what will take place in coming days.

There is a further prayer of Moses in connection with the incident of the golden calf that we need to consider. It is in Ex. 32.30–34, and introduces us to another aspect of the matter: the possibility that Moses' life be taken for their sin.

> On the morrow Moses said to the people, 'You have sinned a great sin. And now I will go up to the Lord; perhaps I can make atonement for your sin'. [31] So Moses returned to the Lord, saying, 'Ah now! this people has sinned a great sin, and they have made for themselves gods of silver. [32] But now, if you will forgive their sin, but if not, blot me out of your book which you have written'. [33] But the Lord said to Moses, 'Whoever has sinned against me, I will blot out of my book. [34] But now, go, lead the people where I told you. Behold my angel will go before you [singular]. And on the day of punishment, I will punish them for their sins.' (Ex. 32.30–34)

Now we cannot be completely sure just what the writer had in mind when he wrote these words. The words of v.32, 'But now, if you will forgive their sin, but if not, blot me out of your book . . .' are not easy to understand, and in fact the original Hebrew here is not totally straightforward.[18] The question is this: is this verse talking about Moses not wishing to live any longer if his people cannot live,[19] or is the intended sense that Moses is actually offering his life for the sin of the people? If it is the latter then we have here the thought of Moses offering himself to suffer *vicariously* on behalf of his people in their sin. My own judgment is that the language of v.30, with its 'perhaps I can make atonement for your sin', suggests that we are dealing with just such a matter of vicarious suffering, and that Moses is speaking about his possible attempt to do something *for* his people rather than merely *with* them. In this situation of what is acknowledged to be a serious sin (both vv.30 and 31 speak of a 'great sin') Moses appears to offer his life that the sinners might live.

But what happened as a result of this intercession by Moses? The matter seems to be left open, and the text is rather vague. Perhaps this vagueness is intentional, for there is a grappling with great themes here: divine wrath, divine mercy, human sinfulness, intercession, and atonement. On the one hand the Lord still makes threatening noises, still speaking about blotting out of his book whoever has sinned against him (v.33), and yet, on the other hand, Moses is told to go and lead the people on the way ahead (v.34). While Moses is promised that the Lord's angel will go before him (that is, before Moses – singular! – v.34a), at the same time there is the warning of the impending judgment upon Israel: 'And on the day of punishment, I will punish them for their sin' (v.34b). Yet what clearly has happened is that an intercessor has offered his life that his people may be forgiven. One commentator has observed that, '. . . in between Israel was the mediator, who wrestled with God and stood in the breach. Alongside the figure of Moses as the great law giver stands Moses the intercessor, who knowing the full wrath of God, shielded Israel from its full force and secured for his people the renewal of the promise.'[20]

V

So we come back to the picture of Moses given in Ps. 106.23, as the one who stood in the breach between the destroying anger of the Lord and the sinful people:

> And he said he would destroy them
>   had not Moses, his chosen one,
> stood in the breach before him
>   to turn away his anger from destroying them.

Certainly in the case of Moses this ministry of intercession had uncomfortable moments, times of seeming danger. What sort of people undertook, or were called to undertake, such tasks? Some years ago it was a commonplace of Old Testament scholarship that the prophets were called to a ministry of intercession,[21] as well as proclamation, but more recently this has been questioned. It has been pointed out that we do not have a great number of references in the Old Testament to prophets who actually intercede for their people.[22] The evidence as to an intercessory ministry of prophets is in fact somewhat mixed. On the one hand it is as a prophet that Abraham is appealed to that he will pray for Abimelech – who had taken Sarah. The message given through a dream concerning Abraham is that, 'he is a prophet, and he will pray for you and you shall live.' (Gen. 20.7). Yet on the other hand the Deuteronomic picture of a prophet, who will be like Moses of old, makes no mention of a prophet praying (Deut. 18.15–18). Equally, Samuel has a prophetic role, and clearly he prays for his people, and his people expect him to continue to pray for them (I Sam. 12.19, 23). And Amos certainly prays for his people, and like Moses does so in a setting where there has been great sin. Thus Amos is the announcer of a coming judgment of terrible proportions (3.11; 5.2–3; 6.9,14; 7.17; 8.3; 9.10 etc.) But he is also portrayed as interceding for his people, at least in the first two of the five visions (7.1–8.3; 9.1–4) about the coming judgment. In the first vision (7.1–3) it is a locust swarm that, as a divine judgment, is about to eat the grass of the land, and

Amos prays that God will forgive. The second vision (7.4–6) is of a rain of fire, and again Amos intercedes:

> How can Jacob stand?
> He is so small.
> > The Lord relented concerning this . . . (Amos 7.2b–3a, 7.5b–6a)

Amos appeals to the mercy of God on the grounds that Israel is so small. His tone is full of irony: these are the very people who by oppressing and exploiting the poor of the land have made themselves, at least by earthly standards, great and powerful! But in the wider scheme of things they are small, and Amos now ranges himself on the side of these weak ones and appeals for them in the face of the mighty judgment of God.[23]

While Amos *does* intercede for his people, on the other hand Hosea does *not*. Yet throughout the book of Hosea is the people's sin and the Lord's judgment, and ever for this prophet a terrible tension on the part of God between his faithfulness to his people and his judgment upon sin. Hosea speaks of religious corruption and coming disaster (1.2–6, 8f.; 2.2–5, 8–13; 4.1–19; 12.2–10), and yet at times feels that God's love for his people is such that he cannot give them up (11.1–9). Thus one day there could be an ingathering of exiles (11.11) and a renewal of the fertility of the land (2.21–23; 14.5–8). Yet nowhere is this prophet portrayed as one who on his own stands directly in the breach between the divine judgment and the human sin. Nor does he tell his people in imperative commands to return to the Lord, but rather associates himself with those who *together* must return. Thus, speaking in the first person plural, the prophet says,

> Come, let us return to the Lord;
> > for it is he who has torn, and he will heal us;
> > he has struck down, and he will bind us up.
> After two days he will revive us;
> > on the third day he will raise us up,
> > that we may live before him.

The Ministry of Intercession

Let us know, let us press on to know the Lord;
>his appearing is as sure as the dawn;
he will come on us like the showers,
>like the spring rains that water the earth. (Hos. 6.1–3)

With Hosea 14.1 the prophet speaks as one who proclaims the word of the Lord. In the name of the Lord he commands his people to return to their God:

Return, O Israel, to the Lord your God,
>for you have stumbled because of your iniquity.
(Hos. 14.1)

But then he seeks to help them to do so. Perhaps, like Moses, he might have prayed for them. In fact what he does do is to give them the words with which they might approach the Lord. He gives them their words of confession to God:

Take words with you
>and return to the Lord;
say to him,
>'Take away all guilt;
accept that which is good,
>and we will offer
the fruit of our lips.
Assyria shall not save us;
>We will not ride upon horses;
We will say no more "Our God,"
>to the work of our hands.
In you the orphan finds mercy.' (Hos. 14.2f.)

What is this? Is this a different model for intercession? Here is the intercessor giving the sinners the words for their humble approach to God, to ask for his forgiveness. Thus, has intercession become petition? Whereas with Moses there was intercession made by one on behalf of the many, now the one gives to the many their words of confession and petition. Certainly, it represents what we might call a more 'congregational' approach, what the Old Testament might refer to as 'all the assembly' making its prayer. And maybe that was indeed perceived to be more effective, perhaps even necessary, if there was to be a *true* turning to God. While there was a Moses to make powerful intercession, there the danger lurked that were sin to take place again, so intercession might again be made for the sinners! As long as there was a Moses, all would be well! As sin abounded, so might human intercession, as well as divine grace, abound (cf. Rom. 6.1)! It may be that there is something of this in the somewhat unresolved ending to the Ex. 32.30–34 incident we considered earlier, where we are not told whether or not the people were forgiven. Is there perhaps in that story the suggestion that the repentance of the Israelites was not sufficiently heart-felt and radical, that what was needed was repentance on the part of each person. Is this perhaps the significance of Hosea giving to his people their prayer with which they may come in repentance to the Lord?

VI

Certainly, the book of Jeremiah tells of the expectation that the prophet will pray for his people and of this taking place. In Jer. 42 we read of those who came to the prophet to ask for his intercession on their behalf (v.2), how he responds to them (v.4), and about how he reports back to them (v.9). Moreover, Jer. 37.3 records how Jeremiah, *as a prophet*, was requested by Zedekiah to pray for himself and his fellow leaders of the nation. Then in Jer. 14.21 we read how the prophet intercedes for his people in a setting of sinfulness, while 18.20 records how Jeremiah did stand before the Lord to plead for them.

But then in striking contrast is the divine command recorded in the book more than once that the prophet is *not* to pray for his people (Jer. 7.16; 11.14; 14.11, 13; 15.1). Nothing like this is found elsewhere in the Old Testament books of the prophets. The command of the Lord to Jeremiah not to intercede for his people, recorded in 7.16, comes in the context of the condemnation of false worship, the prophet's condemnation of the cult of the queen of heaven, and the force of the command is expressed in the use of a number of words for prayer:

> As for you, do not pray (*hithpallel*) for this people, do not raise a cry (*rinnāh*) or a prayer (*tᵉpillāh*), and do not intercede (*pāgaᶜ*) with me, for I will not hear you.[24]

Again in Jer. 11.14 the command not to pray comes in the context of idolatrous practices, and in 14.11 because of the people's wandering from the Lord. But it is in 15.1 that the command is expressed perhaps the most forcefully, in that reference is made to the names of Moses and Samuel and clearly thereby to their reputations as intercessors of old:

> And the Lord said to me, 'Even though Moses and Samuel stood before me, my heart would not turn toward this people. Send them out of my sight, and let them go!' (Jer. 15.1)

What seems to be intended here is that the sin of 'this people' is now so great that not even the intercessions of Moses and Samuel would be able to save them. Whereas at one moment far back in history the Lord gave command through Moses his servant to the Pharaoh that his people must be allowed to go free, now there is a new command from the Lord that his people must go – but go now, that is, out of the sight of the Lord!

What are we to make of this? Is the Lord's mercy at an end (cf. Ps. 77.8)? Or is it intercession that no longer has the effectiveness it was once believed to have? It seems that we must accept that in the tradition of theological thought that has come down to us in the book of Jeremiah, the sin of the people is regarded as so great and serious that forgiveness cannot any longer be considered possible through the medium of intercession. Now the judgment must take place: no longer could even a Moses stand in the breach! The only hope for the future would lie in a more radical renewal of the relationship between the Lord and his people than anything that an intercessor was able to offer. In the book of Jeremiah, while on the one hand we have the divine command to the prophet *not* to seek the forgiveness of his people's sin through prayer, at the same time we do have expressions of hope for the future (especially in chs 30–31)! Clearly, at least in the completed form of the book, there is envisaged a real future for these sinners, a renewed relationship with God. But it will be a deeply renewed relationship: obedience to a set of instructions and teachings will no longer be an external requirement. In the future envisaged here there will be an inward orientation to God and his will.

> I will put my law within them, and I will write it on their hearts; and I will be their God, and they shall be my people. No longer shall they teach one another, or say to each other, 'Know the Lord,' for they shall all know me, from the least of them to the greatest, says the Lord; for I will forgive their iniquity, and remember their sin no more. (Jer. 31.33b–34)

Jeremiah's command from the Lord that he must not pray for his sinful people is a reflection upon the depth of sin into which they have sunk. It is not that prophetic intercession is at an end, is found wanting, or is no longer effective. It may in this instance be ineffective, but that is because the sin is so great! While it may be going too far to say that in the office of the Hebrew prophet there was the call to intercede for, as well as to proclaim to, the evidence that we have does suggest that many prophets regularly *did* pray for their people. This is not to say that *all* prophets did intercede, but it is to suggest that those who passed on for future generations the traditions and preaching of the great prophets believed that from time to time some of them made intercession for their people.

VII

But before we leave intercession – and the prophets – we should say something about the one spoken of in Isa. 52.13–53.12, whom we are accustomed to refer to as the 'Servant'.[25] This 'Servant' of the Lord is represented not only as being numbered with the transgressors, but as bearing the sins of many, and, further, as making intercession for the transgressors. Here, as well as the sense of solidarity with the sinners, is the intercessor who appears to give his life. The following is the translation of Isa. 53.10–12 in the rendering of NRSV:[26]

v.10 Yet it was the will of the Lord
to crush him with pain.
When you make his life an
offering for sin,
he shall see his offspring, and
shall prolong his days;
through him the will of the Lord shall prosper.

v.11 Out of his anguish he shall see light;
he shall find satisfaction through his knowledge.
The righteous one, my servant,
shall make many righteous,
and he shall bear their iniquities.

v.12 Therefore I will allot him a
portion with the great,
and he shall divide the spoil
with the strong;
because he poured out himself to death,
and was numbered with the transgressors;
yet he bore the sins of many,
and made intercession for the transgressors.

But whose sin is it that is being spoken of in Isa. 52.13–53.12? A central theological theme of the prophet we call Second Isaiah (Isa. 40–55) was that a new beginning awaited the exiles. They had served their sentence, paid their penalty, had received from the Lord's hand double for their sins (Isa. 40.2). In contrast to almost all his prophetic predecessors, this prophet spoke of a future of great joy, peace and prosperity. Moreover, it is the Lord, and the Lord alone, who is portrayed as out of his own faithfulness and love – without human prompting, sacrifice, offering or intercession – forgiving his people their sins. What sins then will the 'Servant' of Isa. 53 bear, and for whom will he make intercession? We can hardly avoid the conclusion that the prophet perceived that in days to come forgiveness of sin would be effected by an intercessor who would himself be closely bound-up with his people, ready not only to intercede for them, but willing further to give his righteous life (v.9) that many might be made righteous (v.11).

Moreover, it would seem that in this vision of how the work of the forgiveness of sin might be effected in the future there is the thought that the Servant will be a Moses-like figure.[27] For it was Moses who said to his people,

> You have sinned a great sin. But now I will go up to the Lord; perhaps I can make atonement for your sin. (Ex. 32.30)

And of the Servant it was said,

> Because he poured out himself to death,
>   and was numbered with the transgressors;
> yet he bore the sin of many,
>   and made intercession for the transgressors. (Isa. 53.12b)

As indeed it was to be in the fulness of time, and we believe now is:[28]

> Who is to condemn? It is Christ Jesus who died, yes, who was raised, who is at the right hand of God, who indeed intercedes for us. (Rom. 8.34)

5

'Man . . . is full of trouble'
Prayers from the Depths

I

One of the last of the many letters that Baron Friedrich von Hügel (1852–1925) wrote was to his niece, Mrs Gwendolen Greene. He knew that his death could not be far away, and he wrote, 'I wait for the breath of God, for God's breath. Perhaps he will call me today – to-night.' And later in the letter comes:

> Keep your life a life of prayer, dearie. – Keep it like that: it's the only thing, and remember, no joy without suffering – no patience without trial – no humility without humiliation – no life without death.[1]

The Baron, in speaking of prayer, spoke also about suffering, trial, humiliation and death; indeed, the suggestion is surely there in his words that without the life of prayer, how will a person be able to deal with suffering, trial, humiliation, and death.

Chapters 12–14 of the book of Job contain Job's long speech at the end of the first round of the speeches of his friends. The tale of Job's sufferings has been told (chs 1–2) and Job has spoken (ch 3). The first of the friends – the Comforters – Eliphaz, speaks (chs 4–5) and Job responds (chs 6–7), followed by the second, Bildad (ch 8). After Job's response to what he has to say (ch 9f.), the third friend, Zophar, speaks (ch 11). Then comes the reply of Job at the end of all this cycle of speeches, and in his long contribution he moves from his own situation of suffering to that of humanity in more general terms. So he says:

> Man, born of woman,
>   is few of days, and full of trouble. (Job 14.1)

It is with times of trouble, and a person's prayers to God at such times, that we are now concerned, and we shall return to Job and the tale of his, and our, sufferings, and to his prayers and his relationship with God. But we shall come back to the book of Job by way of three books of the prophets – Habakkuk, Jonah and Jeremiah. Each of these prophets in his own way might have been able to accept the aphorism of Job for himself, that man, born of woman, is few of days, yet full of trouble! Yet each of them in his own way kept his life, 'a life of prayer'.

II

We turn first to the book of Habbakuk,[2] a book that is of interest to us in that no less than half the verses of the whole book are parts of prayers. That is, over half the book is expressed in the language of prayer. There is no other prophetic book in the Old Testament like it. After the opening title (1.1), we are given the first prayer in the book. It is in 1.2–4, and it is a prayer of 'complaint', in the style of those 'laments' we have already encountered.

> v.2 O Lord, how long shall I cry for help,
>   and you will not listen?
>   Or cry to you 'Violence!'
>   and you will not save?
> v.3 Why do you make me see wrong-doing
>   and look at trouble?
>   Destruction and violence are before me;
>   strife and contention arise.
> v.4 So the law becomes slack
>   and justice never prevails.
>   The wicked surround the righteous -
>   therefore judgment comes forth perverted. (Hab. 1.2–4)

The distress that the prophet experiences here springs from the fact that he cries to God for help, and God seems not to hear. His cry to God is because there is violence in the land, and God seems to do nothing to save those who are suffering as a result of it (v.2). In v.3 the prayer goes on (the prophet making no attempt to keep his feelings to himself!) in complaint to God that he has to observe wrong doing and to look at trouble. Indeed, all around him are destruction, violence, strife and contention! It is indeed a troubled world on to which this prophet looks. But what are the troubles at which he is looking? Verse 4 speaks about the law, instruction, becoming slack, and justice not prevailing; about the wicked surrounding the righteous, and judgments coming forth perverted. Though not all would agree, my own feeling is that the scene is one of internal Judaean corruption and the breakdown of social life, a situation in which the rights of the less fortunate and least powerful of the nation are not being protected.[3] Powerful people are taking advantage of the weak. The 'wicked', I suggest, are wicked people within the nation, and the 'righteous' are those who are without power and influence, and who find themselves both oppressed and also dispossessed. At any rate, the prophet makes what is to him a sad and terrible scene of suffering and injustice the subject of his prayer of complaint to God. Here are mortals around him, and in their day so full of trouble! We might argue that as the prophet was crying out to God over the scene of suffering and injustice, he was thereby praying for those who were suffering, and so was engaged in an act of intercession. That would be a legitimate way of understanding this prayer, but it may also be acceptable to understand it more in petitionary terms: the prophet is praying for himself over what is to him a distressing observation of the sufferings and grievances of others. As he observes the tragic lot of certain members of his nation, he personally experiences a sense of anguish and anger, and protests that God appears neither to hear prayers, nor to make speed to save.

But the prophet receives an answer from the Lord, and this is passed on to those around in the conventional way in which a prophet's word would be expressed, as a word from the Lord. But it is not a word that will bring immediate enlightenment:

indeed, the prophet warns his people that they will be astonished, astounded, for the Lord is engaging in a 'strange work' (1.5). This 'strange work' is nothing less than an invasion of the Chaldeans, 'that fierce and impetuous nation' (v.6). Though the matter has been endlessly debated, I suggest that we should accept that the Chaldeans spoken about here are the historical Babylonians who shortly before 600 BC, in the period of the collapse of the Assyrian Empire, established their rule in Mesopotamia. At that time, Egypt was comparatively weak, and thus the Chaldeans were able to move into Judaean and neighbouring lands in Syria-Palestine. What is truly 'strange' about this work of the Lord is the fierceness and arrogance with which these Chaldeans descend upon Judaeans:

> They all come for violence,
>   with faces pressing forward;
>   they gather captives like sand.
> At kings they scoff,
>   and of rulers they make sport.
> They laugh at every fortress,
>   and heap up earth to take it.
> Then they sweep by like the wind;
>   they transgress and become guilty;
>   and their own might is their god! (Hab. 1.9–11)

But if the prophet complained about the wrongdoing among his own people (1.2–4), how can he now complain about what the Lord is doing, strange though that may seem to be in its violence? It was common for the Hebrew prophets to proclaim that the Lord used the great nations to be his agents in the work of judging his own people.[4] So if the arrival of the violent Chaldeans is really an answer to the problem with internal corruption, then here is a further problem! And I think that we do have to read this book in this way, and to understand that the prophet Habakkuk was troubled both by Judaean injustices and *also* by Chaldean rapaciousness. Not only did this prophet cry out over the matter of corruption and lack of justice among his own people, but he was also calling into question that Hebrew prophetical doctrine that the Lord was using the

Chaldeans as his agents of divine judgment. All this is to say that the prophet Habakkuk is confronted with at least two major theological problems as he looks at his contemporary scene. He feels that he is forced to witness a world-order in which the dominant features are corruption and violence. Moreover, the traditional teaching of the Hebrew prophets about God bringing judgment upon corruption and sin through the rule of another nation only added to this prophet's theological problem.

There is just one more matter to consider in regard to the Judaean internal corruption (1.2–4), and then we may proceed. We may perhaps be able to locate these incidents that Habakkuk observed rather more precisely. The references in 1.6 and 9 seem to be to the forward march of a Babylonian army into Syria–Palestine, and we may point to the Babylonian victory in 605 BC at the battle of Carchemish when the Egyptians were defeated. Now the Babylonians were masters in Syria-Palestine. A year or so later, in 604 or 603 BC, the Judaean king Jehoiakim, who reigned in Jerusalem from 609 to 594 BC became the vassal, the 'servant' (II Kings 24.1) of the Babylonian king, Nebuchadnezzar. This further suggests that the internal Judaean social ills spoken about in 1.2–4 were those perpetrated in Jehoiakim's reign. We read of Jehoiakim shedding much innocent blood (II Kings 24.4), while Jeremiah's words about him were caustic in the extreme (Jer. 22.13–19; 26.1–23). Such ills as these would have been more than adequate grounds for Habbakuk's complaint in 1.2–4.

The prophet's response to this is to pray! It is an agonized prayer, in which the prophet asks how the Lord, who by nature is set against evil, can allow such evil as he now observes, to be perpetrated.

> Hab. 1.12 Are you not from of old,
> O Lord my God, my Holy One?
> You shall not die.
> O Lord, you have marked them for judgment;
> and you, O Rock, have established them for punishment.

v.13 Your eyes are too pure to behold evil,
    and you cannot look on wrongdoing;
Why do you look on the treacherous,
    and are silent when the wicked swallow
    those more righteous than they?

v.14 You have made people like the fish of the sea,
    like crawling things that have no ruler.

v.15 The enemy brings all of them up with a hook;
    he drags them out with his net,
he gathers them in his seine;
    so he rejoices and exults.

v.16 Therefore he sacrifices to his net,
    and makes his offerings to his seine;
for by them his portion is lavish,
    and his food is rich.

v.17 Is he then to keep on emptying his net,
    and destroying nations without mercy?

This is an 'angry' prayer, certainly not expressed in 'polite' language to the Lord. We have met this type of prayer in what we term the 'laments', both individual and corporate, in the book of Psalms. But the tone here is particularly impassioned, and even the elements of praise of the Lord in the opening verse ('old', 'Holy One') are soon turned against the Lord in questions as to the ways in which he appears to have made things in the world and let them continue. The prophet is questioning the Lord over the matter of the injustice in the world he is forced to observe in his day. The prophet poses the question 'why?' to God (v.13), and whereas we might have expected in the final verse the question 'how long?', the tone is if anything sharper, with its suggestion that such things look set to go on forever!

In ch. 2 we hear how the prophet set about waiting for the response of God to his complaints. Habakkuk takes his place of 'watching' (2.1), is commanded to write down what he sees, and is assured that he will be answered. There may well be a delay; he may have to wait; but eventually there will be the answer. In the meantime, he is to be faithful – not acting in the wicked ways he sees around him (vv.4f.) – and is assured, in a series of woes (2.6–19) that the fate of the wicked is sealed. Chapter 2 ends with the assurance that God is in his temple, and all the earth is called to be silent before him (2.20).

The answer, such as it is, comes in ch. 3, and is cast in the main in the form of a mighty theophany. It begins with a recollection of God's work in the past, and prays for a revival of it in the present (vv.1f.). Then in vv.3–7 comes the description of the theophany (the appearance in great power) of the Lord, and the following verses describe God's victory over the forces of evil (vv.8–15). And the result for the prophet of all this is that he is possessed of a new hope and confidence for the future. Moreover, were things to get even worse, were there to be even greater disasters that he must experience, yet he would be able to rejoice in the Lord, and exalt in the God of his salvation (v.18).

> Hab. 3.17 Though the fig tree does not blossom,
> and no fruit is on the vines;
> though the produce of the olive fails
> and the fields yield no food;
> though the flock is cut off from the fold
> and there is no herd in the stalls,
> v.18 yet I will rejoice in the Lord;
> I will exalt in the God of my salvation.
> v.19 God, the Lord, is my strength;
> he makes my feet like the feet of a deer,
> and makes me tread upon the heights.

All this ch. 3 of the book is called, in its superscription, a 'prayer', and the fact that there is such a title in 3.1 must be indicative that the author intended the verses that follow to be clearly understood as prayer. The whole of the book of Habakkuk is dealing with an issue of theodicy: how can the prophet go on believing in a God of power, justice and mercy at the same time as witnessing such crimes against humanity – and injustice between people taking place in his contemporary world? And it seems that the only answer that the prophet can come up with is in the language of worship, in particular of prayer. Indeed, the main statements of the prophet's problems have been expressed in the language of prayers (1.2–4, 12–17), and now the answer is expressed also in prayer! We are surely intended to understand that it is only in prayer that Habakkuk comes to appreciate the continuing presence and victory of the Lord on earth – even though the immediate worldly scene around him may suggest either that God is aloof or is not acting with justice. But it is in prayer that the prophet is portrayed as coming to a renewed appreciation of the majesty, the justice and the saving presence of the Lord. And it is perhaps because such things as this are only glimpsed by believers in prayer, that the matter can be communicated to others through the medium of the language of prayer.[5] Any answer that Habakkuk can give to the questions of life, 'Why?', 'How long?', can only be in the language of prayer, in crying out to God, and in prayerful recollection of what God has done, who he is, and what he will do.[6]

III

I turn now to another of the prophets, to Jonah, where the subject of prayer, I suggest, concerns the difficulties and the burdens of mission, of going out into the world in the name and service of the Lord. While Habakkuk's problem is to do with the seeming injustice of the reign of God in the world, the problem that the book of Jonah handles concerns the demands that the Lord makes on his people when he calls them to go out into the world in his name, and the difficulties they experience as they seek to be faithful in response to his call.[7] The book of Jonah stands apart from other prophetic books of the Old Testament in that it is a narrative *about* a prophet. Moreover it is the story of how a prophet was *not* faithful to the call of God! Thus it has been observed that Jonah is portrayed as an anti-prophet.[8]

The story told in the book can be briefly summarized. Ch. 1.1–3 tells how the Lord calls Jonah to go to Nineveh to 'cry out against it', and about how Jonah seeks to escape

Prayers from the Depths

from God and such a task. So Jonah goes to sea, where there is a violent storm during which, while Jonah is fast asleep, the sailors pray, and the captain suggests that Jonah should be praying too (1.4–6). Jonah confesses that he is running away from his God, and that *he* is perhaps the cause of the storm, and so is thrown overboard (1.7–15). The storm subsides, and the sailors sacrifice and make vows to God (1.15f.). Meanwhile, Jonah is swallowed by a great fish and remains in its belly for three days and three nights (1.17), and while he is there he prays to God (2.1), a prayer of thanksgiving (2.2–9). The fish spews out Jonah on to dry land (2.10). This time when God calls him, Jonah does go to Nineveh, and as a result of his preaching the people repent (3.1–5). No less a person than the king of Nineveh proclaims a fast and calls his people to repentance (3.6–9), as a result of which God changes his mind about destroying Nineveh (3.10). This upsets Jonah, who says he wishes to die (4.1–5). Jonah experiences helpful shade from a plant, but the death of the plant and uncomfortable weather makes Jonah feel thoroughly 'out of sorts', so that he again says he wishes to die (4.6–8). On the basis of this experience, God argues with Jonah that the prophet should understand the Lord's concern for Nineveh, and that he – God – desires that it should be saved (4.9–11).

The book of Jonah is brief, but there are a comparatively large number of references to prayer. Leaving aside the prayer of ch. 2 for the time being, the main people who pray are the sailors, those who are portrayed as being non-Jewish people. In the storm at sea it is the sailors who cry out to their gods, while Jonah sleeps (1.5)! Later, these sailors cry out to the Lord (1.14). It is the captain of the ship who suggests that perhaps Jonah should pray to his (Jonah's) God (1.6). Apart from the prayer in ch. 2, the only reference in the book to Jonah praying is in 4.8f., and then it is in terms of complaint about how difficult life has turned out to be for Jonah.

Then there is the prayer in ch. 2. Though not all would agree, I believe that it is not original to the book, but that there was an earlier version of the book consisting of what we now have as 1.1–2.1 and 2.10–4.11. That is, it did not include the prayer in 2.2–9.⁹ This prayer, in fact, does not fit in the context here very well; in particular it looks back on what *has* already taken place, saying that prayer in distress (vv.2–6) has already been answered (vv.2, 5b, 7b). Further, its language is different from that of the rest of the book (we should note, for example, that the word 'great' does not occur in ch. 2, but it does a number of times elsewhere). Also, the character of Jonah in ch. 2 is different from elsewhere: in the prayer, Jonah comes over as a much better, a more religiously faithful person, than he does in the rest of the book.¹⁰

I would agree with the majority of students who see the book of Jonah – coming as it seems it must from the fifth or fourth centuries BC – as being something of a protest on the part of Jews that they themselves are not taking sufficiently seriously the fact that God's rule and steadfast love did extend far beyond the borders of Israel and over the nations. After all, Jonah does give expression to that from time to time:

> I worship the Lord, the God of heaven, who made the sea and the dry land. (Jonah 1.9)

> For I know that you are a gracious God and merciful, slow to anger, and abounding in steadfast love, and ready to relent from punishing. (Jonah 4.2)

The trouble is that Jonah does not wish to live this out! He does not wish to go to Nineveh, and later when he finds that he cannot escape the call to go there, he hopes for the destruction of the city and its people on account of their sinfulness! And yet, the book portrays the fields as ripe for harvest: consistently the book presents the non-Jewish people as being more religiously orientated than the Jews – and especially their prophet! Not only do heathen sailors pray, but also the Ninevite king responded to Jonah's preaching (3.6–9), as indeed the people of Nineveh did (3.5). Even the animals cried out to God for mercy (3.8)! Needless to say, this response was pleasing to God (3.10).

My own judgment is that the original book of Jonah with its three chapters, and no prayer in 2.2–9, was intended to be a criticism of Jewish people – or at least of certain groups in Jewish society – for not engaging in a mission in the name of God to a wider world. It made up what was a rather stern word of judgment upon them for being too inward looking, not sufficiently outward looking in faith and action.

And this is where, I suggest, the prayer of ch. 2 comes in. I regard this as a section added to the work to speak of encouragement and help for the difficult task of mission that was given by God to the people of Israel. While ch. 2 may at one level be read as a prayer of Jonah from the fish's belly, at another level it may be understood as prayer uttered by a person who was surrounded by dangers and problems, but who was experiencing the deliverance of the Lord, in the very task of engaging in a mission to Nineveh. In a moment of weakness this person, engaged in a mission in the Lord's name, prayed to the Lord (v.7), and thereby came to a new understanding that 'Deliverance belongs to the Lord!' (v.9). But this help that is given to his people for their mission is a help that is secured through prayer to the Lord. Here is Jonah who calls and cries out to the Lord (v.2), and we are told that his prayer did come to the Lord (v.7). The addition of the prayer to the book of Jonah is to suggest that the source of strength for those who go out in the name of the Lord is to be found in the practice of prayer.

We may remind ourselves that when Jesus was deeply troubled about the coming moment of supreme suffering in his ministry, he received strength through prayer: he prayed in the Garden of Gethsemane (Mark 14.32–42), where – rather as it had been when the sailors in the storm prayed to the Lord (Jonah 1.5f.) – the disciples fell asleep. Yet strength was given for human weakness, as St Paul was to discover for himself (II Cor. 12.9f.). We may also note that it was after the practices of fasting and prayer that the prophets and teachers of the church at Antioch laid hands on Barnabas and Saul and sent them out on their mission (Acts 13.1–3). Perhaps we may point to a parallel in the life of the Jesuit missionaries, the Society of Jesus, where there was great emphasis on prayer. The members of the Society, while they were activists, were at the same time much given to prayer, and under orders to do so.[11] This Society, like its monastic predecessors, laid stress upon the three vows of chastity, poverty and obedience, but there was also this emphasis upon the practice of prayer. And these examples from the Christian era, I suggest, may for us go some way to illuminating and illustrating what is a major emphasis in the book of Jonah in its final form of four chapters, the second of which contains the prayer in which a man on mission in the name of the Lord is portrayed as finding not only the strength for his own mission, but also the assurance that 'Deliverance is from the Lord!'.

IV

Jonah is sometimes referred to as a reluctant prophet.[12] Jeremiah was also a reluctant prophet: he was reluctant at the first when he was called, protesting that because of his youthfulness, his speech would not be adequate for the tasks to which he was called.

> Ah, Lord God! Truly I do not know how to speak, for I am only a boy. (Jer. 1.6) [13]

And as the time goes by his reluctance to become a prophet becomes no less, if anything the opposite. The experience of being a prophet seems only to have confirmed his worst expectations as to what it looked like at the beginning. What about this as a protest in prayer to God who has called him to this burdensome ministry?

> Jer. 11.18 The Lord made it known to me and I knew;
> then you showed me their evil deeds.
> v.19 But I was like a pet lamb
> led to the slaughter.
> And I did not know
> that they had schemed against me:
> 'Let us destroy the tree in its sap

> and let us cut him off from the land of the
>   living,
>   that his name be remembered no more.'
> v.20 But you, O Lord of hosts, who judge righteously,
>   who try the affections and the heart,
>   let me see your vengeance on them,
>   for to you I have confided my cause.

What are these troubles that the prophet is experiencing? The prayer (for this seems to be an address to God) begins abruptly with no introduction and no indication as to what lies in the background. But what we do have is some indication in the verses that follow that the people of Anathoth, the village from which the prophet came, seek Jeremiah's life, wishing to silence him as a prophet (11.21–23). What he says is too uncomfortable for them! Moreover, a member of their home village would surely be expected to have some message of hope and comfort, at least for *them*! Not for the last time was the discovery made, 'Prophets are not without honour, except in their hometown, and among their own kin, and in their own house' (Mark 6.4). But do these verses, although they follow it, provide the historical background to the prayer in 11.18–20? We cannot be sure about this, and the whole issue of how the long and complex book of Jeremiah came to assume its present form and shape is difficult, and the subject of much discussion.[14] But we may proceed on the basis that there is a very reasonable possibility that the situation described in 11.21–23 provides the historical background to the prayer in 11.18–20.

But then we need to say something about the prayer. It is the first of a series of passages – we shall look at some others in due course – which give the appearance of coming from something like the prophet's spiritual journal. There is nothing else quite like them among the books of the prophets, though in form they are much akin to those individual laments we considered from the book of Psalms. But the big question is, do they come from Jeremiah and do they record his experience of being a prophet of the Lord? For a long time they were regarded as recorded autobiographical materials, that tell us of the man behind the message. One of the most famous, and most attractive, books written upon the Old Testament followed this approach, and the chapter dealing with these passages is still well worth reading. J. Skinner in his *Prophecy and Religion*, said that these passages,

> lay bare the inmost secrets of the prophet's life, his fightings without and fears within, his mental conflict with adversity and doubt and temptation, and the reaction of his whole nature on a world that threatened to crush him and a task whose difficulty overwhelmed him.[15]

But in more recent years questions have been raised over whether these prayers really do come from Jeremiah, or whether they have rather been *attributed* to the historical prophet of that name. It has been pointed out that the writing of biographies and autobiographies is not a feature of ancient Semitic cultures, and it has further been suggested that we should see these prayers, and indeed very much else in the book of Jeremiah, as owing its existence and present arrangement to editors of the whole work, who wished to portray the prophet, his work and his theology, in a particular light for the benefit and instruction of a later age.[16]

And yet whichever way we regard this material – and we cannot know for sure who is right in this matter, and we each have to make up our minds as to what we feel is the most likely possibility – perhaps the end result is much the same. Whether it is the real experience of the historical Jeremiah, or whether alternatively it is the experience of a certain type of prophet of the Lord, as perceived by the editors of a book, we can still appreciate these very startling prayers, and reflect on their openness and honesty. Certainly, we are not hearing in these passages any expressions of quiet faith and calm assurance in God. Rather, here is a servant of the Lord who is deeply perplexed, and whose calling has brought him much suffering and anguish.

It is time to look at the prayer in vv.18-20 in some detail. Verse 18 speaks of the prophet having his eyes opened to what is going on around him. Certainly life is dangerous, and

Jeremiah of all people is one of the least able to defend himself and deal with such dangers. The prophet portrays himself (v.19) as somewhat naive: he is like a pet lamb, a tame lamb, less able than a lamb reared in the normal way to take care of himself and to know what is being plotted. The result is that he is in real danger from his enemies. Then the prophet gives another picture of himself and his plight: he is like a tree in sap; that is, he is under threat of being struck down while he is still young and inexperienced.

Yet what Jeremiah does have is confidence in the Lord: he is sure that the Lord scrutinizes to the very depths of the motives and intentions of people, and that he judges righteously. He is sure that at the end of the day there will be for him a satisfactory outcome to all these difficulties. He is confident that he will receive a verdict in his favour, and that the wicked will be defeated. Moreover, he wishes to see the Lord's vengeance on these people. While such a cry may be characteristic of Psalms of Lament (e.g. Ps. 17.13f.), and though we can understand that he should have had such thoughts and feelings, such sentiments give real difficulty to those who have been commanded to love their enemies, and in such situations to 'turn the other cheek' (Matt 5.39; Luke 6.29). And yet, in the context of a prayer, we are witnessing here a real sense of openness and candour; the whole of the person, 'warts and all' is presented to God!

We may pass to another of these prayers of Jeremiah, Jer. 15.15–18, to which we should add the reply of the Lord in verses 19–21. We may translate the verses as follows:

Jer. 15.15 You know, O Lord,
> Remember me and visit me,
>> and take vengeance for me on my persecutors.
> Withhold your anger and do not remove me,
>> know that I bear reproach for your sake.

v.16 Your words were found and I ate them,
> and your words became to me a joy
> and the delight of my heart;
for I am called by your name,
> O Lord, God of hosts.

> v.17 I did not sit in the company of merrymakers,
> nor did I rejoice.
> As your hand was upon me I sat alone,
> for you filled me with anger.
> v.18 Why is my pain unending
> my wound incurable,
> refusing to be healed?
> Will you be to me like a deceitful brook
> like waters not to be trusted?

This is another of the personal prayers of Jeremiah, sometimes called the 'Confessions'.[17] It is a cry coming from the prophet's ever deepening agony. There is an increasing sense of bitterness, not only against his enemies, but also against the Lord himself. As far as the Lord is concerned, Jeremiah's complaint is that having started him on this mission (which Jeremiah undertook in a spirit of joy), he now seems to have failed him: the Lord has been to Jeremiah like one of those wadis which have waters in winter but which dry up in the summer (v.18). What also is so painful to the prophet is the fact that his calling has involved him in separation from his fellow people (v.17). To be a prophet of doom caused the death of something within the prophet. Lowth said,

> Jeremy quickly found the joy which he had conceived from the honour of being a prophet was turned to heaviness; all his prophecies contained nothing but denunciations of God's indignation against a sinful people. This makes me, saith he, sit alone, renounce all cheerful conversation, and give myself to solitariness and pensive thoughts.[18]

But what is striking is the harshness of the imagery in which all this is expressed: the prophet has 'unending pain' and an 'incurable wound', and the Lord he had been expecting to be a constant strength and support has apparently failed him. What may also seem striking to us is the fact that all this is expressed to God in prayer. This is not restrained, or quiet, or even 'polite' prayer; but rather all that burdens the prophet's mind is poured out in prayer to the Lord. 'From the depths of the abyss,' says

Calvin, 'and from the jaws of death the servants of God send up a cry to the Lord.'[19]

But the prophet receives a response to his agonized prayer:

Jer. 15.19   Therefore thus says the Lord:
   If you turn back, I will take you back,
      and you shall stand before me.
   If you utter what is precious, and not what is worthless,
      you shall serve as my mouth.
   It is they who will turn to you,
      not you who will turn to them.
v.20   And I will make you to this people
      a fortified wall of bronze;
   they will fight against you,
      but they shall not prevail over you,
   for I am with you
      to save you and deliver you, says the Lord.
v.21   I will deliver you out of the hand of the wicked,
      and redeem you from the grasp of the ruthless.

While this may be a response from God to Jeremiah, in no way is it a response to his complaint. In this way, it is rather like the reply of the Lord to Job, which we shall come to shortly (Job 38–41). If anything, there could be an implied criticism, almost the suggestion that Jeremiah may be tempted to 'trim his sails, to make his message a bit more palatable to his audience'.[20] Certainly, the reply, rather than being one of sympathy for all that the prophet finds himself up against, is instead a challenge to continued faithfulness in service, whatever the personal cost and demand to the prophet himself.[21]

Not, however, that the reply is without hope. The same assurance as the Lord gave to Jeremiah at the time of his call is now given again (1.18f.): God who promised at the beginning that he would be with his servant, assures him of that again. The Lord will be with him, to save, deliver, to redeem (vv.20f.). Though the prophet may still experience people 'fighting' him, yet he will be given strength, he will be made 'a fortified wall of bronze' (v.20.). The prophet must be obdurate – maybe as we might express it 'become thickskinned'. But all this will only be given as long as the prophet is faithful to the Lord: 'If you turn back . . .', 'If you utter what is precious . . .'.

How are we to understand that the prophet received this reply? How are we to understand the abrupt change of mood from complaint in vv.15–18 to the spirit of assurance in vv.19–21? We have already observed this phenomenon in certain of the Psalms of Lament where there is this change of mood towards the end, so that a Psalm that in the earlier part consists of an agonized prayer to God, ends with an expression of confidence that prayer has been heard. It may be that we are intended to understand that the prophet comes to a sense of peace through praying. It is, perhaps, yet another example of the 'wonderful metamorphosis' that Heiler spoke about as taking place when an individual lifted up a need to God in prayer.[22]

There is one other of these laments of the prophet Jeremiah to which we shall turn, one in which there is a wide range of feelings expressed. In Jer. 20.7–13 there is a progression from depths of despair (vv.7–10) to confidence (vv.11f.), and even to a final verse of hymn-like praise (v.13). I offer a translation of these verses:

Jer. 20.7   O Lord, you deceived me, and I was deceived;
             you overcame me, and you have prevailed.
           I have become a laughing-stock at all times,
             everyone mocks me.
   v.8   For whenever I speak, I cry out,
             I shout, 'Violence and destruction!'
           For the word of the Lord has become for me
             a source of abuse and derision all the time.
   v.9   If I say, 'I will not mention him,
             or speak any more in his name',
           it is in my heart as a burning fire,
             shut up in my bones,
           and I am weary with holding it in,
             and I cannot.

v.10 For I hear the whispering of many;
         terror is all around!
      'Denounce him! Let us denounce him!'
         say all my friends,
         watching for my fall.
      'Perhaps he will be deceived,
         and we can overcome him,
         and take our revenge on him.'
v.11 But the Lord is with me as a powerful warrior;
         therefore my pursuers will stumble and not succeed.
      They will suffer great shame, for they will not succeed,
         eternal disgrace which will not be forgotten.
v.12 O Lord of hosts, you test the righteous,
         you see into people's deepest thoughts.
      Let me see your vengeance upon them,
         for I have confided my cause to you.
v.13 Sing to the Lord; praise the Lord,
         for he has delivered the life of the needy,
         from the hand of evildoers.

The prophet is back in a sense of deep distress. The prayer in the form and setting in the book as we now have it is portrayed as arising out of the incident with the priest Pashur. In 20.1–6 we are told that because of the message that Jeremiah preached (he was told in 15.19 that he must continue to preach in this vein!), he was struck by Pashur who put him in the stocks. Historically, this may have been the cause of the prayer, or on the other hand it could be that the incident of Pashur has been set as the preceding incident to the prayer so as to provide an example of the type of experience the prophet had and that led him to make such an anguished prayer to God as we find here.

And this is indeed an anguished prayer: extremely strong words are uttered, and they are against the Lord! In v.17 Jeremiah accuses the Lord of nothing less than 'deception' – a word, it is to be noted, that comes from the Old Testament's legal language for seduction (Ex. 22.15). The prophet appears to be saying that in the course of his working out of his calling as a prophet he feels a sense of betrayal by God in the hostility and bitterness he has experienced. It is as if he was overcome (v.7) by God, and by having crushed out of him any possible resistance has been forced to become a prophet. The consequence of this is that Jeremiah has become an object of fun and a source of derision (v.7b). But then, the word of the Lord has itself become for Jeremiah a source of continual abuse and derision, for the reason that he has been called to proclaim prophecies of 'violence and destruction!' – and never good and peace (v.8)! Though Jeremiah would like to rebel against his calling, yet he feels a sense of compulsion that he must continue as a prophet.

Then life for the prophet has become the more burdensome through the 'whispering campaign'. In addition to the earlier problem of having been a laughingstock (v.7), now has been added whisperings against him – and on all sides! (v.10). There are threats upon his life, and the prophet feels it deeply. It seems that the plotters are looking for an opportunity to denounce Jeremiah, and that moreover it is his friends who are doing so. Perhaps the thought is that those who appear to be friends may in fact be spies in the service of the enemy. Perhaps they are on the lookout for an injudicious word, or a false move, which could lead to his condemnation.

And all this, it is to be observed, makes up the content of a prayer to God. What is striking once again is the candour in his approach to God: what bolder condemnation of God can be imagined than to accuse him of seduction? The Lord may stand over against Jeremiah as one who will rule him, but Jeremiah does not let this happen without a struggle, and he makes his prayer one of deep complaint.[23]

But it is perhaps out of this distressed prayer that we are intended to understand the expressions of hope and confidence in vv.11 and 12. It is because of praying, it is once again through the 'wonderful metamorphosis' that prayer effects, that the prophet can glimpse some hope – although he may soon go back to feeling the burdens and the sense of betrayal. But he does become sure again that the Lord is with him 'as a powerful warrior' (v.11). Although enemies may still be with him, yet the prophet comes to see that they are on a slippery slope: he is sure they will stumble, and suffer great shame, and an unforgettable, endless disgrace. The result of the prophet's praying is not dissimilar to that for the psalmist of Ps. 73 who contemplated the apparent success and well-being of the wicked. As a result of his 'going into the sanctuary' (Ps. 73.17), he came to see that those who appeared to have great human success and well-being had in fact a quite insubstantial hold on life, upon what was of permanent and enduring worth (Ps. 73.18–20). Yet the enemies are still with Jeremiah, as v.12, with his wish for divine vengeance upon them, testifies. This again constitutes a problem for those who have been called to love their enemies – and to pray! – for those who persecute them (Matt. 5.44).

Verse 13 seems to be indicating a sudden change in feeling: after all that has gone before, it makes a very sudden declaration that the Lord *has* delivered 'the life of the needy'. Indeed, the occurrence of that expression ('the life of the needy'), along with the plural imperatives ('Sing to the Lord', 'Praise the Lord'), has suggested to some that this verse did not belong to the original prayer. Who is this number of people who are to sing to and praise the Lord, and why has Jeremiah become 'the needy'? The verse may indeed not be original to the prayer, but then, those who were responsible for passing on to us this prayer must have thought that it would be enhanced by the addition. Whether it is original, or an addition, it is an affirmation of certainty in the victory that God gives, and an expression of the sense of hope and confidence that is to be found through prayer. It testifies to the fact that the 'needy' may find help and strength as they affirm their total dependence upon God (cf. Matt. 5.3), that those who put their trust in the Lord may know a sense of deliverance even in the midst of their despair.

The prayers we have been considering from the books of Jonah and Jeremiah have as their subject the difficulties, problems, burdens, all experienced by those who are called in the name of the Lord to particular aspects of his service. Those prayers relate to the ministry of the Lord, and reflect both the burdens of those ministries, and the source of strength and hope that enable those who are called to remain faithful to their callings.

V

The subject of the prayers in the book of Job is different. Here, the background to the prayers is a more general problem about suffering, a problem that may be experienced by all, whether or not they may be called to particular tasks in the world in the name of the Lord. The theme of the book of Job concerns suffering. Job, who turns to God in prayer – angry prayer indeed for much of the time – stands for every person who, throughout all the ages and cultures of the world, experience great suffering, and who must cry out, at least to someone, 'Why?'

The book of Job falls into three main sections. The first is in the Prologue in chs 1f., where the scene is set. Here we read of Job, a man devoted to God, and in his family and many possessions apparently greatly blessed by God. But then suddenly everything goes wrong for Job, and in rapid succession he loses his animals, flocks, servants and children. No doubt we feel that the picture of the Satan, allowed by the Lord to put Job and his faith to the severest tests, contains elements of harshness and crudity, but perhaps we can accept that this is a part of the art of the storyteller.[24] The storyteller has prepared us for what is to come. In what is supposed to be a just world, a good and just man's life has been shattered by loss and bereavement, by disease and degradation. When Job's three friends come to see him they are so appalled at the depths of his sufferings that they sit beside him on the ground in silence for seven days and nights.

But it is the second part of the book that will really interest us, extending from ch. 3 to 42.6. An extended discussion takes place between Job and his three friends, Eliphaz, Bildad and Zophar: this occurs in three rounds of speeches (chs 3–11;

12–20; 21–28). Then there are more speeches by Job, which end in a challenge to God (chs 29–31), followed by yet more speeches, this time from another friend, named Elihu (chs 32–37). Finally come two speeches by God (38–40.2 and 40.6–41.34), each followed by replies from Job (40.3–5; 42.1–6) in which he humbles himself and submits to God. The third part of the book is brief, an epilogue in two scenes – God's judgment upon Job's friends (42.7–9) and Job's restoration (42.10–17).

But it is prayers, and references to prayer that are our concern. Some of Job's friends are ready with their advice to Job on the subject of prayer, and yet we nowhere hear of any of the friends praying. Eliphaz the Temanite seems sure of his ground as concerning prayer: if only Job will return to the Lord, then his prayer will be heard.

> You will pray to him, and he will hear you,
> and you will pay your vows. (Job 22.27)

As it is, Eliphaz feels that Job has an improper attitude towards God, lacking respect before him. Thus Eliphaz says to Job:

> But you are doing away with the fear of God,
> and hindering meditation before God. (Job 15.4)

The young man Elihu eventually has his (lengthy) say (chs 32–37), and seeks to rebuke Job, counselling him as a sinner to confess his wrongs so that he may come 'into his presence with joy':

> Then he prays to God, and is accepted by him,
> he comes into his presence with joy,
> and God repays him for his righteousness. (Job 33.26)

And yet we do not hear of Eliphaz, or Elihu – or indeed of Bildad or Zophar, the other friends – actually praying! Rather, their interest is in theology, thinking about God. But Job *does* pray: he is a religious person. Yet in no way does he address God in gentle, or even 'polite' manner and terms. Job 6f. is Job's response to the first speech of Eliphaz (chs 4f.). At first, Job's response seems to be addressed to his friends, for he speaks to them as several people, with 'you' in the plural. But by 7.7 there is a change to 'you' in the singular, to one person, and it becomes clear that Job's words are now addressed to God, that is, conversation with friends has turned into prayer to God. And yet it is accusatory prayer (v.11), in which Job accuses God of treating him like a monster that needs to be restrained and watched over (v.12). God tortures him with dreams in the night (vv.13–16), and God even spies on him (vv.17–20)! Could not God let him go to his grave in peace (v.21)?

> Job 7.11 Therefore I will not restrain my mouth;
> I will speak in the anguish of my spirit;
> I will complain in the bitterness of my soul.
> v.12 Am I the Sea, or the Dragon,
> that you set a guard over me?
> v.13 When I say, 'My bed will comfort me,
> my couch will ease my complaint,'
> v.14 then you scare me with dreams
> and terrify me with visions,
> v.15 so that I would choose strangling
> and death rather than this body.
> v.16 I loathe my life; I would not live forever.
> Let me alone, for my days are a breath.
> v.17 What are human beings, that you make so much of them,
> that you set your mind on them,
> v.18 visit them every morning,
> test them every moment?
> v.19 Will you not look away from me for a while,
> let me alone until I swallow my spittle?
> v.20 If I sin, what do I do to you, you watcher of humanity?
> Why have you made me your target?
> Why have I become a burden to you?
> v.21 Why do you not pardon my transgression
> and take away my iniquity?
> For now I shall lie in the earth;
> you will seek me, but I shall not be.

Prayers from the Depths

What is remarkable here is that this deeply accusatory language is addressed to God: this is a prayer, and in it Job is open and honest before God as to how he himself feels about his present predicament and the Lord's involvement (and not for good!) in his life. But what also is surely of significance is that Job did not turn his back on prayer. Further, he has the honesty to express himself to God just as he felt about his relationship with God. Perhaps the experience of which Gerard Manley Hopkins speaks is akin to that of the tortured and angry Job who yet continues to pray to God, but whose prayer can be no other than a battle with God:

> My prayers must meet a brazen heaven
> and fail and scatter all away.
> Unclean and seeming unforgiven
> My prayers I scarcely call to pray.
> I cannot buoy my heart above;
> Above I cannot entrance win.
> I reckon precedents of love,
> But feel the long success of sin.
>
> My heaven is brass and iron my earth:
> Yea, iron is mingled with my clay,
> So harden'd is it in this dearth
> Which praying fails to do away.
> Nor tears, nor tears this clay uncouth
> Could mould, if any tears there were.
> A warfare of my lips in truth,
> Battling with God, is now my prayer.[25]

In comparison, how tame, how polite our prayers have become – that is, if in such agony we have continued to pray! Or, even, for modern people, if we have continued to have any faith in God!

But there are more prayers of Job to come. In 16.1–17.16 is the long speech by Job in response to one from Eliphaz. Parts of Job's speech are addressed to the friends (16.2–6; 17.6–10), while elsewhere he appears to be speaking to himself (16.7–17; 17.11–16), or even to the Earth (16.18–22). But 17.1–5 is addressed to God:

Job 17.1 My spirit is broken, my days are extinct,
          the grave is ready for me.
   v.2 Surely there are mockers around me,
          and my eye dwells on their provocation.
   v.3 Lay down a pledge for me with yourself;
          who is there that will give surety for me?
   v.4 Since you have closed their minds to understanding,
          therefore you will not let them triumph.
   v.5 Those who denounce friends for reward
          the eyes of their children will fail.

His friends have failed; they have turned out to be those who mock and provoke him, rather than friends (v.2). So to whom else can he appeal but God? But he does just that. He feels himself to be totally on his own in life, so that the only one who could lay down a pledge for him must be God himself! Only God himself can offer himself as guarantor of Job's innocence. To this God he clings, continuing to pray to him.

As a final example of Job's continuing to pray to God, we go to the three chapters (29–31) where Job makes his final survey of his case. We do not hear of the friends here: now it is between Job and God.

Job 30.20 I cry to you and you do not answer me;
           I stand, and you merely look at me.
   v.21 You have turned cruel to me;
           with the might of your hand you persecute me.
   v.22 You lift me up on the wind, you make me ride on it,
           and you toss me about in the roar of the storm.
   v.23 I know that you will bring me to death,
           and to the house appointed for all living.

To a God who will not answer him, and who appears to be a cruel persecutor, tossing him around, eventually handing him over to death, to him Job continues to pray. Still he does not abandon prayer.

Eventually, of course, Job does receive an answer to his

prayer, but certainly not the sort of answer that he was expecting. It is not a comforting word to one who suffers deeply, but it is a powerful speech of the mighty Lord. And yet just because it is a speech of God to Job, it changes things dramatically for the sufferer. In response to this long speech of the Lord (38.1–40.2), Job makes but brief reply:

Job 40.3   Then Job answered the Lord:
    v.4   See, I am of small account;
            what shall I answer you?
        I lay my hand upon my mouth.
    v.5   I have spoken once, and I will not answer;
        twice, but will proceed no further.

Then follows yet another speech of the Lord (40.6–41.34), and to that Job responds humbly and submissively:

Job 42.1   Then Job answered the Lord:
    v.2   I know that you can do all things,
        and that no purpose of yours can be thwarted.
    v.3   Who is this that hides counsel without knowledge?
        Therefore I have uttered what I did not understand,
            things too wonderful for me,
            which I did not know.
    v.4   Hear, and I will speak;
        I will question you, and you declare to me.
    v.5   I had heard of you by the hearing of the ear,
        but now my eye sees you;
    v.6   Therefore I despise myself,
        and repent in dust and ashes.

Job's satisfaction comes in no way through any increase in knowledge, but rather because he has met God. His friends with their talk and their theology have not been able to help him. Nevertheless, Job, we are told in the Epilogue to the book (42.7–17), did pray for his friends (42.8) – prayers, it seems, more speedily answered than Job's agonizing petitions for himself! But the book portrays any sense of satisfaction and release to which Job comes as that which has come out of his continuing to pray to God.

He has found the answer to his problem. For at bottom this was not a matter of theodicy, but a problem of fellowship. He has not learned the cause of his sufferings or the explanation of the apparent injustices of the world, but he has found God again . . . Therefore Job declares that he has found a new understanding of God compared with which his former knowledge was but as the knowledge of rumour compared with sight.[26]

And that rediscovery is portayed in the book as having been gained through prayer. 'We cannot come to God,' says Luther, 'except through prayer alone, for he is too high above us.'[27] And perhaps we may feel that something of the truth of that statement is borne out in the stories and traditions that have been handed down to us concerning Habakkuk, Jonah, Jeremiah and Job. *They* came to God – and it was through prayer.

6

'For *him* shall endless prayer be made'
Praying for the Nation's Leader

I

It is early in the morning, yet still in darkness, and the hour of battle draws near. It will be the battle of Agincourt, and King Henry V soliloquizes on the burdens of kingship:

> Upon the king! let our lives, our souls,
> Our debts, our careful wives,
> Our children and our sins lay on the king!
> We must bear all. O hard condition,
> Twin-born with greatness, subject to the breath
> Of every fool, whose sense no more can feel
> But his own wringing! What infinite heart's-ease
> Must kings neglect, that private men enjoy.[1]

There are passages in the Old Testament that reveal a deep concern for the king, that he may live and act aright, with wisdom and righteousness, knowing when to use his power and authority and when not. Some of these passages contain prayers for the king, and noteworthy among them are some of the so-called 'Royal Psalms'. It will be recalled that one of the groups of biblical Psalms that Hermann Gunkel discerned had no special characteristics is style, but what they do have in common is a concern with the person or the office of the king. Gunkel called them the 'Royal Psalms'.[2] Some of them are in fact prayers for the king, one such being Ps. 72.[3]

The first four verses of Ps. 72 contain a prayer that the king may be endowed with justice and righteousness:

> Ps. 72.1 Give the king your justice, O God,
>   and your righteousness to a king's son.
> v.2 May he judge your people with righteousness,
>   and your poor with justice.
> v.3 May the mountains yield well-being for the people,
>   and the hills righteousness.
> v.4 May he deliver justice to the poor of the people,
>   give deliverance to the poor,
>   and crush the oppressor.

The king's twin responsibilities are stressed here: prayer is made that he may be given God's justice and righteousness (v.1), in order that he may judge the Lord's people with righteousness and the poor with justice (v.2). When the king thus acts, it is believed that there will be well-being, peace and righteousness (v.3). Thus, how much benefit for all will there be when the king acts with justice and righteousness! And however exalted may be the role or the calling of the king, he remains a human being, a man in need of the prayers of his subjects. Indeed, both they and he stand in need of prayer for the king.[4]

This prayerful concern that a human king may be granted by God the qualities and gifts necessary for the successful exercise of his high office is also to be seen in the prayer in I Kings 3.6–9. This is a prayer uttered by Solomon on his accession to the throne, made in response to the Lord's appearance to him in a dream that contained the invitation to ask what the Lord should give to him. So we read that Solomon prayed:

> You have shown to your servant David my father great faithfulness, for he walked before you in faithfulness and righteousness, and in uprightness of heart towards you. And you have kept for him this great faithfulness, and have given him a son to sit upon his throne this day. [7] And now Lord my God, you have made your servant king in place of David my father, but I am a little youth; I do not know how to go out or come in. [8] And your servant is in the midst of your people who you have chosen, a great people that cannot be counted or numbered for multitude. [9] Give to

your servant an understanding heart to judge your people, to discern between good and evil; for who is able to govern this great people of yours? (I Kings 3.6–9)

Some of the Royal Psalms contain references to the king being invited to make a request to God (see Pss. 2.8; 21.2,4; also 20.4), and perhaps we should understand this prayer in that way. Solomon, in the face of his great and new tasks asks for the gifts of wisdom and ability to govern his people. He asks for an 'understanding' heart, so that he may 'judge' God's people, and also have the ability to 'discern' between good and evil (v.9). The word translated 'judge' here (*špt*) indicated both the ability to 'judge' what is right and what is wrong, but also 'to govern, rule'. It is indeed a high ideal of kingship that is being prayed for here: to be a king is not a matter of using unbridled power and authority, but it is to exercise an authority and gift (both of which are to be sought from the Lord) to judge and to govern, to discern between good and evil. Further, the prayer acknowledges that successful kingship depends upon those things that God gives: it is God who has made Solomon king (v.7)! Solomon himself is a 'servant', a 'youth': he does not have power of his own to function as a king, although he has been given definite and considerable responsibilities.[5] Thus we are not surprised that Solomon is portrayed here as praying and asking for the necessary gifts for the exercise of his kingship!

This prayer that we have been considering is in the books of Kings, themselves part of what scholars have come to refer to as the 'Deuteronomistic history', the extensive theological work, cast in the form of a history, that is made up of the books of Joshua, Judges, I and II Samuel, and I and II Kings, to which reference has been made earlier.[6] Our prayer certainly reflects some deuteronomic emphases,[7] and we may regard it as expressing aspects of the Deuteronomistic historian's view of the institution of kingship: that kingship is not merely about power, but is a gift of God and a service to God for which God's gifts are needed.

But we also come across this prayer, though in a modified

form, in the Chronicler's work. This is another great theological work, again in the form of an immense history of God's people, in this case from the very earliest times until the days of the Babylonian exile. It is likely that the main parts of the books of Chronicles are to be dated around or after the time of Haggai and Zechariah 1–8, sometime after the completion of the Second Temple in 515 BC – but before the time of Alexander the Great (who reigned from 336–323 BC).[8] It seems that the Chronicler had a number of sources of material upon which he drew as he prepared his work, the most extensive of which are our books of Samuel and Kings. Frequently, the Chronicler betrays his particular interests when he deviates from that source, either by addition or subtraction.[9]

The prayer we are considering is to be found in II Chron. 1.8–10 and compared with the prayer in I Kings 3 it is considerably compressed. It reads:

> And Solomon said to God, 'You have shown great faithfulness to David my father, and you have made me king in his place. [9] Now, Lord God, may your promise to David my father be confirmed, for you have made me king over a people as numerous as the dust of the earth. [10] Now give to me wisdom and knowledge to go out and come in before this people, for who can govern this great people of yours?' (II Chron. 1.8–10)

In particular v.8 in this prayer drastically shortens I Kings 3.6f. Whereas elsewhere the Chronicler refers to Solomon as 'young and inexperienced' (I Chron. 22.5; 29.1) – and that is a dominant theme in I Kings 3.6f. – here he is portrayed as ready to assume his kingly responsibilities. Nevertheless, in spite of this emphasis upon his 'maturity' for his new role, there is the prayer to God that he may be given the gift of wisdom. It is as if the Chronicler is saying that even though the person particularly chosen by God may be mature and ready for high office, *still* he stands in need of God's gift of wisdom. Only thus will he be enabled to fulfil his high calling and be able to govern God's people. Whereas the prayer in I Kings 3.6–9 asked for an understanding heart to judge the people, to discern between good and evil, that in II Chron. 1.8–10 asks for wisdom and knowledge to go out and come in before the great people. This suggests that the Chronicler is laying emphasis upon the high responsibility that Solomon is charged with as he becomes king. It is a characteristic of the Chronicler that he presents people as helpless and lacking strength on their own, but knowing a strength when they depend upon God. That is particularly so in the case of the king, and it is instructive to take note of the occurrences of prayer in the books of Chronicles. In these two books there are twenty-one prayers, or references to prayer, but the vast majority are uttered by kings. There are six references to, or prayers of, David (I Chron. 16.35; 17.16–27; 21.8; 21.17; 21.26; 29.10–19); three of Solomon (II Chron. 1.8–10; 6.14–42; 7.12–18); one of Asa (II Chron. 14.11); two of Jehoshaphat (II Chron. 18.31; 20.5–12); three of Hezekiah (II Chron. 30.18f.; 32.20; 32.24); two of Manasseh (II Chron. 33.12f. and 18f.). The remaining four prayers in Chronicles are from Jabel (I Chron. 4.10); Reubenites and others (I Chron. 5.20); Judah (II Chron. 13.14); Levitical priests (II Chron. 30.27). Further, of the total of seventeen prayers on the part of kings, only seven are paralleled in the books of Kings! That is, the Chronicler in his work has kings praying (or kings being referred to as praying) on an extra *ten* occasions compared with those parts of the Deuteronomistic history from which it seems he worked, and adapted for his own purpose. Thus it is clear that the Chronicler has a lively sense of the importance of prayer, at least on the part of kings, and it would seem that he is concerned to stress the fact that if a king is to reign aright, and if the people are to be led aright, with the necessary acknowledgment of their dependence upon God, then there must be this element of prayer on the part of the king.

But, to return to the prayer of Solomon in I Kings 3.6–9, and which the Chronicler has shortened and adapted for his own purposes in II Chron. 1.8–10; in both these forms in which it is found it ends in similar words:

> for who is able to govern this great people of yours? (I Kings 3.9)

For who can govern this great people of yours? (II Chron. 1.10)

Who indeed is sufficient for these things (compare II Cor. 2.16)? Both the Deuteronomistic historian and the Chronicler portray Solomon as somewhat daunted by the task of kingship now lying before him. It is because he realizes the greatness of the task before him and in contrast his own frailty and insufficiency that Solomon (according to both these accounts) prays for the necessary gifts. It will be when Solomon fails to ask in a sense of wonder 'who can govern this great people of yours?', when he begins to think that he is able to do these great tasks, that things for his kingship will begin to go so disastrously wrong![10]

We turn now to a prayer of Solomon's father, David. Once again, the prayer is recorded both in the Deuteronomistic history (II Sam. 7.18–29) and by the Chronicler (I Chron. 17.16–27), and again the Chronicler has introduced some changes which call for comment. We go first to the prayer as it is found in II Sam. 7, a chapter which expresses a particular style of kingship. II Sam. 7 speaks about the divine choice and appointment of David and his successors as kings over God's people.[11] Verses 1–7 tell how David had a desire to build a 'house', that is, a temple, for the Lord in Jerusalem, but vv.8–17 go on to say that it is actually God who will do the building! But it will be a 'house' for David, that is, a dynasty of kings. It is after these verses that the prayer comes, much of which is taken up with praise and thanksgiving to God for the greatness of his deeds in connection with his people, and with David and his house (dynasty). Eventually the prayer comes round to petition:

And now, Lord God, you are God, and your words are true and you have promised to your servant this good thing. [29] And now, may it please you to bless the house of your servant that it may be for ever before you, for you, Lord God, have spoken and with your blessing the house of your servant will be blessed for ever. (II Sam. 7.28f.)

R. E. Clements speaks of this prayer as having, 'some of the most perceptive and fascinating insights the Old Testament has to offer concerning the divine promises to the house of David . . . It is essentially a prayer of petition asking God to keep the word already promised through the mouth of the prophet Nathan . . .'[12] Thus the prayer exalts God, remembers the frailty and humanity of David, and acknowledges that the king, exalted though he be among humans, yet stands in need of the grace of God. It affirms that without the fulfilment of the divine promises there would be no real kingship. While the oracle of Nathan in vv.8–17 constitutes something of a theology of Israelite kingship, both trying to keep the institution in check yet also conceding its great importance, the prayer in vv.18–29 emphasizes the sheer grace on the part of God and reminds all concerned – and in particular the house of David! – that the king was still indeed a human.

The Chronicler's version of this prayer (I Chron. 17.16–27) for much of the time keeps close to the prayer as found in II Sam. 7, but does exhibit some distinctive changes, amongst which is the ascription of a more exalted place to David than is given in II Sam. 7. With II Sam. 7.19 and 20 compare I Chron. 17.17 and 18. Yet it is in I Chron. 17.27 (II Sam. 7.29) that there is the greatest change: instead of the 'may it please you to bless this house . . .', the Chronicles text has, '. . . it has pleased you . . .'. Further, instead of the Samuel text, 'have spoken and with your blessing the house of your servant will be blessed . . .', Chronicles has, 'have blessed, and it will be blessed for ever'.

Thus there is a sense in which the petition at the close of the prayer in II Sam. 7 has in the Chronicler's treatment become praise. While the II Sam. 7 prayer goes some way to emphasize the humanity of the Israelite monarch, the Chronicler almost seems to give a more exalted view of the kingship. It may well be that what we are observing here is the Chronicler's emphasis on the importance of David. It has frequently been noted that the Chronicler has a tendency to glorify the figure of David and his kingship, while at the same time apparently having less interest in David the man. For the Chronicler, David is less a real man of flesh and blood than he is a divinely chosen king who rules over God's people.[13] Yet, even such an exalted ruler as this needs divine help, and, as we have already observed, the Chronicler records many instances of prayer on the part of the kings of ancient Israel. As, indeed, in many a generation a king in the face of high monarchical responsibility has called to God in prayer. An example of this is found in a prayer attributed to William III (1650–1702):

> O Lord, in confidence of thy great mercy and goodness to all that truly repent and resolve to do better, I most humbly implore the grace and assistance of the Holy Spirit to enable me to become every day better. Grant me the wisdom and understanding to know my duty and the heart and will to do it. Endue me, O Lord, with the true fear and love of thee, and with a prudent zeal for thy glory. Increase in me the graces of charity and meekness, of truth and justice, of humility and patience, and a firmness of spirit to bear every condition with constancy and equality of mind.[14]

II

But we began with Ps. 72, itself a prayer for the Israelite king, and to it we must now return. In vv.5–7 the Psalm moves into prayer for a long life for the king:

Ps. 72.5 May he live while the sun endures,
and as long as the moon,
from generation to generation.
v.6 May he be like the rain on the mown grass,
like showers that water the land.
v.7 May righteousness blossom in his days,
and well-being abound
until the moon is no more!

This is intercession, asking God that the king may have long life, but the note of petition is also there on the part of those who pray for the king: may life flow from him (v.6), and may righteousness and peace for them abound through many years (v.7)!

The theme of long life for the king is also to be seen in Ps. 21, especially v.4, with its,

> He asked for long life; you gave it to him – length of days for ever and ever.

The same theme is present in Pss. 61.6f. and 132.8–10,[15] and it is the general subject of many prayers for eastern rulers, as, for example, is witnessed in this daily prayer of a Hittite king:

> But to the king and the queen, to the princes and to the Hatti land grant life, health, strength, long and enduring years and joy! Grant everlasting fertility to their crops, vines, fruit-bearing trees, cattle, sheep, pigs, mules . . .[16]

According to the Old Testament, a day came for King Hezekiah when it looked as if his life would come to an end. Indeed, he was told by the prophet Isaiah to set his house in order, because, rather than recover from his illness, he would die (II Kings 20.2). Thus Hezekiah turned his face to the wall and prayed to the Lord:

> Remember now, O Lord, I implore you, how I have walked before you in faithfulness with a whole heart, and have done what is good in your sight. (II Kings 20.3)

The prayer is found in almost verbatim form in Isa. 38.2f.[17] In II Kings 20.5 we read that in a short time the Lord had both heard the prayer and also granted Hezekiah further years of life. Hezekiah is portrayed as a pious king who in the face of crisis turns in prayer to his Lord. In spite of what we are told was uttered by the prophet Isaiah (II Kings 20.1), the narrative proceeds on the assumption that Hezekiah is innocent, and thus he is spared death. It is the king alone who prays here; the prophet Isaiah merely announces and brings signs (II Kings 20.1, 4–11).

Now the Chronicler has quite drastically shortened his account of this incident:

> In those days Hezekiah became sick to death, and he prayed to the Lord, and he spoke to him and gave him a sign. (II Chron. 32.24)

The incident that in II Kings 20.1–11 occupied no less than eleven verses is here reduced to the span of just one verse, and we have no mention of the prophet Isaiah! Here is portrayed the God who is ready to answer prayer: Hezekiah prays and is healed, rather in the way set out by the Chronicler in his programmatic verse in II Chron. 7.14:

> ... if my people who are called by my name humble themselves, pray, seek my face, and turn from their wicked ways, then I will hear from heaven, and will forgive their sin and heal their land.

Another example of what may be regarded as a prayer for 'life' is in I Kings 13.6, a part of what must be admitted is a difficult chapter to understand.

> And the king said to the man of God, 'Entreat the favour of the Lord your God, and pray for me.' And the man of God entreated the Lord, and the hand of the king was restored to him, and it became as it was before. (I Kings 13.6)

It must be said that here there is a pronounced miraculous aspect to the prayer which the king asked of 'the man of God' (as the young man is consistently named in this chapter, in contrast to the old man from Bethel who equally consistently is called a 'prophet'). It has been pointed out that the narrative in I Kings 13 displays similarities with other prophetic stories, especially the ones in I Kings 20, and possibly comes from the same Northern prophetic milieu as the Elijah and Elisha stories. Certainly the style of prayer here, with a somewhat 'miraculous' resulting healing, is reminiscent of the prayers we have already considered in connection with Elisha.[18]

Praying for the Nation's Leader

III

The principal factor that lay behind the beginnings of the Israelite kingship was the aggressive movement of other peoples into Israel's lands, and the main problem here was the Philistines. The Israelites needed a national leader, capable of leading them to victory against such aggressive neighbours. Thus came about the kingship of Saul, though to be sure the Old Testament contains a number of varying assessments as to the wisdom or otherwise of the nation taking this step. Not all thought that kingship was a good thing! We certainly hear of Saul leading his people to victory over the Philistines (I Sam. 13f.), over the Ammonites (I Sam. 11), and also over the Amalekites (I Sam. 15). And indeed, one of the functions of the king was to rule over his people, to rule successfully so that other rulers would not have power over Israelite people. It is not surprising, therefore, that our Royal Psalm, Ps. 72, has some verses that contain a prayer asking that the rule of the Israelite king may be secured over his people and beyond, so that they may live in security. May other peoples be subject to his rule! In Ps. 72.8–11 we read:

Ps. 72.8 May he rule from sea to sea,
from the river to the ends of the earth.
v.9 Before him, may his foes bow down,
and his enemies lick the dust.
v.10 May the kings of Tarshish and the islands render him tribute,
and the kings of Sheba and Seba bring a gift.
v.11 May all kings fall down before him,
all nations serve him.

The expression 'from sea to sea' in v.8, though it could be understood in the sense 'from the Red Sea to the Sea of the Philistines' as in Ex. 23.31, more probably means something much vaster. In Hebrew thought the earth was suspended over the cosmic waters and surrounded by them (see Pss. 24.2; 88.6; 136.6), and thus 'from sea to sea' may be simply a way of saying 'the whole earth'. It would seem that these verses, then, contain a prayer for the world-wide rule of the king. Of course, it seems like a very grandiose request, but then we are dealing in this Royal Psalm with a vision of the ideal king, one whose rule will in a human setting represent the universal rule of God.

From a rather less idealized, and no doubt more realistic, setting there are various other prayers in the Royal Psalms for the successful rule of the king – even perhaps for his survival. For instance, in Ps. 18.3 and 6 there is the king in distress calling upon God:

> I call upon the Lord, who is worthy to be praised,
>   and I shall be saved from my enemies.
> In my distress I called upon the Lord;
>   to my God I cried for help.
> From his temple he heard my voice,
>   and my cry reached his ears. (Ps. 18.3,6)

The well-known 'Pilgrimage Psalm', Ps. 84, has an 'interruption' for a brief prayer for the king: it asks that God's blessing may be upon the one who 'shields' his people from their enemies:

> Behold our shield, O God;
>   look on the face of your anointed. (Ps. 84.9)

And it is there also in Ps. 144, in the prayers in verses 5–8 and 11-15 where in the terms of theophany (the appearance of God to people[19]) the helpful intervention of the Lord is sought. Again, the theme is present in another of the Royal Psalms, Ps. 20, a Psalm that in general terms may be described as a prayer for victory. This is particularly emphasized in vv. 5 and 9:

> May we shout for joy over your victory,
>   and in the name of our God
>   set up our banners.
> May the Lord fulfil all your petitions.
> Give victory to the king, O Lord;
>   answer us when we call. (Ps. 20.5,9)

Now with such prayers as these we may legitimately associate

Praying for the Nation's Leader

various prayers before battles that we find in the books of Kings and Chronicles. For instance, there is the reference to prayer in II Kings 13.4:

> And Jehoahaz besought the Lord and the Lord hearkened to him, for he saw the oppression of Israel, for the king of Syria oppressed them.

This incident is not treated by the Chronicler, but that need not occasion much surprise, as the Chronicler was selective in what he took up and used, or adapted, from his sources. But in the above verse, we have language and phraseology that is reminiscent of the book of Judges, where we read about the people of Israel sinning, being overrun by their enemies, crying to God for help, being sent a deliverer, being delivered from their oppression.[20] In this instance, the Lord 'heard' the prayer made by King Jehoahaz, heeded the request and gave a saviour.

This helpfully prepares the way for us to consider another prayer that comes from a time when God's people were under siege. This is in II Kings 19.15–19, and the king who prays here is Hezekiah, in the time when Jerusalem was besieged by the Assyrian king Sennacherib. Unfortunately, this prayer is set in a rather complex block of material that has been much discussed by scholars.[21] It is necessary for us to give some attention to these complexities, but the trouble will be worthwhile for by doing so we shall be enabled to see some rather different approaches to prayer being set forth.

In 705 BC the death of the Assyrian ruler Sargon opened the way for King Hezekiah of Judah to think about mounting a revolt against the Assyrian rule over his country. In spite of preparations such as the fortification of Jerusalem and other cities, and the provision of a new water supply to the capital city that would bring the waters of the Gihon spring right into the city, to within the new western wall (II Kings 20.20; II Chron. 32.4–5, 30),[22] the punishment soon came. It seems to have taken place in 701 BC, and while the abundance of material in the Old Testament has led some to suggest that there were in fact *two* campaigns of Sennacherib,[23] the majority view is that there was one, about which we now have a number of accounts. This is the approach here. In the Old Testament we read about this incident in three places: II Kings 18–20; Isa. 36–39; II Chron. 32.1–21.

The material in II Kings 18–20 is largely paralleled by Isa. 36–39, and it is widely accepted that II Kings 18.13–16 and 18.17–19.37 are themselves parallel accounts of the same events of 701 BC. II Kings 18.13–16 is generally referred to as Account A, and 18.17–19.36 as Account B, the latter itself being made up of two versions : B1 in 18.18–19.9a and 36–37, and B2 in 19.9b–35. Further, all this material is paralleled by the Chronicler's account in II Chron. 32.1–21.

Account A tells how in the fourteenth year of Hezekiah's reign Sennacherib captured cities of Judah, so that Hezekiah rendered to him, while he was in the Judaean city of Lachish, gold, silver and other treasures. Thus, it seems we are intended to understand, Jerusalem was spared and Hezekiah continued to reign there. In this account we do not hear of any prayer being made.

In Account B1 we hear of Sennacherib's emissaries coming from Lachish to Jerusalem, of boastful speeches on the part of the Rabshakeh (a high ranking Assyrian officer), and the mocking of Hezekiah's dependence both upon Egypt and upon his Lord God. Hezekiah resorts to the house of the Lord (19.1), and seeks the prayers of the prophet Isaiah (19.4). Isaiah assures Hezekiah that he need not fear, for Sennacherib would hear a rumour and return to his own land where he would die (19.5). We further read how Sennacherib heard about Tirhakah of Ethiopia (19.9a) and (assuming that 19.36f. completes this account) how he returned to Nineveh where he met his death. Thus, while there is a reference to prayer in this account, there is no miraculous or supernatural intervention on the part of God, and the forced withdrawal of Sennacherib is due to human agencies, namely, the news coming from other parts of the Assyrian empire.

Account B2 is widely regarded as being a parallel variant of B1: indeed B2 does in some respects follow B1. However, in B2 the boastful claims of Sennacherib are sent to Hezekiah by letter, which he spreads before God in the house of the Lord

(19.14). There then follows a prayer on the part of Hezekiah (19.15–19):

> And Hezekiah prayed before the Lord and said, 'Lord God of Israel, you are enthroned above the cherubim, God alone of all the kingdoms of the earth; you have made the heavens and the earth. [16] Incline your ear, Lord, and hear; open your eyes, Lord, and see; and hear the words of Sennacherib which he has sent to mock the living God. [17] Truly, Lord, the kings of Assyria have laid waste the nations and their lands, [18] and have given their gods into the fire; for they were no gods but only the work of human hands, wood and stone; so they perished. [19] And now, Lord our God, save us we pray from his hand, that all the kingdoms of the earth may know that you alone, Lord, are God. (II Kings 19.15–19)

The prayer opens with the theme of adoration of God, with the affirmation that he is the creator of the heavens and the earth (v.15), turns to invocation and then goes on to speak of the mocking words about God employed by Sennacherib (vv.16, 17). Then the petition follows in v.19 after the 'and now': 'may the Lord save us from the hand of Sennacherib, that all the kingdoms of the earth may know that the Lord alone is God!' Hezekiah is portrayed as putting his whole trust in the Lord, who responds to this prayer at some length, through a prophecy of Isaiah (II Kings 19.21–34). This response is made up of three oracles: the first (v.28) directed to Sennacherib, the second (vv.29–31) to Hezekiah, and the third (vv.32–34) more generally to any who will hear. The common theme is that Sennacherib will not succeed, but on the contrary will return to his own land. Thus comes v.35 with its striking climax to the story, namely:

> That night the angel of the Lord went out and struck down one hundred and eighty-five thousand in the camp of the Assyrians; and when they arose in the morning, they were all dead bodies. (II Kings 19.35)

Thus Hezekiah's prayer is portrayed as leading to both the

reassuring oracles from Isaiah, and the dramatic, indeed miraculous, *dénouement* of the whole incident, and the defeat of the Assyrians.

The Chronicler (II Chron. 32.1–21) has considerably reworked this whole incident. While the Kings B1 account had Hezekiah going in to the house of the Lord and exhorting the prophet Isaiah to pray (II Kings 19.2–4), and while the Kings B2 account gives the extended prayer of Hezekiah (II Kings 19.15–19), in the Chronicler's treatment these two 'prayings' are conflated, thus:

> Then Hezekiah the king and Isaiah son of Amoz the prophet prayed about this and cried out to heaven. (II Chron. 32.20)

Here both king and prophet pray – though whether they pray separately, or together in the style of what we would recognize as a 'prayer meeting', we are not told! But a more significant difference in the Chronicler's account over against the two accounts in Kings is the fact that the Chronicler has Hezekiah first of all take practical and military steps to deal with the crisis. Thus Hezekiah attends to the water supply (vv.3f.), the fortifications and the weapons (v.5), and the military organization of the people (v.6). Even so, these details are followed by the assertion that the real source of hope lies not in such human activities but in trust in the Lord: '. . . with us is the Lord our God, to keep us and to fight our battles' (vv.7f.). And it is only after such practical steps have been taken, and confessions of faith made, that it is recorded how king and prophet prayed and cried to heaven. The result of all this is the visit of the angel of the Lord[24] who slays a more modest number of Sennacherib's soldiers – but those slain are yet the mighty warriors, commanders and officers!

Now this represents a different way of regarding prayer from that envisaged in the Kings B2 account. Here in the Chronicler's account, though the victory is portrayed as being God's, it does not have quite the dramatic results that have been seen earlier: there have been the human and military preparations made, and the praying does not have within it quite the drama as is to be observed in the B2 account in the Deuteronomistic history.

All in all, in the various records that we have of this historical incident, there are portrayed a number of different approaches to, and theological understandings of, prayer. While the Kings B2 account contains a style of prayer that is associated with a dramatic, even miraculous, divine intervention, the Kings B1 account emphasizes an answer to prayer being given through a secondary cause, while the Chronicler appears to lay stress upon the association of prayer to God, along with appropriate human activity. And the II Kings Account A does not make *any* mention of prayer. We shall return in our final chapter to a consideration of this variety of approaches to, and understanding of, prayer in the Old Testament.

In the meantime we may briefly draw attention here to a number of other prayers in the books of Chronicles that are presented as being in times of battles. There are a number of these,[25] one of which reads as follows:

> And Asa cried to the Lord his God, and he said, 'O Lord, there is no difference for you between helping the strong and the weak: help us, Lord our God, for we rely upon you, and in your name we have come against this multitude. O Lord, you are our God: let no mortal prevail against you.' (I Chron. 14.11)

The setting of this prayer is a battle (which the Deuteronomistic historian does not mention) between Zerah the Ethiopian, with his army of (so we are told) a *million* men and three hundred chariots, and Asa of Judah, with his army of three hundred thousand Judaeans and two hundred and eighty thousand Benjaminites (vv.8f.). Brief mention is made of the drawing up of battle lines at Mareshah (v.10), and then follows Asa's prayer, immediately after which comes the notice, 'So the Lord defeated the Ethiopians before Asa and before Judah, and the Ethiopians fled' (v. 12).[26] The emphasis is upon the powerlessness of people apart from God (a fact emphasized by the victory of the much smaller army over the greater) – and the strength and victory on the part of those who turn to the Lord. Here there is but small mention of human preparation for the battle.

Another example is to be found in the Chronicler's treatment of the reign of Jehoshaphat:

> And Jehoshaphat cried out, and the Lord helped him. (II Chron. 18.31)

In I Kings 22.32 Jehoshaphat, in the heat of battle, cries out, in the sense, it would appear, of distress, even desperation. The Chronicler has expanded his text at this point, and now the king's cry is clearly directed to God, and moreover is a prayer. Further, it is a prayer that God hears: sufficient aid is given with the result that Jehoshaphat is spared. This is another example of a familiar theme in the Chronicler's work, namely the help that is available from God, especially in a military context, and as a response to prayer.[27]

A final example of this emphasis of the Chronicler on what strength is available to people through prayer may be drawn from II Chron. 20.5–12. This has an extended prayer, too long to be set out here. It comes in another battle scene and again concerns Jehoshaphat in the face of a numerically very great foe (v.12). It is an elaborate prayer, cast in the form of a 'complaint' (lament) with its recitation of past favours (vv.6f.), a protestation of innocence along with a statement of trust (vv.8f.), a complaint (vv.10f.) and a plea (v.12). The prayer, said to have been uttered in the house of the Lord (v.5),[28] is answered in an oracle of salvation by the mouth of a Levite named Jahaziel (v.13–18). It has been pointed out how Jehoshaphat is portrayed by the Chronicler as equipping and manning the fortified cities (17.2, 12, 19) and recruiting an army of no less than a *million* warriors (17.14–19), but at the same time, 'the pious king is expected not only to possess military strength but to forego its use and to rely only on God for protection'.[29] But this may not be quite so paradoxical as Japhet suggests, for it is another example of the association and blending of prayer and action with, at least in the Chronicler's presentation, a particularly marked emphasis upon the need of prayer, and the great benefit that comes from praying.

IV

But human kings do wrong, and commit sin – and Israelite kings were no exception. Not, however, that any of the Royal Psalms contain any expressions of prayerful confession of sin to God. This, of course, is understandable: the Royal Psalms are giving expression to nothing less than an *ideal* of Israelite kingship. This is what kings are, and how they behave, in a theoretical and ideal way. But other parts of the Old Testament, being perhaps not so convinced about the God-given nature of the monarchy as were those who were responsible for the composition of the Royal Psalms, see things rather differently. Elsewhere, kings are portrayed in less idealized light, in more 'down to earth' terms, and are presented to us, like Cromwell in his portrait, 'warts and all'. In some such instances, though not in all, we shall come across a prayer of confession on the part of the monarch. To such prayers of penitence we now turn.

Chapters 21–24 of the second book of Samuel seem to make up an appendix to the book.[30] Chapter 24, which appears to look forward to the building of the temple in Jerusalem, begins with an account of a census that King David took (vv.1–9). We would hardly see anything wrong in such an act. We would regard it as an exercise designed to assess human resources – something of a human stewardship campaign. But in ancient Israel, such an act would have been regarded in some circles as a sin, for it betokened an apparent dependence upon human strength and not upon God. In so far as it was a denial of the strength and help that was available solely from God, it would have been held to be a sin. And David did indeed come to acknowledge his misdeed in effecting his census (v.10). So he prays his prayer of confession to the Lord:

> And David said to the Lord, 'I have sinned greatly in what I have done. And now, O Lord, take away I pray the iniquity of your servant, for I have behaved very foolishly.' (II Sam. 24.10)

Here we have confession ('I have sinned greatly . . .'), petition ('And now, O Lord, take away . . .'), along with acknowledgment of folly ('. . . for I have behaved very foolishly.') David acknowledges not merely a lack of prudence in ordering the census, but comes to perceive that it was a sin, in the sense that there was a distrust in God and his might, a misplaced trust in human resources. In what has been termed 'a sign of grace',[31] God is portrayed as offering a choice of three punishments. Then, in the context of the chosen punishment, comes another prayer from David:

> And David spoke to the Lord when he saw the angel who was smiting the people, and he said, 'Behold, I have sinned and I have done wickedly, but these sheep what have they done? Let your hand, I pray, be against me and against the house of my father.' (II Sam. 24.17)

In this prayer David is portrayed as accepting full responsibility for the sin, even going 'so far as to invite the judgment of the Lord on himself and his family . . . in order that *these sheep* may be spared'.[32] Thus he pleads for his people. Further, as the text now stands there is a marked emphasis upon the Lord's changing his mind, which in fact is portrayed as having taken place *before* (v.16) David's prayer of penitence (v.17)! Some accept this order of events,[33] whereas others regard v.17 as referring to a time *prior* to that of v.16.[34] The Chronicler keeps this sequence of events, having the Lord relent in I Chron. 21.15 *followed by* David's prayer of confession in v.17. There are considerable differences between the texts of the prayers in II Sam. 24.17 and I Chron. 21.17, but the Chronicler's longer prayer does not materially change things apart from, if anything, laying greater emphasis on the cause of the plague being David's sin. Again, the Chronicler has emphasized that God's grace stands in the forefront.

Yet the most striking instance of repentance in a prayer of a king occurs in the Chronicler's treatment of Manasseh. The Deuteronomistic historian, portraying Manasseh as representing the very depths into which Israelite kingship could sink, could see no redeeming features in his reign, and could even portray the later exile as being due (in spite of the good reign of Josiah which followed: II Kings 22f.) to the evils of Manasseh

Praying for the Nation's Leader

(II Kings 21.1–18). The Chronicler's treatment of Manasseh's reign is very different (II Chron. 33.1ff.). Like the Deuteronomistic historian he speaks of the king's apostasy (II Kings 21.1–9; II Chron. 33.1–10), but then goes on to add what is otherwise unattested, namely his being led away as a captive of the Assyrians to Babylon, his repentance there, his subsequent restoration to his throne, and the carrying-out of a partial reform of the cult (II Chron. 33.11–20). The historicity of these added details has been the subject of much discussion,[35] but more significant for our present purposes is the fact that, whether or not this actually happened, the Chronicler *has* included this material. Why has he done so? Clearly, he is adding material on the theme of exile and restoration, and stressing human repentance and divine mercy.[36] Thus the Chronicler speaks of Manasseh – complete with his manacles – being taken captive to Babylon:

> And in his distress he entreated the Lord his God, and humbled himself greatly before the God of his fathers. [13] And he prayed to him, and he accepted his entreaty, and he heard his plea, and restored him to his kingdom in Jerusalem. And Manasseh knew that the Lord was indeed God. (II Chron. 33.12f.)

Sara Japhet has pointed out that the Chronicler's chapter on Manasseh has a chiastic structure, at the pivot of which are the above two verses.[37] The whole chapter goes thus:

(a) v.1 Introduction: Manasseh is king
  (b) vv.2–8 Manasseh's transgressions
    (c) vv.10–11 Punishment : exile to Assyria
      (d) vv.12–13 Repentance and delivery
    (e) v.14 Manasseh's earthly enterprises
  (f) vv.15–17 Religious restoration
(g) vv.18–20 Conclusion: death and burial

Presumably, the fact that the notices of the king's prayers, his repentance and restoration, stand at the pivotal position in the literary composition point to their central significance for the Chronicler. To be noted here are not only a series of verbs concerning prayer and repentance, but also the fact that penitential prayer and an act of repentance go together. Altogether, there is an unmistakable emphasis on the reality of divine forgiveness that flows from true human penitence and repentance. Further, it should not be overlooked that in vv.18f. are *further* references to Manasseh's prayer and repentance!

> And the rest of the acts of Manasseh, and his prayer to his God, and the words of the seers who spoke to him in the name of the Lord God of Israel, these are in the annals of the kings of Israel. [19] And his prayer and the response to him, all his sins and unfaithfulness, and the sites where he built high places and set up the asherah and the images before he humbled himself, these are written in the records of the seers. (II Chron. 33.18f.)

Thus, clearly, the Chronicler makes emphasized reference to the humility and the prayer of confession of Manasseh, to the fact that prayer and repentance go together, as well as to the divine forgiveness, which in more general terms he believes is available for those who humble themselves, pray, seek the Lord and turn from their wicked ways (compare II Chron. 7.14).[38]

V

It may reasonably be asked what significance there is in this series of prayers for, or of, kings of many centuries ago for those who live for the most part no longer under the rule of monarchs. While clearly there is interest in these prayers of a historical nature (either politically or religiously), what is there for us today?

Generally the Old Testament has a high view of kingship, for the most part believing the institution to be ordained by God. Further, in the case of some kings it was believed that they had been chosen and appointed by divine decree (see esp. II Sam. 7). But at the same time, the Israelite and Judaean kingship did not come to have attached to it the more extravagant claims of divinity known in some of the nations round about.[39] In ancient

Israel, while the king was certainly an exalted person, he was at the same time a human being. In fact, while there can have been few more exalted human beings than the Israelite king, yet this same person stands in need of prayer not only at the point at which he ascends the throne, but also throughout his reign. Any life that he has – and certainly any gift of long life – will be dependent upon the grace of God, and this gift will ideally be sought in prayer. But it is particularly for the military sphere of his responsibilities that prayer will be made, and certainly the Chronicler portrays the king, as he defends his realm from the encroachments of the enemy, as standing in need of that strength of God which a person may seek from the Lord by prayer, and which in the Chronicler's view, God is so ready to give. We may well feel a difficulty in associating ourselves with all these prayers for success in battle, and question what significance such prayers may have for our lives. But we perhaps need to understand the thought that lies behind them, namely that for any great enterprise in life we must have the blessing and strength of God. It is a principle given expression in various parts of the scriptures. It is there in Second Isaiah:

> He gives power to the faint,
>   and strengthens the powerless. (Isa. 40.29)

But it is also there in St Paul:

> I can do all things through him who strengthens me. (Phil. 4.13)

The Old Testament texts we have been considering remind us of the belief that such divine strength may be sought through prayer.

Further, a king, being a human being, is prone to sin, even to sin grievously, and like others will need to seek divine forgiveness through prayer. David, as we have seen, needed to do this (II Sam. 24.17), but the most remarkable example of a king who successfully sought forgiveness through prayer is to be observed in the Chronicler's treatment of the reign of Manasseh (II Chron. 33). Not only does the Chronicler present a very different understanding of the reign of Manasseh than does the Deuteronomistic historian (II Kings 21), but also presents the king as having been enabled to gain a new lease of life as a result of his humbling himself, and making his prayer of confession.

All this is to say that in the thought of the parts of the Old Testament we have been considering in this present chapter, there is the conviction that no one, however exalted their status or role in life may be, is above the need to pray for themself and to seek the prayers of others as they exercise their responsibilities in life. And if even kings are not beyond the need of prayer, how much more is that so for those with less exalted callings in life – both then and now? Many people today may well feel that their tasks and responsibilities, while not great, are yet demanding. They may well know their need of reserves of strength and wisdom whose source will be found to be the same as those for the kings of ancient Israel, namely, God. Like the kings of old they will pray for strength, wisdom, and forgiveness – and ask for the prayers of others, that such gifts may be given. And many today will, like those kings in the thought of the author of the Royal Psalm, ask that as they labour faithfully, so may they make their own contribution (perhaps in its way very small, but nevertheless significant) to the harmony of nature and the well-being of all life (Ps. 72.1–4).

But at another level there is the continuation of these prayers for kings in our present-day prayers for rulers of nations, and their governments. For, as people in ancient times looked to their kings, so we today look to rulers and governments to work towards a world order in which there is justice and righteousness for all, and in particular for the least privileged members of society. Thus, today:

> We pray for the peoples of the world and their leaders . . . that they may seek justice, freedom and peace for all.[40]

But long ago, Cromwell (1599–1658) made such a prayer his own:

> Strengthen us, O Lord, to relieve the oppressed, to hear the groans of poor prisoners, to reform the abuses of all

professions; that many be made not poor to make a few rich; for Jesus Christ's sake.[41]

And since then many have made a central place in their prayers for intercessions on behalf of national rulers and leaders. Thus, for instance:

> Sovereign Lord of men and nations, we pray for rulers and statesmen who are called to leadership among their fellow countrymen; give them vision to see far into the issues of their time, courage to uphold what they believe to be right, and integrity in their words and motives; and may their service to their people promote the welfare and peace of mankind; through Jesus Christ our Lord.[42]

And finally, let us try to imagine that moment in ancient Israel when one king died and another acceded to the throne. That must surely have been a moment when hope was kindled again, and when prayer was made, that the new king might indeed rule with success, wisdom and righteousness, and enjoy longevity of reign. With that thought in our minds we may contemplate the following prayer. It is a prayer for a time of General Election of a government, and it was written by a Bishop of Oxford.

> O Lord, we beseech thee to govern the minds of all who are called at this time to choose faithful men and women to serve in the great Council of the nation; that they may exercise their choice as in thy sight, for the welfare of all our people; through Jesus Christ our Lord.[43]

7

'My house shall be called a house of prayer'

The Place of Prayer

I

Critics of English literature are generally agreed as to the greatness of T. S. Eliot's series of poems, *Four Quartets*.[1] The poems are intensely religious, but they concern a religion that is localized in time and space. While the *Four Quartets* represent four seasons and four elements, the imagery of each is based on a particular localized setting. The setting of the last of these poems is Little Gidding, the place where, in the seventeenth century, Nicholas Ferrar and his family established a small religious community – later pilloried as 'The Arminian Nunnery'.[2] It must have been the chapel at Little Gidding that Eliot had in mind when he wrote:

> . . . You are not here to verify,
> Instruct yourself, or inform curiosity
> Or carry report. You are here to kneel
> Where prayer has been valid.[3]

Throughout the ages men and women have sought holy places, places where it is believed that 'prayer has been valid'. Such a search is reflected in parts of the Old Testament, and our concern in this chapter is with the place, the locality, of prayer, in particular, but not exclusively, the temple in Jerusalem.

However, it has to be said that the vast majority of the Old Testament texts that concern prayer, depict it as taking place irrespective of a particular building. Indeed, prayer took place long before the people of Israel had a temple – or other religious building. Cain is portrayed as praying without the benefit of a building (Gen. 4.13f.); the servant of Abraham on his matrimonial mission that we considered earlier made his prayers at the well at Nahor (Gen. 24.12–14) – and certainly Moses had to make his intercessions without temple (Ex. 32.11–14, 30–34 etc.)! Nevertheless, life for those who had come out of Egypt is portrayed as being blessed with the desert tabernacle (Ex. 25–31, 36–40), an elaborate tent that served as a shrine during the period of the desert wanderings. Thus, the wandering Israelites are portrayed as having a 'holy place' where the presence of God was believed to be.

II

Apart from this tabernacle, we are also told about the tent of meeting (Ex. 33.7–11; Num. 11.16–30; 12.1–16),[4] where Moses enjoyed a time of intimacy with the Lord. There, we are told, the Lord spoke with Moses. While we do not read specifically of Moses speaking with God, yet the speech of 'friends' is mentioned:

> Now Moses used to take the tent and pitch it outside the camp, far off from the camp; he called it the tent of meeting. And anyone who sought the Lord would go out to the tent of meeting, which was outside the camp. [8] Whenever Moses went out to the tent, all the people would rise and stand, each of them, at the entrance of their tents and watch Moses until he had gone into the tent. [9] When Moses entered the tent, the pillar of cloud would descend and stand at the entrance of the tent, and the Lord would speak to Moses. [10] When all the people saw the pillar of cloud standing at the entrance of the tent, all the people would rise and bow down, all of them, at the entrance of their tent. [11] Thus the Lord used to speak to Moses face to face, as one speaks to a friend. Then he would return to the camp; but his young assistant, Joshua son of Nun, would not leave the tent. (Ex. 33.7–11)

One of the most striking statements in this passage occurs in verse 11: 'Thus the Lord used to speak to Moses face to face . . .' This certainly seems to be referring to occasions of very great intimacy between Moses and God! And the talk of such intimate fellowship is yet more remarkable when we set it alongside what is said in verse 20 of the same chapter. There we read:

> 'But,' he [God] said, 'you cannot see my face; for no one can see me and live.' (Ex. 33.20)

What is being indicated in verse 20 concerns the overwhelming greatness of God, so great, so holy, that a human could not possibly look upon it and survive.[5] Yet the Lord, we are told in v.11, 'used to speak to Moses face to face'. In an attempt to reconcile these statements we can appeal to different literary sources: we may suggest that they come from different theological traditions, each having rather different conceptions of God. But another way of regarding these verses is to understand them as expressing the paradoxical facts that God is both far beyond us and yet at the same time close to us: he is both transcendent and immanent; his holiness sets him totally apart from us, and yet he makes himself available for us.[6] And bound up in this paradox of the transcendence and immanence of God is the gift of prayer, one of the principal means whereby a person, or a group, may come into intimate communion with the holy and majestic God. Not, of course, that prayer is explicitly spoken about in Ex. 33.11: the language here concerns the Lord speaking to Moses, face to face – there is no mention of Moses speaking to God.

Nevertheless, the following verses (Ex. 33.12–23) *will* speak about Moses praying to God, and of God's promise that he will, under certain conditions, reveal himself to his servant. But where does *this* praying of Moses take place? We are not told. It could be back on the mountain, the setting of the earlier materials, or alternatively it could be in the tent of meeting – the tent that we have been hearing about in the preceding verses (7–11). And indeed, the setting of the prayer of vv.12–23 could be in this same tent. Moreover, in the present form of the book of Exodus – that is, with 33.7–11 leading on to 33.12–23 – those responsible for this arrangement may well have intended us to understand that the prayer of vv.12–23 did take place in the tent of meeting, in which case that tent was, on at least some occasions, a place of prayer. We cannot be sure about this [7] – either about what happened from a historical point of view, or just what the editors of this material intended us to think. Perhaps we have to leave the matter there, and be content to go on to what we can be more sure about.

III

When we come to speak of the temple at Shiloh we are indeed on surer ground. Although we may not know when, or by whom, this temple was built and established, we do hear of it in I Sam. 1.9, and in 3.3 we read of the presence of the ark there:

> and Samuel was lying down in the temple of the Lord, where the ark of God was. (I Sam. 3.3)

When and where this ark came from – once again! – we do not know, but at some stage prior to its being installed in the temple at Shiloh it could perhaps have become a container for the two tablets of the law (I Kings 8.9). We read of its being carried by the sons of Levi during the wilderness wanderings (Deut. 31.9), and over the Jordan by the priests (Josh. 8.1). But, more importantly, the ark served as a representation of the presence of God on earth with his people, and the fact that this ark was housed in the temple at Shiloh must have given to that place an enhanced importance and significance as a point at which earthly and heavenly realms were believed to meet. It was to this temple that Elkanah went, so we are told, year by year to worship and to sacrifice (I Sam. 1.3). And it was here that Hannah prayed to the Lord (I Sam. 1.10), her prayer of some agony of spirit that was somewhat misunderstood by Eli the priest. What he mistakenly thought was drunkenness was in fact Hannah's silent prayer (I Sam. 1.12–16; see pp.23ff above).

Later, after Hannah had borne her son, Samuel, she took him to Shiloh to present him to the Lord, and there she prayed (so we are told) once again, but this time, not surprisingly, her prayer was one of thanksgiving (I Sam. 2.1–10).

Although there may be these recorded instances of Hannah praying at the temple of Shiloh, there is no mention in the traditions concerning this temple that speak of it specifically as a place of prayer – as some parts of the Old Testament, as we shall see, do about the later temple in Jerusalem. We are not surprised that the setting of Hannah's prayer should be this holy place, a place that no doubt had an enhanced reputation as a religious and holy site due to the presence there of the sacred ark. Such a holy place would presumably have been a favoured place for prayer: it was here that the Lord appeared to Samuel, and as well as the ark being housed in it, there was the lamp of God (I Sam. 3.3). Moreover, the Lord continued to appear at this temple (I Sam. 3.21). Nevertheless, we do not read that the people went there in order to pray, or of any instruction or advice that prayer was to be made there.

We have to confess our ignorance as to how long this temple stood at Shiloh. It does not seem that it was long-lived. In two parts of the Old Testament we have reference to its demise, but at what precise historical moment it came to an end is not easy to determine with certainty. In Jer. 7.12 we read:

> Go now to my place that was in Shiloh, where I made my name to dwell at first, and see what I did to it for the wickedness of my people Israel.

There is also a reference to Shiloh in Ps. 78.60f.:

> He abandoned his dwelling at Shiloh,
>   the tent where he dwelt among mortals,
> and delivered his power to captivity,
>   his glory to the hand of the foe.

It is interesting that in the latter reference there is the description of the Shiloh temple as a 'tent': presumably the thought is that those functions that the desert tent of meeting fulfilled as a place of meeting between God and his people were now subsumed within (if not replaced by) the temple at Shiloh. It may be that the destruction of the Shiloh temple took place around 1050 BC, in that time when the Philistines were successful in overrunning the Israelites. It was this very threat and menace of the Philistines that threw the Israelite tribes into such a time of turmoil and change, a time that was to call forth the main aspects of the ministry of Samuel, and to bring about the need for a king to rule over the tribes of Israel.[8]

IV

The first king of Israel was Saul, the son of Kish, who ruled from about 1020 to 1000 BC. He was hardly a successful king: although he did do much to free his people from the threat of the Philistines and the Ammonites, yet at the same time there is a sense of tragedy about this man who for some reason or other comes to be rejected as king.[9] Whether we are to understand this rejection as coming from God (as I Sam. 10.8 understands it), or whether from the prophet Samuel (as I Sam. 14.33–35 and I Kings 3.3 see the matter), we can hardly now decide. What is clearer is that while the authority of Saul waned, that of his rival David steadily increased (II Sam. 3.1). After the death of Saul, while Saul's son Ishbosheth ruled over the northern tribes of Israel, David became king of Judah in the south, establishing himself in Hebron (II Sam. 2.1–11). But soon the northern tribes offered *their* kingship to David (II Sam. 3–5), and thus David became king over 'all Israel'. The success story continues: he defeated Israel's main enemies, in particular the Philistines, and then, most significantly, captured the city of Jerusalem from the Jebusites, and made it his own, the 'city of David' (II Sam. 6). Henceforth Jerusalem, or Zion (II Sam. 5.7), was both the political capital of 'all Israel', and also the religious centre and symbol of faith in the Lord God of Israel.

It comes as no surprise to us that David should have wished to build a temple in Jerusalem. No doubt there was a desire that there should be a worthy successor to the Shiloh temple, which in all probability had been destroyed by this time. Further, a temple in David's new capital city would have done much to give a sense of legitimization to this new place. What had been until recently a 'foreign' city now became an Israelite city, indeed *the* Israelite city. Moreover, around this time it would seem that there arose the belief that the Lord had chosen both Mount Zion as his dwelling place and the house (dynasty) of David to rule over Israel. Such a belief in this dual election of place and dynasty is reflected in Ps. 132.11–14:[10]

> The Lord swore to David a sure oath
>   from which he will not turn back:
> 'One of the sons of your body
>   I will set on your throne.
> If your sons keep my covenant
>   and my decrees that I shall teach them,
> their sons also, forevermore,
>   shall sit on your throne.'
> For the Lord has chosen Zion;
>   he has desired it for his habitation:
> 'This is my resting place forever;
>   here I will reside, for I have declared it.' (Ps. 132.11–14)

The God who had made his dwelling here, surely needed a worthy temple in this place! Thus we are not surprised that David wished to build a temple in Zion, Jerusalem (II Sam. 7.1–3). Yet for some reason or other it was not to be. There is recorded in II Sam. 7 a word of the Lord (an oracle) to David brought to him via the ministry of the prophet Nathan, to the effect that David was not to build a 'house' (temple) for the Lord, but rather the Lord would build David a 'house' (dynasty) (II Sam. 7.4–17). In more matter of fact terms, it could have been the case that David did not 'get round' to building this temple: quite simply, he was otherwise occupied throughout his reign.

Whatever were the actual historical circumstances that prevented David building a temple in Jerusalem, the task was carried out by his son, and successor to the throne, Solomon.

This temple was a mighty edifice that according to the books of Kings put the nation in debt (I Kings 5.10f.; 9.10f.). The Chronicler's account is more enthusiastic about the whole enterprise; it makes no mention of the debt, and says that the work was carried out by foreign workers (II Chron. 2.17f.; 8.7–10).[11] In general terms, there were three major parts to the temple: the porch (the *ûlām*), the temple or place (the *hêkāl*), and the holy of holies (the *d^ebîr*). The last named, the holy of holies, or inner sanctuary, was considered by some to be the place where God dwelt, and here the ark of the covenant was placed (II Kings 6.23–28). There were also special temple furnishings, such as the bronze pillars, the bronze sea and much else.[12] There were also a number of altars placed in the temple,[13] and it is clear that a significant aspect of the temple worship was to do with the offering of the different sacrifices. In the account of the dedication of the temple, we read of the bronze altar being too small for all the offerings made that day (I Kings 8.62–64). Yet just prior to this note about these sacrifices has been an account of Solomon's prayer of dedication of the temple (I Kings 8.14–61), but no mention is made of sacrifice! All the emphasis in the prayer is on the subject of *prayer*, and to this we now turn.

V

This prayer of Solomon is very lengthy, being in fact the longest prayer in the Old Testament. As well as occurring in I Kings 8.14–61, it is also to be found in II Chron. 6.3–42. These two forms of the prayer are very similar, though in the latter part there are differences to which we must pay attention. We shall begin by considering the prayer as it is found in Kings, observing first its arrangement and structure. I have said that this is a lengthy prayer, and it has to be said that the treatment of it here will be correspondingly lengthy. This is not only because this is an important and significant prayer, but also because there are different ways of 'looking at' it. We shall be investigating the prayer by two 'methods'.

The composition opens in 8.14–21 with a prayer of adoration of God that focusses upon the mercies of the Lord to the people of Israel and the house of David. The prayer of dedication proper begins with 8.22–30; again there is the adoration of the great God with whom there is no equal, whose dwelling is in heaven, but who has chosen David and his house. In a sense of wonder, the question is asked whether this great God can dwell on earth – much less in this temple! – but Solomon prays that prayers offered in the temple may be heard in heaven.

Then in v.31 the main part of the prayer commences, and it is in effect a prayer about prayers that people will make to God from a variety of different situations. Solomon prays that in a series of hypothetical circumstances the prayers of the people may be heard and answered by God. These possible situations that may give rise to prayer are:

1. I Kings 8.31–32 When an offence is committed by a person against another.
2. vv.33–34 When there is an attack by an enemy.
3. vv.35–36 When there is drought.
4. vv.37–40 When there are natural disasters.
5. vv.41–43 When a foreigner comes and prays.
6. vv.44–45 When people pray towards the city God has chosen.
7. vv.46–51 When people are captives and they pray to God.

The prayer closes with two further sections. First in vv.52–53 there is a final plea that God will hear the prayers of those who though far away pray to him, and secondly in vv.54–61 there is an extended prayer of blessing. In this, God is blessed (praised) for his goodness to his people, and his continued blessing upon the present generation is prayed for.

Now, when we consider this prayer as a whole, we can see that it has a regular pattern and shape. That is, the central block of the seven hypothetical situations when people may pray to God, along with the two opening sections, and the two closing sections, give a satisfying and balanced literary 'shape'. We may represent this 'shape' and overall pattern of the prayer as follows:

A: vv.14–21 Adoration
   B: vv.22–30 Adoration
      C: vv.31–51 The seven petitions
         1. vv.31–32 Personal offences
         2. vv.33–34 Enemy attack
         3. vv.35–36 Drought
         4. vv.37–40 Natural disasters
         5. vv.41–43 The foreigner praying
         6. vv.44–45 Praying towards the city
         7. vv.46–51 Captives praying towards the city
   B^1: vv.52–53 Final Plea
A^1: vv.54–61 Adoration and blessing

This exhibits a satisfying wholeness and balance: there is introduction, continuation and conclusion. Moreover, the main central part of the prayer consists of prayers in the seven hypothetical situations of distress. The number seven in the Old Testament is a particularly significant and sacred number, and this fact suggests that the present form is due to a conscious arrangement on the part of some individual or group.

We now need to give some attention to our 'method' in studying the prayer. Thus far, we have been considering it in the form in which it has been handed down to us. To regard it in this way is, in the language of literary studies, to adopt a *synchronic* (from the Greek for 'same time') approach. This approach is to look at a text, a piece of writing, as it stands at one particular point in its history, usually (as here) in its final form, that is, the form in which we find it in the canon of scripture.

But there is another way of approaching texts, and that is to employ what has been called the *diachronic* (from the Greek for 'through time') approach. In this, the interest and the emphasis is on the *history* of the composition of the text. Many of the biblical texts – and this is especially the case with the Old Testament – were composed from sources that have been added to and expanded. This process has sometimes taken place over a long period of time. Further, behind this process of addition and expansion there lies the work of a succession of authors and editors (redactors). Sometimes, as for example in the case of the book of Jonah (as I suggested in Ch. 5 above) we can see where the expansion of the text took place: in that particular instance I argued that ch. 2 was added at some later stage to the original work, consisting of what we now know as chs 1, 3 and 4. In this way, my approach with Jonah was *diachronic*, whereas, by contrast, my approach to the book of Ruth in an earlier chapter (Ch. 4) was *synchronic*. My reason for handling the book of Ruth synchronically was simply because the story of that book seems to be whole and complete in the form in which it has been handed down to us, exhibiting no real 'seams' between parts that might have been added at later stages to those that were 'original'.[14]

But to return to Solomon's prayer. So far, I have considered this synchronically, that is, from the point of view of its final form. But this same text may also be studied diachronically, as some parts of it do appear to have come from later stages than others.[15] This is to be seen in particular in the petitions to God in the seven hypothetical circumstances of distress. We can well imagine that the historical setting of the first five of these petitions is indeed that of Solomon's kingdom, or at least of that of a successor of his in the period up to the conquest of Jerusalem in 586 BC, when many Judaean people were deported to Babylonia (II Kings 25). But it is different when it comes to the sixth petition (vv.44–45): this would seem to presuppose conditions where God's people are away in exile. Now their prayer and supplication are towards the city which God has chosen, and the temple – which is indeed depicted as still standing. In fact, at the time that the people of Jerusalem were taken into exile, the temple was destroyed (II Kings 25.9). Thus, it would seem that these verses must come from a time earlier than the exile, but that the writer expected that the exile would take place.

In the seventh petition (vv.46-51) the historical setting is unmistakably exilic: this is indicated by references to the people being given up to an enemy, and having been carried away captive to the land of the enemy (v.46). In this situation, those concerned are envisaged as making their supplication and prayer towards the land which had been given to their fathers, towards the chosen city, towards the temple – which is again still depicted as standing. Even in this situation, may God hear in heaven his dwelling place, and maintain their cause, forgive them, and give them compassion towards those who have carried them away captive.

But there seems to be a further historical situation reflected in the final plea in vv.52f. (B¹): here there is no mention of the temple or the city as the focus of the prayer. It now looks as if the temple has been destroyed. Now the burden of the prayer is that in this far-away place to which God has separated these people, may he be alert to the supplications of king and people – that he may indeed hear them when they call.

Thus there are these two ways of regarding and studying this prayer – and also, of course, many other prayers in the Old Testament, especially if they are extensive compositions – the *synchronic* and the *diachronic*. But it should not be thought that one is the 'correct' way of studying the prayer, and the other 'incorrect'. Which approach we take may well depend on how important we feel the original historical settings of the prayer are to us as we study it today. If one is anxious to begin with thinking about the prayer in its original historical setting, then presumably one will feel that a *diachronic* approach should be employed. But then the question may be raised as to how sure one can be about precise historical details. We may be able to locate those exilic parts of the prayer with some precision, but what is one to say about the historical setting of those earlier examples of the seven petitions? Do they really come from that historical moment when Solomon dedicated his new temple, or are they rather the sort of petitions that some theologians felt that leaders and people should be praying and which have been attributed to – put in the mouth of – Solomon? We shall return to this matter of the purpose of this prayer, but for the present may notice this problem of locating such written materials in precise historical settings, and that it is this particular difficulty that in large measure has led to the recent burgeoning of the more literary approaches to the Old Testament, and to looking at texts *synchronically*.¹⁶

Thus there are good reasons why we might wish to look at Solomon's prayer *diachronically*, endeavouring where we feel it is possible – but hopefully ready to be agnostic where we cannot be sure – to speak about the historical settings of the various parts of the prayer. This will help us to understand why it is that different parts of the prayer carry rather different emphases. Such an approach should help us to see how those who at some later stage came to the earlier composition should have added further material to the prayer in order to reflect something of their new situation, something about the world in which they lived. Such considerations may helpfully serve to remind us, when we come to appropriate such a prayer for our own lives, that we too are living in very different days, with very different social and historical backgrounds, from that of Solomon – or even from those of the Jewish people who were in exile in Babylon. Like those Judaean or Jewish people of old we are still indeed prone to sin, and we should surely pray to God for forgiveness – but we live neither in Solomon's kingdom, nor in exile in Babylon. We are living in a very different world today, and moreover our religious situation is not the same, for however much our praying may be influenced by prayers from the Old Testament, yet *our* prayers will be made in the name of our Lord Jesus Christ.

We have said that it may be the difficulty of determining historical, social and political matters which causes us some problem, even disaffection, with the *diachronic* approach – and, we may add, with the whole of what may generally be labelled the 'historical critical' approach to the Old Testament.¹⁷ At the same time, other considerations may lead us in the direction of reading and studying this prayer of Solomon in a *synchronic* way, that is, in the form that we now have it in the Bible. We may quite simply feel that, because it is in this form that the church has accepted it into the canon (that is, 'rod', 'rule') of scripture, then this is the form that *we* should be accepting and reading. *This* is the prayer that has been given to us, and *this*, we may feel, is the prayer we should be reading and studying, rather than some possibly earlier forms which were not (in those forms) accepted into the canon of scripture. There is yet another reason why we may wish to regard the final form of the prayer as the one that is to be read by us: it may be, quite simply, that the Lord speaks to us through this scripture, that we feel some word is being said to us about our faith in God, our life in Christ, our pilgrimage in the power of the Holy Spirit. That may not necessarily have come as we dissected the prayer into its historical segments, but rather as we read the prayer in its final form. We may not express it in this way in our Bible Study Group, but God's word to us for our lives, or for our group, or for our church, may come to us through our reading of this long prayer in I Kings 8.14–61, as we read it *synchronically*.

VI

But we need to give attention to the contents of the prayer: these display a wide range of concerns.

In the first place, the prayer is uttered to the God who is incomparable and infinite. Thus Solomon begins:

> O Lord, God of Israel, there is no god like you in the heavens above or on the earth below . . . (I Kings 8.23)

And he continues:

> But will God indeed dwell on the earth? Even the heaven and the highest heaven cannot contain you, much less this house that I have built. (verse 27)

This is an expression of adoration and wonder: God is so very great, far beyond anything that human beings can understand or imagine. We are reminded of a prayer of David, uttered, so the Chronicler records, at the time when all the preparations had been completed for the building of the temple:

> Blessed are you, O Lord, God of Israel our father for ever and ever. Yours, O Lord, is the greatness, the power, the

> glory, the splendour, and the majesty; for all that is in the heavens and the earth is yours; yours, O Lord, is the kingdom, and you are exalted as head over all. Both riches and honour come from you, and you rule over all; in your hand are power and strength; and in your hand it is to make great and to give strength to all. (I Chron. 29.10b–12)[18]

While Solomon's prayer, like David's, may begin on this theme of the greatness and incomparability of God, the thought moves on: this great God is actively concerned with his people of earth. Indeed, he has not only had, but continues to have a relationship – in fact, a covenant relationship – with them:

> ... keeping covenant and steadfast love with your servants who walk before you with all their hearts, who have kept with your servant David my father what you declared to him; you promised with your mouth and have this day fulfilled with your hand. (I Kings 8.23b–24)

At a later stage the main content of the prayer will place considerable emphasis on human sin and failure (vv.31-53), but what we may consider to be remarkable is this mingling together in the one prayer of these themes of the incomparability of the Lord, his covenant relationship with – and thereby his commitment to – his chosen people, and their continued propensity to sin. Those between whom there is this great 'distance' have been brought 'near' – and at that by the incomparable one![19]

But before the prayer comes to its main centre block of petitions, there is the note of invocation, the calling upon God. We have already encountered this in some Old Testament prayers, in particular the prayers in certain Psalms. In Solomon's prayer it is as follows:

> Regard your servant's prayer and his plea, O Lord my God, heeding the cry and the prayer that your servant prays to you today, that your eyes may be open night and day toward this house, the place of which you said, 'My name shall be there', that you may heed the prayer that your servant prays towards this place. Hear the plea of your servant and of your

people Israel when they pray towards this place; O hear in heaven your dwelling place; heed and forgive. (I Kings 8.28–30)[20]

What is particular about this invocation lies in the fact that the prayer asks that God's eyes may be upon the temple, the place where he has said 'My name shall be there' (v.29). The book of Deuteronomy seems to be at pains to express with great care any thought on the subject of God's dwelling on earth. Deuteronomy stresses that God can never be represented in human and concrete form (Deut. 5.8), and seeks to express that sense of his presence in the temple by means of its 'name theology': the people of Israel have communion with God in that place God has chosen, where he will 'make his name dwell' (Deut. 12.5, 11 etc.). While Deuteronomy does not say that that place is the temple in Jerusalem – for to do so would have been anachronistic in a work that is presented as a great sermon of Moses as his people are about to cross the River Jordan and advance into the promised land – clearly it is.[21] Deuteronomy's 'name theology' seeks to give theological expression to the concepts of greatness, transcendence, otherness and universal sovereignty of God, and yet to speak of him as immanent, 'with' his people – 'present', in a sense, with them. By means of this expression, God is portrayed both as other-worldly and also as having some personal presence on earth. In Solomon's prayer this theme is developed with the thought of the temple as a place of prayer, a particular place where God has caused his name to dwell, a place from which God in his transcendence and otherness is addressed. At times in this prayer, people are spoken of as praying actually within the temple (vv.31, 33, 43), whereas at other times prayer is made 'toward' the temple (vv.30, 35, 38, 42, 44, 48).

So the prayer comes to its central section: the petitions to God from the series of possible situations in which people may find themselves. In this wide range of circumstances where there is difficulty, people will turn to God in prayer. Solomon prays that *those* prayers may be heard. We need to consider these possible situations in turn:

1. I Kings 8.31–32: The situation envisaged here is where a person has been accused of a crime of which they say they are innocent. Num. 5.11–31 and Ex. 22.7–12 give the background to the practice of such a person swearing an oath as to their innocence. The prayer asks that such a petition may be heard by God, and that he will vindicate the innocent and condemn the guilty. We may say that this is an intercession, asking that in a specific instance justice may prevail.

2. vv.33–34: The situation envisaged here is where sin has occurred, which has resulted in military defeat by an enemy. We should note that the Deuteronomistic historian makes the assumption that the cause of the defeat was an earlier sin on the part of those who have been defeated. When such defeated people pray to God their prayer of petition (and confession?), may they be forgiven!

3. vv.35–36: Here is a similar possibility, but rather than military defeat, the crisis is now drought, an event interpreted by the Deuteronomistic historian as having been caused by the sin of the people. The prayer here is that when such afflicted people pray towards the temple, at the same time confessing the Lord's name and turning from their sin, may God hear in heaven and may he forgive them.

4. vv.37–40: Again, this is a situation where sin has occurred, now giving rise to a number of possible natural disasters. Corporate sin may bring about – so the writer here argues – famine, pestilence or plague. Clearly, any one of these would create havoc among large numbers of people. When those people pray to God (there is no mention here of confessing God's name and turning from sin), may he hear in heaven his dwelling place, and forgive.

5. vv.41–43: This is rather different, and the envisaged setting is *not* one in which sin has occurred. Rather, now is supposed a foreigner – that is, a person who has been attracted to the Jewish religion and its worship – hearing of the greatness of the God of Israel and making his prayer

of petition in the direction of the temple. May *his* prayer be heard by God in his dwelling place in heaven.
6. vv.44–45: Like the previous instance, this also is one where petitionary prayer is made. But now it is corporate, and made by Israelite people. When they go out to battle and make their prayers in the direction of the temple, may God hear in heaven and 'maintain their cause'.
7. vv.46–51: We turn back now to another possible situation of sin. Now we read of people having been given over into the hands of the enemy, and this strongly suggests to us that this part of the prayer comes from a time after the people of Judah and Jerusalem had begun to experience exile following the fall of Jerusalem in 587/586 BC. Certainly now they cannot make their prayer for themselves and for their forgiveness *in* Jerusalem. But if they 'come to their senses' (v.47), and repent and plead with God, and confess that they have sinned, praying *towards* their land, the city and the temple, may they be forgiven and may their captors have compassion upon them.

VII

Now what is remarkable about this prayer is its great emphasis on the temple as a place of prayer, or as a place *towards* which prayer is to be made. Although the Deuteronomistic historian speaks of the bringing of the ark to the temple being accompanied by great sacrifices (I Kings 8.5) – and also that there were further and numerous sacrifices following the prayer of dedication (I Kings 8.62ff.) – there is no mention of the sacrificial cult in this long prayer. That is, this prayer does not speak of the temple as a place of sacrifice, although it is clear that sacrifice *did* take place there.[22] This fact is the more striking when we recall that although one of the purposes of the sacrificial system was to secure the divine forgiveness of sin,[23] here in Solomon's prayer, forgiveness (and four out of the seven possible instances of prayer concern situations where forgiveness of sin is sought) is to be secured by prayer. In this prayer, it is prayer rather than sacrifice that is envisaged as the basic medium of communication between God's people and their Lord, and also as their means of seeking his forgiveness.

Nevertheless, as we have observed, there is material both before and after this prayer that speaks of sacrifices being offered (I Kings 8.5, 62ff.), and it would seem that the Deuteronomistic historian, who put all these materials together, must have been aware of the fact that side-by-side here are portrayed different ways of approach to God, and of the securing of divine forgiveness for human sin and failure. It is thus surely not so much a matter of prayer, in the Deuteronomistic historian's view, having replaced sacrifice as the means of seeking forgiveness, but that in at least some circles in ancient Israel there were perceived to be these two ways of securing it.

In a more general sense, elsewhere in the Old Testament prayer and sacrifice appear to be regarded as alternative forms or aspects of worship, and not as mutually exclusive. Isa. 56.6f. speaks of the temple both as providing the setting where sacrifice is offered, and also as being a house of prayer:

> And the foreigners who join themselves to the Lord,
>   to minister to him, to love the name of the Lord,
>   and to be his servants,
> all who keep his sabbath, and do not profane it,
>   and hold fast my covenant -
> these I will bring to my holy mountain,
>   and make them joyful in my house of prayer;
> their burnt offerings and their sacrifices
>   will be acceptable on my altar;
> for my house shall be called a house of prayer
>   for all peoples. (Isa. 56.6f.)

Ps. 141.2 seems to be asking that prayer may be acceptable as a replacement for sacrifice:
> Let my prayer be counted as incense before you,
>   and the lifting up of my hands as an evening sacrifice.

Perhaps prayer and sacrifice are intended to be seen as equally valid in Prov. 15.8, though what in this verse makes their effect different is the wickedness or the uprightness of the worshipper:

> The sacrifice of the wicked is an
>   abomination to the Lord,
> but the prayer of the upright is
>   his delight.

Finally, we may observe that in Jonah 2.7–9 we again have this placing of prayer and sacrifice alongside one another in the manner of alternative modes of worship, but we also have here – and this conveniently brings us back to a prior theme – the aspect of prayer being directed towards the temple:

> As my life was ebbing away,
>   I remembered the Lord;
> and my prayer came to you,
>   into your holy temple.
> Those who worship vain idols
>   forsake their true loyalty.
> But I with the voice of thanksgiving
>   will sacrifice to you;
> What I have vowed I will pay. (Jonah 2.7–9)

While in no way at all did the Deuteronomistic historian wish the great temple in Jerusalem either to be identified with God, or to be regarded as the place where God had his residence, even so he was aware of a particular divine presence ('name') in that place. It must have been this divine presence in the temple that made it the place either in which, or towards which, prayer was to be made. Thus was the temple a focus for prayer, a point of intersection between the earthly and the heavenly realms.

In the I Kings 8 version, the prayer of Solomon ends with verses 52–61, vv.52–53 being a final plea that God will indeed hear the prayers of his people when they call upon him, especially in view of the fact that it is God who has separated them out from the nations to be his own people – as he promised through Moses when he brought the ancestors of these people out of Egypt. Verses 54–61 make up a final expression of adoration of God and a prayer that he will continue to be with his people and maintain their cause.

VIII

It is now time to turn to the Chronicler's version of this prayer of Solomon. This is to be found in II Chron. 6.3–42, and for much of the time it follows the I Kings 8 text closely.[24] But when we come to the end of the prayer there are considerable changes, for the Chronicler omits so much of I Kings 8.50–53. Much of this omitted material is about Moses and the exodus of the people of Israel from Egypt. It is in fact taken up and used by the Chronicler in a speech of Hezekiah in II Chron. 30.6–9, but in the context of the prayer of Solomon, he seems to wish not to use it. This is perhaps because he desires to stress the contemporary moment; rather than 'dwelling on the past' with Moses and the exodus, he stresses the fact that in his day the promise of God to David has truly been fulfilled.

Further, in place of this material about Moses, the Chronicler has added a quotation from Ps. 132.8–10. This is in II Chron. 6.41f.:

> And now you arise, Lord God, go to your resting place, you and the ark of your might. Let your priests, Lord God, be clothed with salvation; let your saints rejoice in goodness (v.43). O Lord God, do not turn away the face of your anointed; remember your faithfulness to David your servant.[25]

We may say that the Chronicler is wishing to emphasize two matters here in his quotations from Ps. 132 (and a very useful quotation it is to him in this context!). In v.42 in the first place, he is able to speak about the final resting place of the ark, the ancient symbol of the presence of God with his people. The ark is now in the temple (see I Chron. 15.1–16.43), now signifying in a renewed way the presence of God with his people – in particular in the house of prayer, in the place of intersection between earth and heaven towards which prayer henceforth is to be made. Then in the second place, in v.43, in the words of the somewhat free use (the order of the two lines has been reversed!) of Ps. 132.10, he stresses the importance of the succession of kings of the house of David: it is to these in the present day that the Lord's promises are made, and presumably the Chronicler has in mind the importance of the place that the king held in the relationship between God and his people.

Here then is the Chronicler setting out his programme for his people as a further stage of national life is re-established with the completion and dedication of a new temple in Jerusalem in 515 BC. Solomon's temple had been destroyed by the Babylonian army in 587/586 BC (II Kings 25.9, 13–17), and on the return of Judaean people from their exile it was a matter of urgency on the part of some of their leaders that the temple should be rebuilt speedily. Eventually, this task was carried out by Zerubbabel (II Chron. 36.23; Ezra 1.1–4; 6.15). Although the form of the Chronicler's work is a great history of the people of Israel that runs from the days of Adam (I Chron. 1.1) right up to the reign of Zedekiah and the exile in Babylon (II Chron. 36.11–21),[26] it seems that his purpose in writing was to set forth his vision for the re-establishment of the national and spiritual life of the nation after the exile. In all probability the Chronicler wrote his work sometime in the period between the dedication of the temple of Zerubbabel in 515 BC and the time of Alexander the Great (who reigned from 336–323 BC). Certainly the Chronicler's work displays a lively interest in the Temple cult, in the ministries of Levites and singers, and for this and other reasons would seem to reflect the concerns of the period after the temple rebuilding.[27] But it is clearly a work that comes from the Persian period: there is no hint of all that would take place with the military conquests of Alexander the Great from 336 BC onwards. Thus, although the Chronicler may be writing in II Chron. 6 of Solomon's temple and kingship, he is in fact thinking about Zerubbabal's temple (that is, what we call the second temple) and he has a vision of the day when the Israelite kingship would be restored. Clearly a central part of his vision of this restored community is of a great temple in the midst of its great city Jerusalem, a place of prayer, a place in which the ancient symbol of God's presence, the ark, resides, a place where it is clear that God's promises to King David are seen truly to be fulfilled.

IX

But it was not to be quite as the Chronicler envisaged it. The kingship never was re-established, and the temple was not to last as long as perhaps the Chronicler thought it would. It seems that the temple cult was established again in the days of the prophets Haggai and Zechariah, and apart from the time of desecration from 167-164 BC in the days of the Greek ruler Antiochus IV, it provided a focus for the religious life of the nation. Indeed, the temple was greatly extended by the Roman ruler Herod the Great (37–4 BC) from 20 BC. The 'new' temple precincts were twice the size of the old ones, but the finishing touches had hardly been put on it when it was destroyed by the Romans in AD 70.[28] After that, there would not be a temple, to be there as a house of prayer for the people of Israel and all the nations.

There was, however, to be an alternative place of Jewish worship, namely, the synagogue. In the New Testament Gospels we read of synagogues at Nazareth (Matt 13.54; Mark 6.2; Luke 4.16) and at Capurnaum (Mark 1.21; Luke 7.5; John 5.59). Elsewhere in the New Testament it is said that Jesus taught or worked a miracle in a synagogue, but the place is not named, while Mark 1.39 says he preached in all the synagogues throughout Galilee. In the Acts of the Apostles we read of synagogues in a series of cities outside Palestine.[29] Clearly, by such times the synagogue was an established institution. But it has to be said that much about the history and the liturgy of the Jewish synagogue is quite unclear to us.

In the first place we have to say that the origins of the synagogue are shrouded in mystery. There is no Old Testament text that speaks unambiguously about a synagogue, and we do not know where it was that the institution took its origin. The most common suggestion is that the synagogue originated in exilic communities (either in Babylon or elsewhere) and served to make-up for the lack of the Jerusalem temple. This is indeed a possibility, but no more than that! Further, we do not know whether the rise of the synagogue was due to the need on the part of the Jewish people for a meeting place for social, or educational, or worship needs – or a combination of some, or all, of these.[30]

Whatever were the original needs of Jewish people that brought about this institution, it is clear that the synagogue did become among other things a house of prayer.[31] It would seem from the evidence of archaeological discoveries that there was a concern that the orientation of the synagogue should be towards Jerusalem, though in some cases it was the front of the building that was thus orientated, but in others it was the shrine where the scrolls were kept. This facing towards Jerusalem was a reflection of the concern that prayer should be made towards that city and its temple, a concern we have observed in I Kings 8, Dan. 6.10 and elsewhere. Certainly, the institution was to give rise to the prayer known as the Eighteen Benedictions,[32] and, as the centuries went by, a series of Jewish Prayer Books.[33] And while, of course, prayers could be said in any place, whether or not there was a building, a crisis for Jewish religion occurred with the destruction of the Temple by the Romans in AD 70. That 'house of prayer' was no more. We must count it as providential that for the Jewish faith there was to be the institution of the synagogue to become something of a successor to the Jerusalem temple as a national shrine.[34]

Christians, on the other hand – while in no way insensitive to and unappreciative of the benefits to be found in physical buildings as places of prayer – recall the words of Jesus as recorded in St John's Gospel, apparently concerned with the Jerusalem temple and its possible destruction:

> Jesus answered them, 'Destroy this temple, and in three days I will raise it up.' The Jews then said, 'This temple has been under construction for forty-six years, and will you raise it up in three days?' But he was speaking of the temple of his body. (John 2.19–21)

While at one level the conversation is about Herod's temple, at a deeper level on the part of Jesus it concerns his own body, through which the final appearance of God to all his people has already taken place, and which was thus the real temple, the true centre for worship (John 4.20–24). C. K. Barrett says that it is possible that John's thought goes further and includes also the conception of the body of Christ, the church, as in the Pauline metaphor of Rom. 12.5, Col. 1.18 and elsewhere. 'In three days Christ raised up his human body . . . and with it the church, which through the Holy Spirit became the Temple of God, the true house of prayer for all nations.'[35]

8

'I have heard your prayer'
Old Testament Prayer

I

Jean Baptiste Marie Vianney (1786–1859), the saintly and celebrated Curé d'Ars, is reputed to have told his catechism classes the following story.

> We had in this parish a man who died a few years ago. One day, coming into the church to say his prayers before going out to work in the fields, he left his mattock at the door and lost all thought of himself before God. One of his neighbours, who worked a few fields away and was used to seeing him every morning, started to wonder why he hadn't turned up. Going back to the village, he had the idea of looking into the church in case he was there, and there he was, of course. 'What have you been doing all this time?' he asked him, and the man replied: 'I looks at God and God looks at me.'[1]

It is a picture of prayer as a natural activity, of conversation taking place between a disciple and his Lord. It reminds us of the tradition of intimacy between Moses and God in the desert tent, 'Thus the Lord used to speak to Moses face to face, as one speaks to a friend' (Ex. 33.11).

There are parts of the Old Testament that speak of prayer in terms of a natural conversation on the part of individuals and groups with God. But alongside such a broad generalization it has to be said that in the Old Testament there is a great variety of prayers, of occasions in which prayers are made, of approaches to prayer, and of understandings of prayer.

Something of this variety has been observed in the preceding pages, but may be brought into sharper focus if we consider the various prayers, types of prayers, and approaches to prayer, as they occur in the so-called Deuteronomistic history, the extensive theological work, permeated to some extent by the central ideas of the book of Deuteronomy, that is made up of Deuteronomy, Joshua, Judges, I and II Samuel, I and II Kings, and which we have already noted a number of times.[2] It is not that this great work, apart from the Deuteronomic theological themes that run through it, exhibits any marked sense of homogeneity, for it is clear that a wide range of different and disparate sources have been employed in its composition. These diverse sources display varying approaches to prayer – as we shall now see in the brief survey of the history that follows.

II

If we turn to the book of Deuteronomy in the first place, we see that there is a prayer at 1.11, itself a part of material that may well have been supplied by the Deuteronomistic historian to serve as an introduction to the whole work of Deuteronomy–II Kings.[3] The prayer in Deut. 1.11 is a prayer of intercession on the part of Moses, asking a future full of blessings for the people of Israel:

> May the Lord, the God of your fathers, make you a thousand times as many as you are, and bless you, as he has promised. (Deut. 1.11)

We may regard this as a generalized prayer of intercession of Moses for his people, supplied by the Deuteronomistic historian for the opening of his work, an example of the type of prayer of intercession that Moses did make for his people. It looks back on what God has promised to his people, and asks that in days to come, such promises might be fulfilled.

The second prayer in Deuteronomy is in 3.23-26. It is a petition in which Moses asks that he may be allowed to go over the Jordan into the new land. This prayer is of interest to us in two regards. In the first place, the Deuteronomistic historian appears here to be 'borrowing' words from another prayer of Moses, his intercessions for his people in the time of their great sin in the desert. This is recorded in Numbers 14.13–19, a prayer that was not recorded by the Deuteronomistic historian at that stage in his narrative (Deut. 1.34), but only now taken up and used in a new setting. In the second place, we may associate this Deut. 3.23–26 prayer of petition with those prayers of distress uttered by prophets such as Jonah and Jeremiah, in which they cry out to God as they face times of stress and conflict in the exercise of their God-given ministry (see Ch. 5 above).

When we come to Deut. 9.20 and 25f. we do have prayers of intercession on the part of Moses, first for Aaron and then for all the people, in both cases in the face of the fierce and wrathful anger of God occasioned by the great sin of the making of the golden calf in the desert. We have already considered this prayer in Ch. 4 above, and noted how it lays a particular emphasis upon all that Moses sought to do before the Lord as the intercessor on behalf of his people. In Deut. 9.25f. there is the mention of Moses lying prostrate before the Lord for forty days and nights, but there is not here (as I have argued that there is in the equivalent prayer in Exodus) the thought of Moses giving himself for the sin of his people.

There are just three more prayers in the book of Deuteronomy. At 21.8 there is recorded a brief intercession, again on the part of Moses, for his people, in a situation when an unsolved crime of murder has taken place, while in 26.7 is the record of a prayer of petition uttered by the people of Israel. This is their cry of distress which they made to their God when they were held in captivity in Egypt, a prayerful cry of distress that is now recorded in the expression of thanksgiving made by Israelites at the ceremony of the offering of the first-fruits (Deut. 26.1–11). What is being celebrated here is the fact that the people of Israel when in distress could indeed pray to their God in the belief that he would hear and respond. This is an acknowledgment both of the absolute dependence of these people upon their Lord, but also of his readiness to hear his people's cry, and his willingness to act for their deliverance. In the following section (26.12–15), which deals with a tithe offering made once every three years – for the benefit of Levites, aliens, orphans and widows, so that they too may eat their fill (v.12) – the people of Israel are to ask God's continued blessing upon themselves. Thus they are to pray:

> Look down from your holy habitation, from heaven, and bless your people Israel and the ground that you have given us, as you swore to our ancestors – a land flowing with milk and honey. (Deut. 26.15)

So, excluding Deut. 1–3, with its two prayers (1.11; 3.23–26) and apparently composed to serve as an introduction to the Deuteronomistic history, in Deut. 4ff. we have only five prayers or references to prayer, three of which are intercessions of Moses (9.20, 25f.; 21.8) and two petitions of the people of Israel (26.7,15).

To our way of thinking, this may appear to reflect a marked lack of emphasis on prayer. It may surprise us, for Deuteronomy stresses that Israel and her God are to have a relationship of intimate closeness; Israel is to 'cleave' to the Lord (Deut. 4.4; 10.20; 11.22; 13.5; 30.20). Indeed, the book of Deuteronomy holds up the vision of the whole of Israel's life as lived in a relationship of closeness with God: the Lord hears Israel's talk (1.34); he closely watches over Israel's march (2.30, 33, 36, 37; 3.2, 3, 18, 22); he speaks to Israel (4.1–40; 9.10); he speaks face to face with Israel (5.1), while for her part, Israel is to love the Lord (6.4), for truly she is his own possession (6.6). Israel is to eat before the Lord (12.7) and to beware of prophets who would take her away from the Lord (13.1ff.).

It is Moses, however, who in Deuteronomy enjoys a particularly close relationship with the Lord: he and God talk together (1.34); when God spoke to Israel, Moses stood between the parties (5.22–27); the Lord spoke to Moses (5.31–33); God commanded Moses what he was to teach Israel (6.1); God speaks with Moses (9.12–14; 10.1; 31.2, 16; 32.48). Such indeed is the closeness of relationship between Moses and God that God himself buried his servant after death (34.6)! It hardly comes as a surprise that for Deuteronomy, no prophet has arisen quite like him whom the Lord knew face to face (34.10). Nor is it surprising that with such intimacy existing between Moses and the Lord, Moses 'besought, implored' God (3.23–26), or that he could pray for Aaron (9.20). But what is perhaps surprising to us is that there is not more in Deuteronomy about the people in general praying to God. If such intimacy between God and his people exists, why do we not have more references to prayer recorded in this book? But this is perhaps to see things in a way rather removed from the ideology of the book of Deuteronomy. Perhaps we today must emphasize prayer, maybe particularly contemplation and meditation,[4] in order to remind ourselves that *all* of life is to be lived out for God, in the sight of God, with him at the centre. The book of Deuteronomy makes the assumption that all of Israelite life is God-centred, and his people must beware that they do not 'forget' him (Deut. 8). Nevertheless, when things go wrong, and when indeed they do 'forget' him, then they will pray to him, or have one who will pray to him on their behalf. But for 'normal' daily life, Deuteronomy has the vision that there is a constant attentiveness to God, an awareness of God's presence within and around – ideals that in our culture and age perhaps have to be sought in various ways, one of which is through prayer.[5]

We may move on to consider the book of Joshua,[6] and we note that in it there are just two instances where we are told that prayer was made – Josh. 7.6–9 and 10.12–14. The first of these comes in the lengthy story of the sin of Achan (7.1–8.29), a sin somewhat difficult for us to understand in that it was occasioned because he did *not* destroy all that had belonged to the defeated enemy. All the booty was believed to belong to the Lord, and therefore must not be appropriated to humans. This is the very thing that Achan did, as a result of which it was believed that the people rendered themselves open to defeat at the hands of the people of the city of Ai.[7] In this dire situation Joshua prayed for his people:

And Joshua said, 'Alas, Lord God, why have you brought

over this people, over the Jordan, to give us into the hand of the Amorites to destroy us? Would that we had been content to dwell beyond the Jordan! (v.8) Lord, what can I say when Israel has turned its back before their enemies! (v.9) For the Canaanites and all the inhabitants of the land will hear this, and surround us, and will cut off our name from the earth. What will you do for your great name? (Josh. 7.7–9)

This is a prayer of intercession, rather like the prayers Moses prayed for his people in the desert. Indeed, in the book of Joshua, the man Joshua is portrayed very much as Moses is in the book of Deuteronomy. Thus, for example, they are each depicted as intercessors for their people in these times of great crisis occasioned by their sin (Deut. 9.25–29; Josh. 7.7–9). In both of these prayers there is an identification of the interests of Israel with the Lord's honour: both intercessors are concerned to say that if things go badly for Israel, so will the Lord's honour not be maintained in the eyes of other peoples (Deut. 9.28; Josh. 7.9).

Behind this story is the belief that the war which Israel was waging with her enemies was in some sense a 'holy war', a war that was being fought by God, because the Israelites were his people.[8] The second prayer in the book of Joshua comes in another 'holy war' incident – the story of the battle of Gibeon (10.1–15). That the battle was won was due to the sun remaining until Israel had success on the field (10.13). Such a happening is known to have been recorded about other situations in antiquity,[9] but here is spoken about to make clear that what was wrought on that day was a mighty deliverance for Israel by God, with only minimal human effort. Thus, as in other holy war incidents, people are told not to fear, there is a miraculous intervention from the Lord – but those who do fear and panic are the enemy. We should perhaps notice that other 'holy war' occurrences take place in that region – I Sam. 14; II Sam. 5.17–25; I Sam. 7.7–12. Of these, it is only in the last incident that prayer is mentioned, as indeed it is in the present one (Josh. 10.14). But we have to say that the theme of prayer in Josh.10 is muted: we hear only that the Lord 'hearkened to the voice of a man', and we are given few details as to who prayed and what they prayed. We do read of Joshua 'speaking' in v.12, but that is not mentioned in v.14, and we have to conclude that in the record of this incident there is no great emphasis on prayer and its effects. And that perhaps has to be our judgment on the book of Joshua in general, for it could be that the earlier incident we considered (Josh. 7–8) was more concerned about pointing to parallels between Joshua and Moses than it was about speaking of prayer.

We now turn to the book of Judges,[10] the central section of which (2.11–16.31) is characterized by a fairly standardized mode of presentation of the material. We read about deliverers and judges, and about recurring cycles of sin, punishment (being handed over to an enemy), a crying out to God, God raising up a deliverer, the enemy being subjugated with the result that the 'land had rest'. Whereas the various episodes are so different, this 'framework' remains in essentials the same. It is the *crying out to God* part of these incidents that is of interest to us.

In the book of Judges we have the situation that there is no Moses (or even a Joshua) who will offer prayers of intercession on behalf of a sinful people. Now it is the people themselves who will cry out (z^cq, s^cq) to God. Not only was this a time when we are told that every man did what was right in his own eyes (Judg. 17.6; 21.25), but when perhaps also each person had to make their own prayers. We have already noted that the Hebrew verbs 'cry out' (z^cq, s^cq) are generally employed where there is acute distress on the part of those who are praying (see Ch. 2 above), and these words are used to describe Israel's plea to God in their time of suffering in Egypt (Ex. 2.23f.; 3.7, 9; Deut. 26.7). Here in Judges the people *cry out* to God in a situation of subjugation by a foreign power, interpreted in the book of Judges as a punishment for their sins of apostasy and idolatry. In Judges 3.9, 15, 30; 4.3, 23; 6.6; 10.10, we read of Israel 'crying to the Lord' and of their being delivered.

However, there are three rather different stories in the book of Judges, and these call for some comment. In Judg. 6.36–40 we read about Gideon asking for a sign of the Lord, and of his being granted one. In this incident Gideon appears to talk with the Lord in terms of considerable intimacy, in ways reminiscent of the 'call' narratives of certain of the Hebrew prophets: Moses (Ex. 3.1–12); Isaiah (Isa. 6); Jeremiah (Jer. 1). Though the language of prayer might not be used here, is it in fact prayer that is taking place when Gideon converses with God?

Then in Judg. 13–16 we have a series of stories about Samson – something indeed of a rogue, but clearly portrayed as being divinely inspired and employed. The news of and preparation for his birth both stress this. Not only do his parents receive a divine visitation to tell them of his forthcoming birth, but in a spirit of piety his father prays that they may be further visited, so that they may be guided in their upbringing of the child. So Manoah entreated (*'tr*, see Ch. 2 above) the Lord for guidance (Judg. 13.8f.). In his life, in a moment of crisis, Samson called on (*qr'*, see Ch. 2 above) the Lord (15.8f.), and at the end of his life – in that moment of death when he was to slay more Philistines than he slew in his life – Samson once again calls on (*qr'*) the Lord to strengthen him (16.28). But especially as regards the birth of Samson, we note that there is a marked similarity with that of Samuel – in each case there is the barren wife, the prayer, the divine intervention, and the birth of a son who is dedicated as a Nazirite.

But before we come to the chapters that record the prayer for and the birth of Samuel (I Sam. 1ff.), there is a final section in the book of Judges (chs 19–21) which tells of the civil war of the twelve tribes against Benjamin. Perhaps it is intended to speak of the nadir of the fortunes of Israel, now so much in need of a king to fight its battles, and to give its people a national cohesion. The book of Judges ends with a prayer in which God is asked why there should be such tragedy in Israel at this time:

> And the people came to Bethel, and sat there until evening before God, and they lifted up their voices and wept bitterly. And they said, 'Why, Lord God of Israel, has this happened in Israel that there should be this day one tribe lacking in Israel?' And on the morrow the people rose early and built there an altar and offered burnt offerings and peace offerings. (Judg. 21.2–4)

The books of Samuel speak of the establishment and growth of the institution of kingship in Israel. Samuel was something of a bridge personality spanning the old age of the judges and the new era of the kings. We have already seen how the birth narrative of Samuel is suffused with prayer, and also how Samuel came to be regarded as an intercessor, somewhat after the order of Moses (see Chs 1 and 4 above). Samuel is portrayed in I Samuel as fulfilling a number of roles, and some of the material regards him as a kingmaker. Thus Saul became the first king of Israel, and after him came David. David's kingship was more developed than Saul's, and his rule much more widespread. He ruled Israel and Judah, as well as conquering Jerusalem and making it his capital city. Not only were the Philistines subdued, but David conquered various neighbouring states: Edom, Moab, Ammon and Syria.[11]

But then, at the close of David's life there was the burning question of who was to succeed him in his various kingships. One part of the Old Testament that does seem to have a particular concern with this succession to the kingship is the so-called 'Succession Narrative'.[12] At least to some extent it is concerned with what certain individuals or groups saw as the vital matter of ensuring a smooth transition from the kingship of David to that of the appropriate, even divinely designated, successor. This Succession Narrative is of interest to us as it has a number of prayers.

This Narrative comprises basically II Sam. 9–20 and I Kings 1–2, and according to L. Rost in his study of the work, its key theme is expressed in I Kings 1.20, 'And now, my lord the king, the eyes of all Israel are upon you, to tell them who shall sit on the throne of my lord the king after him.'[13] There are seven prayers in the Succession Narrative: (1) II Sam. 12.13, a prayer of confession of David; [14] (2) II Sam. 12.16, David's intercession for the child; (3) II Sam. 14.17, a petition of a woman; (4) II Sam. 15.31, David's petition that the counsel of Ahithophel to Absalom be made foolish; (5) II Sam. 18.28, Ahimahaz's thanksgiving for David's deliverance from Absalom's force; (6) I Kings 1.47, intercession on the part of David's servants; (7) I Kings 1.48, David's thanksgiving that one of his offspring will sit on his throne, and that he has been permitted to see this.

It has been pointed out that in the Succession Narrative there is a marked emphasis on the fact of God's indirect involvement with, and intervention in the affairs of the world, and especially in the matter of the succession to David's throne.[15] All through these events God is present, and yet at the same time there is an unmistakable picture of events that seem to have been put into effect as a result of human actions. Apart from his direct sending of Nathan in II Sam. 12.1ff. and inflicting the baby with a fatal illness (12.5ff.), God here is portrayed as working through secondary causes.

Rost compared the Succession Narrative with the Ark Narrative (I Sam. 4–6):[16] in the latter there is (in contrast to what is found in the Succession Narrative) considerable emphasis upon the Lord's direct involvement in the world. But it should be noted that in the Ark Narrative there is only one reference to prayer, and that concerns David blessing the people on the occasion of the ark having been brought safely to Jerusalem (II Sam. 6.18). In no instance in the Ark Narrative is prayer mentioned as a means of communication between people and God, and nor is there any hint that by means of prayer any course of action is effected or changed.

Now, as has been observed above, there are in the Succession Narrative a number of prayers. One of these occurs in II Sam. 15.31 in a scene dealing with David's enforced departure from his city as a result of the seizure of power by his son Absalom (II Sam. 15.13–31). This prayer was uttered by David at the summit of the Mount of Olives – a location with a particular significance, a place we are told 'where God was worshipped' (v.32). Here David learned that Ahithophel was amongst the conspirators with Absalom, and so he prayed, 'O Lord, I pray, turn the counsel of Ahithophel into foolishness' (v.31). In the succeeding verses we hear how through a series of events the prayer was answered and how, eventually, David regained his throne.[17] It does seem that the author of this work wished to portray that in a mysterious manner the good and satisfactory outcome to the whole issue of the succession depended both upon what God did, and also upon what certain people did. Moreover, he seems to have been at pains to suggest that within that somewhat mysterious nexus of forces there were prayers at certain crucial moments.

Another prayer, coming at the moment when events appear to have turned out well for David, is at I Kings 1.47. This is an intercession on the part of some, unnamed, servants of David, who ask for God's blessing upon David and Solomon. It should be noted that two further prayers (II Sam. 18.25; I Kings 1.48) are prayers of thanksgiving, the first for David's deliverance from the hand of Absalom, and the second that it has been possible for the king to pass his throne to his chosen son. Yet it should not be thought that prayer in the Succession Narrative is portrayed as being a means whereby humans may always and in any circumstances be able to secure divine intervention for the particular course of action they desire: indeed, when in II Sam. 12.16 David intercedes for Bathsheba's child, the prayer is not answered as David had asked. Moreover, the humans are shown in their frailty in this finely-told story: the prayer in II Sam. 12.13 is a confession of sin on the part of David, while the element of flattery lurks near the surface in the woman's petition in II Sam. 14.7.

If it is possible to see any common thread in the prayers in the Succession Narrative it is, as would be expected, on the theme of David and his designated successor. But the whole matter of the succession is portrayed here in a subtle way as being, mysteriously, inexplicably, both the work of God and also the result of various human acts. Further, prayer is involved in that process, perhaps intended to represent the way in which human action and divine purpose are held together.

But how different is such an approach to prayer from that which we have observed in another block of materials in the Deuteronomistic history, in the Elijah and Elisha cycles (I Kings 17–19; 21; II Kings 1–10.36; 13.14–21) (see Ch. 1 above). Certainly in the case of the prayers connected with events in the life and ministry of Elisha, there is to be observed what we may feel is a rather crude way or regarding prayer. Elisha prays, and what is prayed for is granted by the Lord! Minimal human effort appears to be associated with such prayers, and God is portrayed as being available to deploy his almighty powers in accordance with the will of anyone who is praying. We have noted how the prayers of Elisha are usually in the context of healings and granting of sight. In the case of Elijah's prayers we again have the 'medical' theme, but augmented to some extent by prayers of petition, and also 'complaint' in connection with his calling as a servant of the Lord.

Finally, in this survey of the principal prayers in the Deuteronomistic history, we revisit briefly the accounts that tell of the deliverance of Jerusalem in 701 BC, in the days of Hezekiah, from the power of the Assyrian army. We saw earlier, in Ch. 6 above, how the different accounts of these events set forth a variety of approaches to prayer. What has come to be referred to as Account A (II Kings 18.13–16) speaks of Jerusalem being spared, but we noted that this account makes no reference to prayer. Account B1 (I Kings 18.18–19.9a and 36– 37) is certainly different: it speaks of Hezekiah resorting to the house of the Lord (19.1) and seeking the prayers of the prophet Isaiah (19.4), and of the city being delivered: not through any supernatural event, but rather because the Assyrians departed overnight from Jerusalem, having received unfavourable news from other parts of the empire. Then there is Account B2 (II Kings 19.9b–35): it tells of an elaborate prayer that Hezekiah, in the temple, prayed to God (19.14–19). This prayer is portrayed as leading not only to a series of reassuring words from the prophet Isaiah, but also to a dramatic ending to the whole crisis, namely the striking-down of a hundred and eighty-four thousand in the camp of the Assyrians, so that the welcome sight that greeted the besieged inhabitants on the following morning was the spectacle of these Assyrians, dead (II Kings 19.35)![18]

This brief survey of the prayers in the Deuteronomistic history has surely demonstrated what a wide range of forms, approaches to, and theologies of prayer is to be found in this work. But such variety is to be seen throughout the Old Testament. We need now to try to highlight some aspects of this rich diversity, and thus seek to draw together some themes that we have encountered in this study.

III

In some parts of the Old Testament there is a good deal about the role and ministry of the intercessor. Moses, we might say, is the Old Testament's intercessor, *par excellence*. In times of deep crisis for his people, when their whole future is portrayed as hanging in the balance, Moses takes upon himself (or is called to take upon himself) the task of praying on behalf of the sinners. But the ministry of intercession is also to be seen with Samuel (in his case in days when his people pass through times of rapid change), while in the book that bears his name, Joshua is depicted as a new Moses, still interceding for his people, now in a new situation, and a new age. But intercession in the Old Testament is not portrayed as taking place only in great and stirring times such as those of the desert wanderings and the conquest of the land, but in much more ordinary and 'homespun' situations. An example of this is found in the drama of Ruth, where there are those who take it upon themselves to pray for others, so that for those who pass through difficult circumstances there may be a good and beneficial outcome.

This intercessory theme is also to be found in the New Testament: Luke 22.32 concerns Jesus interceding for Peter; John 17 for his disciples; Luke 23.34 for his executioners. In the life of the church we read of the faithful praying for Peter when he was in prison (Acts 12.5); of Paul (or whoever) praying for the Ephesians (Eph. 1.16); of what people are to do when anyone is ill (James 5.13–17). At a later date, it is intercession that makes up a part of what Egeria is witnessing when she writes:

> As soon as dawn comes, they start the Morning Hymns, and the bishop with his clergy comes and joins them. He goes straight into the cave, and inside the screen he first says the Prayer for All (mentioning any names he wishes) and blesses the catechumens, and then another prayer and blesses the faithful. Then he comes outside the screen, and everyone comes up to kiss his hand. He blesses them one by one, and goes out, and by the time the dismissal takes place it is already day.[19]

Further, Christians believe that as well as these intercessions on the part of humans, there is also the intercession of the risen and ascended Christ. Thus Paul writes:

> Who is to condemn? It is Christ Jesus, who died, yes, who was raised, who is at the right hand of God, who indeed intercedes for us. (Rom. 8.34)[20]

Yet it needs to be stressed that belief in the ascended Christ's intercession for us has not led the church to denigrate or derogate from the ministry of human intercession. That is to say, in the Christian church the Old Testament model of intercessory ministry is retained, alongside, and as a part of, that of Christ.[21]

IV

But what the Christian church is perhaps in danger of neglecting is something that is centrally present among the Old Testament prayers. It is the 'cry' of anguish. In its less strident forms we have seen it in the 'cry' of Israel in her distress in Egypt (Ex. 2.23). But it is also present in the book of Deuteronomy with its hope that the historical cry will be remembered annually, and so continued thanks will be given that the Lord heard his people's cry (Deut. 26.7). Further, the 'cry' of the people is heard in the book of Judges, in those moments of periodic crisis when all hope seemed to be gone. Then it is that the people of Israel 'cry' to the Lord, as a result of which a deliverer is sent. Luther may be said to translate this into a Christian context in a verse of his Christmas hymn *From heaven above to earth I come*:

> This is the Christ who far on high
> Has heard your sad and bitter cry;
>   Himself will your salvation be;
>   Himself from sin will set you free.[22]

But the crying out to God in prayer is also present, as we have seen, in Habakkuk, where the prophet cries out to God on behalf of his suffering people. It is there too in the book of Jonah, and also in the experience of Elijah in his attempt to be faithful in the ministry to which it is believed God calls an individual, (see Chs 1 and 5 above). But above all, it is to be found in the personal cry of distress of a person who in spite of their sufferings is determined to cling on to God. This is to be seen in its most sustained form in the book of Job, where we have a series of outspoken prayers of agony, in which Job becomes more forthright with God, the more his problems continue, the darkness deepens around him, and the divine silence continues. To our peril we neglect and cease to employ the mode of this agonized and assertive cry to God, the condition that Bunyan spoke of that 'provokes him to groan out his requests unto the Lord',[23] what we might call a wrestling with God, a wrestling in which we acknowledge both God as seemingly antagonistic but also as our only sure hope.[24] So indeed there must be the clinging on to him in the darkness and doubt – until he does appear again. We have also seen this prayer in the book of Psalms in the 'complaint' (or the 'lament'), a prayer that betokens the hanging-on in trust to him who is believed to be most precious (see Ch. 2 above). Of course, we need to be aware of the dividing line between this 'crying' to God and 'murmuring' about him and his ways, as the people of Israel did in the wilderness (Ex. 15.2–27; 16.1–8; 17.1–7 etc.). G. W. Coats reminds us that 'The lament question and the murmuring accusation appear in the same mould. But the one is an act of faith, the other rebellion. Must the lamenter not always be cautious, lest his lament pass over into revolution?'[25] Real though that danger may be, yet a greater danger for us could be that in our search for what we suppose piety to be, and the feeling for a sense of delicacy before God, and the expression in words of address to the divine, all that are aesthetically suitable, we neglect to be properly honest with God in our prayers. Not all prayer, if it be true prayer, a full reflection of the experience of the moment and of our relationship with God, can be expressed in words redolent of the the style of *The Book of Common Prayer*. Not always can we pray thus:

> Lighten our darkness, we beseech thee, O Lord; and by thy great mercy defend us from all perils and dangers of this night; for the love of thy only Son, our Saviour, Jesus Christ.

What sort of darkness is that? That surely is the darkness which in a few hours we may confidently expect the dawn to scatter. How different is that darkness which Hopkins experienced!

> I wake and feel the fell of dark, not day.
> What hours, O what black hours we have spent
> This night! what sights you, heart, saw; ways you went!
> And more must, in yet longer light's delay.

And in such darkness he prays:

> No worst, there is none. Pitched past pitch of grief,
> More pangs will, schooled at forepangs, wilder wring.
> Comforter, where, where is your comforting?
> Mary, mother of us, where is your relief?[26]

A range of prayers in the Old Testament reminds us of our need of the diversity in prayer today – if indeed our prayers are to be true reflections of life's diverse experiences and of our on-going relationship with God and with one another. Moreover, the range of Old Testament prayers is to be observed not only in their various themes and moods, but also in so far as they are informal cries or more formal compositions. As we have seen, both types are found in the Old Testament, and both have their place in the life of prayer of individuals and the church (see Ch. 3 above).

V

The Old Testament presents the ideal of a life, all of which is lived out in the sight of God. The norm is that God is known in all situations in life: when he cannot be found, then is the time to cry out to him, as Job and some psalmists did, and ask (demand if necessary) his appearance. But in more normal life his presence with his people, and their relationship with him, is assumed. This, I suggest, may account not only for the fact that Old Testament prayer is generally of the 'prophetic' type rather than the 'mystical' – to use the categories of Heiler[27] – but also that some books such as Deuteronomy make what may appear to us to be only small mention of prayer. 'Mystical' prayer, that is meditation or contemplation, may be needful for us, in order to remind us that all of life is to be lived out in fellowship with God. In general, the Old Testament assumes this life of fellowship with God as the normal way of life. But there will be times when people have forsaken God, and then a Moses will plead with God that they be permitted to return (e.g., Ex. 32.11–14), or a Hosea will give them a prayer with which they may approach God once more (Hos. 6.1–3).

There are, of course, some books of the Old Testament that make little or even no mention of prayer. Some of these need not unduly surprise us: some books are concerned with a limited number of themes and thus understandably do not make any explicit mention of prayer. This may explain the absence of prayers and references to prayer in Song of Songs, Obadiah, Nahum and Esther. If Ecclesiastes 5.2 refers to human speech[28] (which in my judgment it does) then here is another book with neither words of nor reference to prayer. But then this fact is perhaps not surprising when we consider the general approach of the book, as expressed towards the end:

> The end of the matter; all has been heard. Fear God, and keep his commandments; for this is the whole duty of everyone. (Eccles. 12.13)

We have already observed the comparative sparseness of prayers in Joshua and the so-called Ark Narrative, but we may also observe that there is little about prayer in Micah (only 3.4 and 7.7), Zephaniah (3.10) and Malachi (1.9). Yet we might have expected the book of Haggai, concerned as its eponymous hero is to rebuild the temple, to have at least one reference to prayer! In comparison, how much does Nehemiah pray over his building of the Jerusalem walls (see Ch. 3 above)! Nevertheless, we may feel that belief in the reality of prayer is there on the part of those who passed these stories and oracles on to us;

certainly, no part of the Old Testament literature *denies* the
reality of prayer, or denies that God is ready to hear the prayers
of his people. The book of Job witnesses to the reality of the
life of prayer and the life of faith even when all is suffering and
darkness around, and even when the God to whom prayer is
being made appears neither to hear nor respond.

At the same time, there are those crucial moments in life when
it is clear that prayer must be made: when much is at stake,
when a wrong decision might lead to disaster, then prayer must
be made. Thus we can understand the occurrence of prayers in
the stories we have about kings, and those accounts of prayers
for the nation. In particular, we have seen that in the
Chronicler's theological presentation of the history of Israel, we
are given more prayers and references to prayer than are
to be found in the Deuteronomistic history (see Ch. 6 above).
It has been observed that the Deuteronomistic history is
essentially a pessimistic work, with little hope for the future. Its
overall concern is to explain the catastrophes of the exiles of
722 and 587 BC, and any hope for the future is somewhat
muted. In comparison, the Chronicler's work is a more hopeful
presentation of the life of Israel, that seeks to portray a hope
of restoration after the disaster of the exile.[29] So the Chronicler
is concerned for Israel as the national and religious life is re-
established after the exile: he is particularly concerned that at
this crucial moment Israel goes in the 'right' way, that it is
obedient to the will of God. How important, then, is prayer,
and the seeking of divine guidance and strength for the new
age! In order to 'preach' this message the Chronicler presents a
series of 'lessons' from the past, a series of stories in which, as
we have seen, prayer plays no insignificant part.

The same concern to stress the importance of prayer is to
be observed in the so-called Succession Narrative that deals
with the issue of the transition of the kingship from David to
whoever is to be his successor. Again, at this crucial moment
in the life of the nation there is the stress on the importance
of prayer, and the linking of the divine will and action with
those of the human participants in events.

VI

The earlier consideration of these prayers in the Succession Narrative highlighted the fact that in that work there is a distinctive theological understanding of prayer. We may go further than this, and say that within the Old Testament there is no single understanding of prayer, but rather a diversity of theological approaches to it. Moreover, it is clear that we shall not find warrant in the pages of the Old Testament for the 'correctness' of one understanding of prayer against another. The stories of Elisha, for example, set forth a type of prayer that we may feel verges on the magical: a person prays to God, the prayer is granted, and the wish fulfilled. As we have observed in the prayers of Elisha, many are concerned with healings – and in such situations in those days, perhaps all that people could do was pray. But we have come across other instances where it was deemed that all that was necessary for the desired end to be achieved was to pray to God (e.g., II Kings 19.9b–35). But there are other traditions of theological thought in the Old Testament that speak of prayer being made, but when the resulting situation has been secured through the actions of a third party (e.g., II Kings 18.18–19.9a and 36f.). Or again, there is that strand of thought that stresses that prayer and action must go together, an approach that is most obvious in the book of Ruth, and in the Succession Narrative, but which we have encountered in various other places (see e.g., II Chron. 32.1–21). Indeed, in our consideration of prayers in the different parts of the Deuteronomistic history earlier in this chapter, we noted this varied approach to and theological understanding of prayer. Moreover, in certain parts of that work we have observed a marked absence of prayer, for example in the Ark Narratives (I Sam. 4–6). Yet in the events that that narrative portrays, God is perceived to be present: he is active in those worldly events that his people are experiencing. But we hear little of prayer being made to him. Different is the Succession Narrative, which acknowledges human beings as in need of God and of his helpful presence and action in the world, but who at the same time are themselves capable of adult, mature, logical action in the face of the great issues of the day that confront them.

Whilst it is the proper approach in a work of this nature, concerned as it is with a study of prayer in the Old Testament, to stress that there are these different theological approaches to prayer alongside one another, it is at the same time reasonable to regard some approaches as less theologically sophisticated than others. We may perhaps feel that it is a mature and responsible style of Christian discipleship in the world that is reflected in those paradoxical words of Dietrich Bonhoeffer: 'The God who lets us live in the world without using the working hypothesis of God is the God before whom we stand continually.'[30] We may further feel that the most appropriate general style of prayer for such a life of discipleship in the world – in which we seek to stand before the God who calls us to adult and mature faith – is of the type we have observed in the Old Testament in such works as the Succession Narrative, and the book of Ruth. While no doubt for us there will indeed be occasions when 'all we can do is to pray',[31] we may feel that for the less desperate and, hopefully, more normal situations it is more appropriate that our prayers are accompanied by deeds and actions.[32] Thus will there be *both* prayer and action.[33]

Diversity in the Old Testament presentation of prayer is also to be seen in the multiplicity of *forms* of its prayers. Some are long and elaborate, such as those in the books of Daniel, Ezra and Nehemiah that we considered in Chapter 3. Others are brief and simple (e.g., I Kings 19.4). In between these extremes are those represented in the book of Psalms, no longer brief cries to God, and yet not displaying all the extent and movement through themes of those found in the late books.[34]

But there is variety in the *settings* in which all these prayers are made. Prayer may be offered from the temple (e.g., I Kings 8.14–61), or alternatively from a home (e.g., Dan. 6.10); it may be made on the field of battle (e.g., II Chron. 18.31) or simply in a field (e.g., Gen. 4.13f.). And prayer would come to be made in the synagogue, and in various other places where a person happened to be, often directing the prayer towards Jerusalem. Indeed, the Old Testament affords us the vision of all who wish to do so being able to pray to God. Even those who are blatantly unrighteousness are not told that they *cannot* pray – merely that it cannot be guaranteed that their prayers will be heard (e.g., Isa. 1.15)!

VII

In no part does the Old Testament give us any 'teaching' about prayer. The nearest approach to any 'teaching' on the subject is the disquisition on prayer contained in Solomon's prayer at the dedication of the temple (I Kings 8.14–61; II Chron. 6.3–42). But this is not the same as the 'teaching' on prayer as found in the New Testament in response to the disciples' request, 'Lord, teach us to pray', and as given in the Lord's Prayer (Luke 11.1–4; Matt 6.9–13), or even as presented by the Gospel writers in those sections of their gospels where words about prayer are gathered together.[35]

One distinctive feature of New Testament prayer, as compared with the Old Testament, lies in the matter of the address to God. The common form of address to God in Old Testament prayers is 'Lord', 'Lord God', 'Lord, our God', or the like. In some of the New Testament prayers we have God addressed as 'Father' (Greek *pater*) (e.g., Mark 14.36; Matt 6.9; 11.25,26; Luke 23.34, 46; John 11.41; 12.27f.; 17.1, 5, 11, 21, 24, 25). Even more striking is the address to God in Jesus' prayer in Gethsemane, expressed by 'Abba' (Mark 14.36).[36] 'Abba' is an Aramaic word (Aramaic being the language in general use in the first century AD in Palestine, especially in Galilee), a familiar term for 'father'. In Judaism it was used as a title for rabbis (teachers) and as a proper name, but hardly ever for address to God. 'It denotes childlike intimacy and trust, not disrespect',[37] and its intimate style of address to God is reflected in St Paul's use of it in Rom. 8.15 and Gal. 4.6. It could be that it was a form of address commonly used by Jesus in prayer, and it is further possible that Jesus taught his disciples to address God in this intimate way in their prayers.[38]

In the formality of approach and address to God in Old

Testament prayers it is as if the transcendence (the 'otherness') of the great God is being emphasized. This transcendence of God is given marked emphasis in such prayers as that of Solomon at the dedication of the temple:

> For will God really dwell upon the earth? Behold, the heaven and the highest heaven cannot contain you, much less this house which I have built. (I Kings 8.27)

R. E. Clements says about this prayer:

> God is omnipresent and utterly transcendent to the visible world – 'heaven and the highest heaven cannot contain him'; he is omniscient – 'for thou, thou only, knowest the hearts of all the children of men'; he is utterly and impartially righteous – 'condemning the guilty . . . vindicating the righteous'.[39]

Many years ago, a German scholar, Rudolph Otto, wrote about the peculiar quality of the religious life and experience, that it is a trembling awe before the overwhelming and fascinating mystery of the divine.[40] It is there in the book of Isaiah:

> In the year that King Uzziah died I saw the Lord sitting upon a throne, high and lifted up, and the skirts of his robe filled the temple. Above him stood the seraphim. Each had six wings: with two he covered his face, with two he covered his feet, and with two he flew. And one called to another and said:
> 'Holy, holy, holy, is the Lord of hosts,
> his glory fills the whole earth.'
> And the foundations of the thresholds shook at the voice of him who called, and the house was filled with smoke. And I said:
> 'Woe is me, for I am ruined,
> for I am a man of unclean lips,
> and I dwell among a people of unclean lips,
> for my eyes have seen the King, the Lord of Hosts.' (Isa. 6.1–5)

The wonder of the gift of prayer is that a human, indeed a

sinner, may approach this omnipresent and transcendent God. The Puritan preacher Richard Sibbes (1577–1635) spoke about our approach to the awesome majesty of God, and about the necessity of doing so through the mediation of Jesus: 'Be sure not to go to a naked God: for so he is a consuming fire, but go to him in the mediation of him whom he loves . . .'[41] Yet in prayer, the awesome and majestic God – omnipresent, transcendent, omniscient – seeks to be attentive to those who approach him, thus making himself 'immanent' ('close') for his people, near to them in their need, or whatever is their condition at the time when they pray to him. The issues of the greatness of God and yet his nearness to us in prayer are perhaps reflected in Charles Wesley's lines:

> Omnipresent God, whose aid
>   No one ever asked in vain,
> Be this night about my bed,
>   Every evil thought restrain;
> Lay thy hand upon my soul,
>   God of my unguarded hours;
> All my enemies control,
>   Hell, and earth, and nature's powers.

Thus Solomon's prayer has not only:

> For will God really dwell upon the earth? Behold, heaven and the highest heaven cannot contain you, much less this house which I have built. (I Kings 8.27)

but also:

> Regard your servant's prayer and his supplication, Lord my God, hear the cry and the prayer which your servant prays before you today . . . (I Kings 8.28)

In the Old Testament there is presented to us a whole series of occasions when prayer was made, and when prayer was heard. It thus witnesses to the reality of a life of prayer in the context of the daily life of the world. It does not seek to portray prayer as a means of manipulating God, though we may perhaps feel that some of its prayers come dangerously near to doing so! Nor, for the most part, does it regard prayer as the means to effect a 'magical' change in a person's situation. But it does portray prayer as an appeal to the God of love and compassion, that he may have mercy on this person or group, and that the God of power and might may defend or strengthen others. In no place does the Old Testament seek to give any explanation as to *how* this may be, but it does truly point to the reality of prayer, and affirms that more often than not prayer does make a difference to the situation of those on whose behalf the prayer is being made.

VIII

There is both continuation and development of this Old Testament tradition of prayer, not only in the New Testament tradition,[42] but also in the prayer life of Judaism.[43] To attempt a consideration of either of these developments is beyond the scope of this work, but as this study comes to an end it may reasonably be asked: What is the abiding contribution of the Old Testament to the life of prayer today, in particular to the prayer-life of Christians? That contribution surely lies in the witness of the Old Testament to the sheer reality and possibility of prayer in the midst of the varied and manifold life of the world. In a range of settings, in different historical situations, prayers of praise and confession, of petition and intercession, of complaint and thanksgiving, are offered by many different peoples, individuals, groups, leaders, and rulers.

T. F. Torrance, in an essay on the Scottish theologian John Baillie (1886–1960), and in particular on his life of prayer, speaks about Baillie's book *A Diary of Private Prayer*.[44] Torrance observes that a central feature of the prayers in this book, 'is their contemporary setting in people's life and work'.[45] Might not one of the sources that flowed in to enrich the faith and thought of the author of those prayers have been the Old Testament, with its many prayers and references to prayer in such a wide variety of human and worldly settings? For the Old Testament witnesses to the fact that in the midst of life we may pray to the Lord God, and that further, our prayers will be heard:

> Then the word of the Lord came to Isaiah: 'Go and say to Hezekiah, "Thus says the Lord, the God of your ancestor David: I have heard your prayer . . ."' (Isa. 38.5)

Thus, a psalmist wrote, and the people sang:

> Praise is due to you,
>   O God, in Zion;
> and to you shall vows be performed,
>   O you who answer prayer! (Ps. 65.1–2a)

Abbreviations

EQ	*Evangelical Quarterly*, London
ET	English Translation
ExpT	*Expository Times*, Edinburgh
GNB	Good News Bible
HUCA	*Hebrew Union College Album*, Cincinnati
JB	Jerusalem Bible
JBL	*Journal of Biblical Literature*, Atlanta
JSOT	*Journal for the Study of the Old Testament*, Sheffield
JTS	*Journal of Theological Studies*, Oxford
LXX	Septuagint
NIV	New International Version
NRSV	New Revised Standard Version
REB	Revised English Bible
RSV	Revised Standard Version
SBL	Society of Biblical Literature
SJT	*Scottish Journal of Theology*, Edinburgh
TDOT	*Theological Dictionary of the Old Testament*, ed. G. Botterweck and H. Ringgren, Grand Rapids
TynB	*Tyndale Bulletin*, London
VT	*Vetus Testamentum*, Leiden

Notes

Introduction – 'Made in the image of God'

1 I am indebted to O. Cullmann, *Prayer in the New Testament*, London 1995, p.151, note 60, for this, originally in D. Soelle, *Atheistisch an Gott glauben*, Olten and Freiburg 1988, p.109.
2 On defining prayer, see Ch. 2 'What is Prayer? In Search of a Definition' by A. Wierzbicka, pp.25–46 in L. B. Brown, et al., *The Human Side of Prayer: The Psychology of Prayer*, Birmingham, Alabama 1995.
3 D. Z. Phillips, *The Concept of Prayer*, London 1965, p.3. This, as Phillips explains, is a parody of a quotation from Augustine's *Confessions* (Book 11:14), an example of some of the difficulties we have when we try to give an account of concepts with which we are perfectly familiar, in the example from Augustine, 'time'.
4 J. Macquarrie, *Principles of Christian Theology*, London 1966, p.437.
5 F. Heiler, *Prayer: A Study in the History and Psychology of Religion*, tr. S. McComb, Oxford 1932, p.xiii.
6 In general this represents Reventlow's basic definition of prayer as far as the Old Testament is concerned. See H. G. Reventlow, *Gebet im Alten Testament*, Stuttgart 1986, p.89. We can hardly adopt D. R. Ap-Thomas's definition of prayer ('Some Notes on the Old Testament Attitude to Prayer', *SJT* 9 [1956], pp.422–29, p.422) as 'man's attempt to get God to meet a particular need', as that would exclude prayers of praise, thanksgiving and complaint. At the same time, I am aware of the danger of over-comprehensiveness in the definition I adopt: some passages in the Old Testament are perhaps better described as 'conversations' with God, rather than as 'prayers' – for example, the 'conversation', surely, of the man and the woman with God in the garden (Gen. 3.9–13). For a discussion about the definition of prayer, at least as far as the Old Testament is concerned, see S. E. Balantine, *Prayer in the Hebrew Bible: The Drama of Divine-Human Dialogue* (Overtures to Biblical Theology), Minneapolis 1993, pp.30f.
7 On these methods see, e.g., J. H. Hayes and C. R. Holladay, *Biblical*

Exegesis: A Beginner's Handbook, London 1987; J. Barton, *Reading the Old Testament: Method in Biblical Study*, London 1984; R.J. Coggins, *Introducing the Old Testament*, Oxford 1990. On the literary approach see in particular, D.M. Gunn and D.N. Fewell, *Narrative in the Hebrew Bible*, Oxford 1993.

8. B.S. Childs, *Biblical Theology of the Old and New Testaments*, London 1992, p.78.

9. To speak of *Old* and *New* Testaments is, of course, to approach the former from the perspective of the latter. For those who come to the former from the Jewish perspective, it is no doubt more appropriate to refer to them as 'the Hebrew Bible', or '*Tenakh*' (*Torah* [Law], *Nevi'im* [Prophets], *Kethubim* [Writings]). For different perspectives on scriptures, see S. Bigger (ed.), *Creating the Old Testament: The Emergence of the Hebrew Bible*, Oxford 1989, pp.31–50.

1. 'And Cain said to the Lord'

1. The Hebrew text of Gen. 4.8 does not say where this took place, but the Greek (and some other) translations of the Hebrew add, 'Let us go to the field'. It may be that the words have been omitted in the Hebrew.

2. This is to say that I do not regard the conversation between Adam and the Lord in Gen. 3.9ff. as a prayer. In that story God is portrayed as being visible, existing in human form, taking his walk in the garden in the cool of the day. This, I suggest, is 'conversation'. Prayer I regard as taking place when a human being makes an address to an invisible deity. On this matter, and for a definition of prayer, see Introduction, pp.4f. above.

3. For further reading about Gen. 1–11 and 12–36, see J. Rogerson, *Genesis 1–11* (Old Testament Guides), Sheffield 1991, and R.W.L. Moberly, *Genesis 12–50* (Old Testament Guides), Sheffield 1992.

4. Such a 'short story' is called by scholars a 'novella'. See, e.g., G.W. Coats (ed.) *Saga, Legend, Tale, Novella, Fable: Narrative Forms in Old Testament Literature*, Sheffield 1985.

5. This is the understanding of S.E. Balantine, *Prayer in the Hebrew Bible: the Drama of Divine-Human Dialogue*, (Overtures to Biblical Theology), Minneapolis 1993, pp.64–71, who cites Gen. 32.9–12 as an example of 'Prayer as a means of caricature'. Balantine says, 'As a whole verses 3–21 [of Gen. 32] present a sequence of activities that describe Jacob's movements from planning to praying, and back to planning again. It is the picture of one who intends to leave nothing to chance, or perhaps, nothing to God' (p.69). But is that not to take seriously the association of prayer and action?

6 G. von Rad, *Genesis*, London 1963 (revised ed.), p.313.
7 C. Westermann, *Genesis 12–36*, tr. J.J.Scullion, London 1985, p.509.
8 *Origen's Treatise on Prayer*, tr. E.G. Jay, London 1954, pp.114–15.
9 On the 'Joseph Story' see, R.W.L. Moberly, *Genesis 12–50* (Old Testament Guides), Sheffield 1992, pp.33-36; G.W. Coats, *Genesis: With an Introduction to Narrative Literature* (The Forms of Old Testament Literature), Grand Rapids 1983, pp.263ff.
10 See Westermann, *Genesis 12–36*, p.189. The Greek version (LXX) has sought to harmonize these two blessings into one.
11 G. von Rad (*Genesis*, p.412) says, 'For the believer can never speak generally and abstractly about God but only about definite revelations and experiences that exist in his own sphere of life.'
12 R. Alter, *The Art of Biblical Narrative*, London 1981, p.84, says, 'All in all, it is just the sort of prayer that a simple, sincere country wife, desperate in her barrenness, would utter.'
13 See L. Eslinger, *Kingship of God in Crisis: A Close Reading of I Samuel 1–12*, Sheffield 1985, pp.99–112, on Hannah's prayer of thanksgiving.
14 R.E. Clements says that it is praise to God which is the most important and central goal of all prayer. He asserts, 'Praise is the greatest form of prayer because through it we come to a true and proper understanding of our place in the world and of the infinite possibilities which God has set before us' (R.E. Clements, *The Prayers of the Bible*, London 1985, p.14).
15 Other instances of prayer and healing of illness may be cited: Num. 12.9–15; II Kings 4.32–37; 5.1–14; 13.21; 20.1–11; cf. Isa. 38.1–22.
16 See G.H. Jones, *I and II Kings* (New Century Bible), Volume II, London 1984, pp.310f.
17 J.A. Montgomery and H.S. Gehman, *The Books of Kings* (International Critical Commentary), Edinburgh 1951, p.305.
18 G.H. Jones, *I and II Kings* (New Century Bible), Volume II, London 1984, p.330.
19 J. Skinner, *I & II Kings* (Century Bible), Edinburgh, no date, p.237.
20 We may perhaps helpfully be reminded of some words of J. Macquarrie, 'This means that all magical ideas of prayer must be rejected, and of course they ought to be. Religion and faith have nothing to do with attempts to manipulate the world by occult means' (*Principles of Christian Theology*, London 1966, p.439).
21 Bunyan waxes eloquent on the subject of prayer coming from unscrupulous lives:

> When men regard iniquity in their hearts, at the time of their Prayer before God. *If I regard iniquity in my heart, the Lord will not hear my prayer*, Psal. 66.18. For the preventing of temptation, that by the misunderstanding of this, may seize thy heart; when there is a secret

love to that very thing, which thou with thy dissembling lips dost ask for strength against. For this is the wickedness of man's heart, that it will even love, and hold fast that, which with the mouth it prayeth against; and of this sort are they, *that honour God with their mouth, but their heart is far from him*, Ezek. 33.31.

J. Bunyan, 'I will pray with the Spirit' (otherwise, 'A Discourse Touching Prayer'), *Miscellaneous Works of John Bunyan*, Vol. II, ed. R. L. Greaves, Oxford 1976, p.273.

2. 'O Lord, hear my prayer'

1. R. E. Prothero, *The Psalms in Human Life*, new edition, London 1904, p.177. Prothero quotes 1632 as the date of Herbert's death: more commonly it is given as 1633.
2. Ibid., p.10.
3. H. Gunkel, *Die Psalmen*, Göttingen 1926, reprinted 1968 and 1986; H. Gunkel and J. Begrich, *Einleitung in die Psalmen*, 2 Vols, Göttingen 1928–33.
4. R. Murray, *The Cosmic Covenant*, London 1992, p.192, n.7.
5. P. C. Craigie, *Psalms 1–50* (Word Biblical Commentary), Waco 1983, p.162.
6. On the psalms of lament, see C. Westermann, *Praise and Lament in the Psalms*, Edinburgh 1981. See also, now, C. Westermann, *The Living Psalms*, Edinburgh 1989, pp.21ff., 65ff.
7. The Hebrew is *rinnāh* ('ringing cry'): on this word see J. F. A. Sawyer, 'Types of Prayer in the Old Testament. Some Semantic Observations on Hitpallel, Hithannen, etc.', *Semitics*, 7 (1980), pp.131–43, esp. pp.134f.
8. The Hebrew is *t^epillāh* ('prayer'). See Sawyer, 'Types of Prayer', pp.133f.
9. 'He expresses the night-time in regard of God's visitation, because that when he was withdrawn from the eyes of men, he saw more clearly the vices which otherwise would have lain hid. Like as again . . . the darkness of the night lays the conscience more open, by taking away all coverings, and the affections disclose themselves more freely . . .', J. Calvin, *A Commentary on the Psalms*, tr. A. Golding, revised and ed. T. H. L. Parker, Vol. I, London 1965, pp.174f.
10. *King Lear*, V, iii, 322–3, Arden edition, London 1972. I am indebted to S. E. Balantine, *Prayer in the Hebrew Bible: The Drama of Divine-Human Dialogue* (Overtures to Biblical Theology), Minneapolis 1993, p.146, for this illustration, though he ascribes the speech to Albany, as is the case in some editions of the play.
11. Westermann, *Praise and Lament*, p.262.

12 See W. Brueggemann, 'The Costly Loss of Lament', *JSOT* 36 (1986), pp.57–71.
13 Hebrew *qārā'*.
14 Westermann, *Praise and Lament*, p.268, says, 'The threefold character of the lamentation reveals an understanding of man in which the existence of an individual without participation in a community (a social dimension) and without a relationship with God (a theological dimension) is totally inconceivable. Using modern categories, we would say that the three elements of the lamentation presuppose an understanding in which theology, psychology, and sociology have not yet been separated from each other.'
15 This is an exceptionally difficult verse to translate; thus the various translations are very different.
16 The second part of v.14 may be translated in a way that understands the thought about the enemy and their destruction continuing. Thus NRSV:
   May their bellies be filled with what you have stored up for them;
   may their children have more than enough;
   may they leave something over to their little ones.
17 A. Weiser, *The Psalms* (Old Testament Library), London 1962, p.181; P. Craigie, *Psalms 1–50* (Word Biblical Commentary), Waco 1983, p.164.
18 J. Calvin, *A Commentary on the Psalms*, I, p.183.
19 F. Heiler, *Prayer: A Study in the History and Psychology of Religion*, tr. S.McComb, Oxford 1932, pp.259f.
20 The Hebrew words are: *hithannēn* (from the root *ḥnn*) 'to make supplication'; *teḥinnāh* 'supplication'; *taḥᵃnûnîm* 'supplications'. On these words see Sawyer, 'Types of Prayer', pp.138f.; *TDOT* V, pp.22ff.
21 The Hebrew is *šwʿ*.
22 In the translation of GNB there appears to be only one line, whereas others have lines one and two: in fact GNB has combined the sense of these two lines, with their rather different words for prayer, and rendered, 'Hear me when I cry to you for help'. This does perhaps reasonably convey the *sense* that the psalmist intended, whatever one may feel about it as a translation of the original.
23 On these prayers in Habakkuk and Jonah, see Ch. 5 below.
24 'This petition for retribution on the evildoers may not be in accord with twentieth-century Christian thought, but it was reasonable enough in its own setting. This prayer is not an expression of a vindictive personal revenge, but it is rather a longing for divine justice and for a society where a man can trust his fellow, and where they can serve the same Lord' (A. A. Anderson, *Psalms* (New Century Bible), Vol. I, London 1972, p.230).

25 J. Calvin, *A Commentary on the Psalms*, Vol. I, p.325.
26 See Ch. 6 below for prayers for the king.
27 The Hebrew words are z^cq and s^cq. On these words see *TDOT*, IV, pp.112–22; R. N. Boyce, *The Cry to God in the Old Testament* (SBL Dissertation Series), Atlanta 1988. There does not seem to be any particular pattern in the occurrence of one form of this verb against the other.
28 G. F. Hasel, *TDOT* IV, p.115.
29 G. F. Hasel, *TDOT* IV, p.120.
30 The Hebrew is *pāgā^c*. On this word, see Sawyer, 'Types of Prayer', pp.135f.
31 The Hebrew is *^{c}atar*. On this word, see Sawyer, 'Types of Prayer', pp.137f.
32 The Hebrew is *hillah panim*. See *TDOT* IV, pp.407–409; Sawyer, 'Types of Prayer', pp.136–7.
33 Hebrew *nā'*.
34 This usage is carried over and sometimes found in (archaic) English, for example in Longfellow's (1807–1882) 'The Wreck of the Hesperus':
   Then up and spake an old sailor,
      Had sailed the Spanish Main,
   'I pray thee, put into yonder port,
      For I fear a hurricane.'
See *The Oxford Book of Narrative Verse*, ed. I. and P. Opie, Oxford 1983, p.211.
35 See R. E. Prothero, *The Psalms in Human Life*, London 1904; art. 'Psalms' in G. S. Wakefield (ed.), *A Dictionary of Christian Spirituality*, London 1983, pp.322f.
36 C. Westermann, *The Living Psalms*, Edinburgh 1989, p.23.
37 A. Weiser, *The Psalms*, p.774.
38 Quoted by H. J. Kraus, *Psalms 60–150: A Commentary*, Minneapolis 1989, p.467n.
39 In Ps. 40 some scholars think we have what were originally two Psalms, vv.1–10 being an Individual Thanksgiving, and vv.11–17 an Individual Lament. Others argue that it was originally one composition: this view is perhaps the more commonly espoused of the two these days. But this need not concern us here, as our interest lies in vv.1–10 as an example of an Individual Thanksgiving Psalm.
40 See, for example, Weiser, *Psalms*, pp.337f.
41 *The Rule of St Benedict*, ch. 20, tr. J. McCann, London 1976, p.32.

3. 'O Lord, hear; O Lord, forgive'

1. For details, see P. R. Davies, *Daniel* (Old Testament Guides) Sheffield 1985, pp.33f.
2. For details, see H. G. M. Williamson, *Ezra and Nehemiah* (Old Testament Guides) Sheffield 1987, pp.45f.
3. See G. H. Jones, *I & II Chronicles* (Old Testament Guides) Sheffield 1993, pp.86–94.
4. A. Lacocque, *The Book of Daniel*, tr. D.Pellauer, London 1979, p.113.
5. A. A. Anderson, *Psalms* (New Century Bible) Volume 2, London 1972, p.845. On the hours of prayer in the time of Jesus, see J. Jeremias, *The Prayers of Jesus*, (Studies in Biblical Theology, second series), London 1967, pp.69ff.
6. For further details about times of and posture for prayer, see D. R. Ap-Thomas, 'Some Notes on the Old Testament Attitude to Prayer', *SJT* IX (1956), pp.422–29; 'Notes on Some Terms Relating to Prayer', *VT* 6 (1956), pp.225–41.
7. *Mishnah*, tr. H. Danby, Oxford, 1933, Berakoth 4.1
8. See the discussion by E. G. Jay, tr. *Origen's Treatise on Prayer*, London, 1953, p.40; P.Bradshaw, *Daily Prayer in the Early Church*, London, 1981.
9. See Jay, *Origen's Treatise*, pp.36–38.
10. *Origen's Treatise*, pp.114f.
11. *Mishnah*, Berakoth 4.5,6.
12. On prayers of 'blessing', see S. E. Balantine, *Prayer in the Hebrew Bible* (Overtures to Biblical Theology), Minneapolis 1993, pp.199–224; P. D. Miller, *They Cried to the Lord: the Form and Theology of Biblical Prayer*, Minneapolis 1994, pp.281–303.
13. Frequently, it is Deuteronomic elements that are borrowed: some would see here a continuing influence of Deuteronomistic perspectives in the piety of Judaism. See S.E.Balantine, *Prayer in the Hebrew Bible* (Overtures to Biblical Theology) Minneapolis 1993, pp.103f.
14. See also Num. 14.18; Neh.9.17; Pss.86.15; 103.8; 145.8; Joel 2.13; Nahum 1.3; Jonah 4.2. On the passage as an Israelite statement of faith, a 'creed', see, e.g., J. I. Durham, *Exodus* (Word Biblical Commentary), Waco 1987, pp.453–55.
15. *Book of Common Prayer*, General Confession, Morning Prayer. On this emphasis of Thomas Cranmer (1489–1556) see, e.g., P. Forster, 'Some Reflections on the Theology of Thomas Cranmer', pp.253–272 in M.Johnson, ed., *Thomas Cranmer*, Durham 1990.
16. *George Herbert and Henry Vaughan*, 'The Oxford Authors' edition of Herbert's poems, ed. Louis L. Martz, Oxford 1986, pp.171f.
17. See Ch. 2 above.
18. 'Hence this prayer cannot conclude with a superficial appeal for

deliverance from misery, but must end simply on a note of confession (vv.33ff.) and distress (vv.36f.). It does not jog God's elbow, but leaves him entirely free to act according to his own will.' (D. J. A. Clines, *Ezra, Nehemiah, Esther* [New Century Bible] London 1984, p.199).

19 See, e.g., Ex. 10.16f.; 32.31f.; Num. 21.7; 22.34; Judg. 10.15; I Sam. 12.10; 15.24f.; II Sam. 24.10; Isa. 63.7–64.12.

20 H. G. M. Williamson, *Ezra, Nehemiah* (Word Biblical Commentary) Waco 1985, p.306.

21 Neh. 9.6–11 now forms part of the Jewish morning liturgy, and some would argue that the whole of this prayer (9.5–37) had a considerable influence on the wider liturgy of the synagogue. See L. J. Liebreich, 'The Impact of Nehemiah 9.5–37 on the Liturgy of the Synagogue', *HUCA* 32 (1961), pp.227–37, though S. C. Reif, *Judaism and Hebrew Prayer*, Cambridge 1993, makes no mention of it.

22 D. Bonhoeffer, *Letters and Papers from Prison*, revised and enlarged edition, London 1967, p.199 – though Bonhoeffer was not convinced that the man was praying, merely breaking down.

23 M. Greenberg, *Biblical Prose Prayers as a Window to the Popular Religion of Ancient Israel*, Berkeley and Los Angeles 1983, p.17.

24 Greenberg, loc.cit.

25 E. Underhill, *Worship*, London, third edition 1937, pp.110f. Something of this 'hostility' about which Underhill speaks may be sensed in the following two (Christian) approaches to prayer. One of the reasons that John Cosin (1594–1672) gives for compiling a collection of prayers is, 'that men before they set themselves to pray, might know what to say, and avoid, as near as might be, all extemporal effusions of irksome and indigested prayers; which they use to make, that herein are subject to no good order or form of words, but pray both what, and how, and when they list' (J. Cosin, *A Collection of Private Devotions*, London 1627, from the Preface). But his younger contemporary John Bunyan (1628–88) will have none of this dependence on a prayer book: 'But here now, the wise men of our days are so well skill'd, as they have both the *Manner* and *Matter* of their Prayers at their finger ends; setting such a Prayer for such a day, and that twenty years before it comes. One for *Christmas*, another for *Easter*, and six days after that. They have also bounded how many syllables must be said in every one of them at their publick Exercises. For each Saints day also, they have them ready for the generations yet unborn to say.' (J. Bunyan, 'I will pray with the Spirit' (Otherwise, 'A Discourse Touching Prayer'), *The Miscellaneous Works of John Bunyan*, II, ed. R. L. Greaves, Oxford 1976, pp.247f.)

26 J. E. Goldingay, *Daniel* (Word Biblical Commentary) Waco 1989, p.231.

27 J. A. Montgomery, *Daniel* (International Critical Commentary) Edinburgh 1927, p.368.
28 Thus Montgomery (see note above) says, 'The saint prays as the Church prays, and this prayer is modelled after customary liturgical forms of the Synagogue' (pp.361f.).
29 See B. W. Jones, 'The Prayer in Daniel IX', *VT* 18(1968), pp.488–93. Also, A. Lacocque, 'The Liturgical Prayer in Daniel 9', *HUCA* 47 (1976), pp.119–42.
30 See M. E. W. Thompson, 'Prayer, Oracle and Theophany: The Book of Habakkuk', *TynB*, 44.1 (1993), pp.33–53.
31 N. W. Porteous, *Daniel* (Old Testament Library), London 1965, p.134. Elsewhere Porteous says of the author, 'He is not thinking primarily of the need for Daniel to be illuminated as to the meaning of a passage of scripture; rather, in the crisis of history during which he is actually writing, he desires to give in the words of this prayer expression to the piety of those for whom he is speaking. Without this prayer there would be something essential missing from the book of Daniel' (p.136).
32 *Documents from Old Testament Times*, ed. D. W. Thomas, New York 1958, pp.93–94.
33 H. G. M. Williamson, *Ezra, Nehemiah* (Word Biblical Commentary) Waco 1985, p.179. D. J. A. Clines (*Ezra, Nehemiah, Esther* [New Century Bible Commentary], London 1984, p.142) makes the point that this is one of the few clear references in the Old Testament to *silent* prayer. See also I Sam. 1.13.
34 Surely a prayer after John Bunyan's heart! See note 25 above.
35 Certainly Heiler, as we have seen, found in this spontaneous type of prayer his principal interest: 'Formal, literary prayers are merely the weak reflection of the original, simple prayer of the heart' (F. Heiler, *Prayer: A Study in the History and Psychology of Religion*, tr. S. McComb, Oxford, 1932, p.xviii).
36 H. G. M. Williamson, *Ezra, Nehemiah*, pp.218f.
37 D. J. A. Clines, *Ezra, Nehemiah, Esther*, p.172.
38 J. Blenkinsopp, *Ezra-Nehemiah* (Old Testament Library) London 1988, p.357.
39 Quoted by F. Colquhoun, *God of our Fathers*, London 1990, p.107.
40 On fasting, see, D. Tripp in *A Dictionary of Christian Spirituality*, ed. G. S. Wakefield, London 1983, pp.147f.
41 That is, assuming that Ezra came 'before' Nehemiah – as the Old Testament portrays him as doing, and now, it appears, more widely accepted by scholars. For an outline of the issues see, e.g., H. G. M. Williamson, *Ezra and Nehemiah*, 1987, pp.55–69, and the Commentaries of Blenkinsopp, Clines, and Williamson mentioned above.

42 Clines (*Ezra, Nehemiah, Esther*, p.162), quoting W. Rudolph, speaks of Nehemiah obeying his motto *ora et labora*, while Blenkinsopp (*Ezra-Nehemiah*, p.248) speaks about 'a Cromwellian combination of prayer and military vigilance'.

4 'Moses besought the Lord'

1 For recent commentaries on the Book of Ruth, see, for instance, E. F. Campbell, Jr, *Ruth* (Anchor Bible), New York 1975; R. L. Hubbard Jr, *The Book of Ruth* (New International Commentary on the Old Testament), Grand Rapids 1988; J. Gray, *Joshua, Judges, Ruth* (New Century Bible), revised edition, Grand Rapids and Basingstoke 1986.
2 For further details see, M. E. W. Thompson, 'New Life Amid the Alien Corn: The Book of Ruth', *EQ* LXV (1993), pp.197–210.
3 The Greek text of the Old Testament (LXX) has a different reading at this point: it has the people as witnesses while the leaders pray. For details, see Thompson, 'New Life Amid the Alien Corn', p.206.
4 E.g., Josh. 7.6–9 (Joshua); 10.12–14 (Joshua); II Sam. 12.16 (David); I Kings 1.36 (Benaniah); 1.47 (King's servants); 17.20f. (Elijah); II Kings 4.33 (Elisha); 6.17–20 (Elisha); 19.4/Isa. 37.4 (Isaiah); Joel 2.17 (priests); Ezra 6.10 (Ezra); II Chron. 30.18f. (Hezekiah) etc.
5 On the 'Ark' see, e.g., the article 'Ark' by G. A. F. Knight, in *The Oxford Companion to the Bible*, ed. B. M. Metzger and M. D. Coogan, New York and Oxford 1993, pp.55f.
6 See R. P. Gordon, *I & II Samuel, A Commentary*, Exeter 1986, pp.106f.
7 'Although Samuel appears again in the narratives that follow, this chapter [I Sam. 12] really contains both a summing up of Israel's fortunes to his day and a reflection on the meaning of her history.' P. R. Ackroyd, *The First Book of Samuel* (The Cambridge Bible Commentary), Cambridge 1971, p.96.
8 On the 'Deuteronomistic history', see A. H. W. Curtis, *Joshua*, (Old Testament Guides), Sheffield 1994, pp.17–21; J. G. McConville, *Grace in the End* (Studies in Old Testament Biblical Theology), Carlisle 1993.
9 See P. D. Miller, *They Cried to the Lord: The Form and Theology of Biblical Prayer*, Minneapolis 1994, pp.263–65.
10 R. Baxter, *The Reformed Pastor*, ed. J. T. Wilkinson, London 1950, pp.75, 90.
11 Deut. 29.23; Isa. 1.9f.; 13.19; Jer. 49.18; 50.40; Ezek. 16.46–50, 53–55; Amos 4.11; Zeph. 2.9; Lam. 4.6; Ps. 11.6; Matt 10.15; 11.23f.; Luke 10.12; 17.29; Rom. 9.29; II Peter 2.6; Jude 7; Rev. 11.8.
12 C. Westermann, *Genesis 12–36: A Commentary*, London, 1985, p.291, and see pp.283f. for others who take this approach.

13 P. D. Miller, *They Cried to the Lord*, p.267.
14 P. D. Miller, *They Cried to the Lord*, p.270, thinks that this is a 'cry' (of prayer) on the part of those in the city who are suffering. But the word 'cry' (see Ch. 2 above on this, especially n.24) may stand either for a prayerful 'cry' to God, or a human cry in a context where there is not prayer. Here it could mean 'outcry', in the sense of 'cry of protest', or 'commotion' etc.
15 J. Baillie, having spoken about our making requests known to God (Phil. 4.6), goes on to say, 'but it is contrary to all true faith to suppose that we may hold him to a particular way of responding. It would be frightening to take upon ourselves that measure of responsibility... As someone has put it: "If God granted me the form of my petition, he would be denying me the substance of my desire."' *The Sense of the Presence of God*, London 1962, p.65.
16 K. Barth in *Church Dogmatics* (Vol.II/1, ET Edinburgh 1957, pp.490ff.), in a section on 'The Constancy and Omnipotence of God', speaks about the immutable God of the Bible who is forever acting in freedom and love. Barth says, 'But it is just at this point that he is the 'immutable' God. For at no place or time can He or will He turn against Himself or contradict Himself, not even in virtue of His freedom or for the sake of His love ... The immutable is the fact that this God is ... gracious and holy, merciful and righteous, patient and wise. The immutable is the fact that He is the Creator, Reconciler, Redeemer and Lord. This immutability includes rather than excludes life. In a word it is life.' (pp.494f.) I am indebted to L. J. Kuyper and his helpful article on this subject, 'The Suffering and the Repentance of God', *SJT*, 22 (1969), pp.257-77, for this reference to Barth.
17 P. D. Miller, *They Cried to the Lord*, p.278.
18 J. I. Durham, *Exodus* (Word Biblical Commentary), Waco 1987, p.432, speaks about, '... a phrase which seems awkwardly incomplete in Hebrew (either a word has dropped out or the narrator is attempting to represent Moses having difficulty saying what he wants to say) ...'.
19 This is how R. W. L. Moberly, *At the Mountain of God: Story and Theology in Exodus 32-34*, Sheffield 1983, p.57, understands it.
20 B. S. Childs, *Exodus* (Old Testament Library), London 1974, p.581.
21 H. H. Rowley, for example, in his *Worship in Ancient Israel: Its Forms and Meaning*, London 1967, p.163, said: 'For the prophet was not only the man who brought the word of God to man. He was also the spokesman of man to God, and as intercessor he figures frequently in the Old Testament.' Rowley cited, as instances of this: Gen. 20.7 (Abraham); I Sam. 12.19 and 23 (Samuel); Ex. 32.11ff., 31f.; 33.12ff. etc.(Moses); Jer. 15.1; 37.3 (Jeremiah).

22 S. E. Balantine, 'The Prophet as Intercessor: A Reassessment', *JBL* 103 (1984), pp.161–73; *Prayer in the Hebrew Bible*, Minneapolis 1993, pp.50ff.
23 See M. E. W. Thompson, 'Amos – A Prophet of Hope?', *ExpT* 104 (1992–93), pp.71–75, for more details about the intercessions of Amos, and a possible explanation for the absence of intercession with the last three visions.
24 For these Hebrew words see Ch. 2 above, notes 5, 6, 27 and the references there.
25 The literature on the 'Servant' and the so-called 'Servant Songs' (Isa. 42.1–4; 49.1–6; 50.4–9; 52.13–53.12) is enormous! As a starting point, R. N. Whybray, *The Second Isaiah* (Old Testament Guides), Sheffield 1983, pp.65–78 may be recommended.
26 The text of Isa. 52.13–53.12 is notoriously difficult to translate. There are words about whose meaning we are unsure. Further, the prophet would seem to be saying something new and radical. Just what he had in mind is difficult for us to know, and all too easily we read into the text what we want to! All too easily Christians read the work and death of Christ into this passage; instead of *translating* the text, we *interpret* it. However, it would generally be agreed that the text does speak of the *death* of a servant. But for a contrary view see, R. N. Whybray, *Thanksgiving for a Liberated Prophet: An Interpretation of Isaiah Chapter 53*, Sheffield, 1978; *Isaiah 40–66* (New Century Bible), London 1975, pp.171ff.
27 On the Servant as a figure like Moses, see G. W. Coats, *Moses – Heroic Man, Man of God*, Sheffield 1988, pp.207–9, esp.p.208: 'The servant is the new Moses, just as for the first Isaiah the leader is the New David.'
28 See the helpful comments by M. Hollings in, *A Dictionary of Christian Spirituality*, ed. G. S. Wakefield, London 1983, p.310: 'Vicarious offering is another facet of intercession – the offering of oneself for another. This is marked especially in contemplative religious orders, among missionaries, those committed to living with the poor, lepers, prisoners. St Thérèse of Lisieux offered each painful step during her last illness for missionaries; Fr Kolbe took the place of another prisoner to die in the gas chamber; Fr Damien, giving himself for lepers, became a leper.'

5 'Man . . . is full of trouble'

1 F. von Hügel, *Letters to a Niece*, London 1928, pp.xlii, xliii.
2 For an introduction to the book of Habbakuk, see R. Mason, *Zephaniah, Habbakuk, Joel* (Old Testament Guides), Sheffield 1994, pp.59–96.

3 See M. E. W. Thompson, 'Prayer, Oracle and Theophany: The Book of Habbakuk', *TynB* 44.1 (1993), pp.33-53.
4 See, for example, Amos 6.14; Hos. 8.14; Isa. 10.5-15; Jer. 5.14-19; 49.37; Ezek. 5.16; Joel 2.25, etc.
5 We may notice that Habakkuk is on his own among the Old Testament prophets in his useage of prayer in such a predominant way. In the article cited in n.3 above, I said, 'It is as if for this prophet the prophetical and woe oracles serve a somewhat subservient function to those prayers that are employed to express what are the most significant parts of the prophet's burden' (p.53).
6 'Such praying [i.e., crying out] is inevitable because of the mystery of who God is – at times unquestionably present, on other occasions inexplicably aloof. Such praying is also necessary. Without it, waiting for relief would threaten to stagnate and leave one in despair. Without it, one's feet could not begin to traverse the path that Habakkuk describes as the way of faith.' S. E. Balantine, *Prayer in the Hebrew Bible: The Drama of Divine-Human Dialogue*, Minneapolis 1993, pp.188f.
7 On this approach to the book of Jonah see, M. E. W. Thompson, 'The Mission of Jonah', *ExpT*, 105 (1993-94), pp.233-36. For introduction to this book see also, R. B. Salters, *Jonah and Lamentations* (Old Testament Guides), Sheffield 1994, pp.12-62.
8 See R. Payne, 'The Prophet Jonah: Reluctant Messenger and Intercessor', *ExpT* 100 (1988-89), pp.131-34.
9 See Salters, *Jonah and Lamentations*, pp.28-40.
10 G. von Rad said that elsewhere in the book (apart from in the prayer) Jonah is 'mulish'! See H. W. Wolff, *Obadiah and Jonah: A Commentary*, tr. M. Kohl, Minneapolis and London 1986, p.130.
11 See, e.g., paragraphs 812 and 638 of St Ignatius of Loyola, *The Constitutions of the Society of Jesus*, tr. G. E. Ganss, St Louis 1970, pp.331, 281:

> The Society [of Jesus] was ... instituted ... through the omnipotent hand of Christ, God and our Lord. Therefore in Him alone must be placed the hope that he will preserve and carry forward what He deigned to begin for His service and praise and for the aid of souls. In conformity with this hope, the first and best proportioned means will be the prayers and Masses which ought to be offered for this holy intention through their being ordered for it every week, month, and year in all the regions where the Society resides.
>
> ... let them [those in houses and colleges of the Society] pray for ... the other members of the Society [who] are working in diverse places among believers or unbelievers, that God may dispose them

all to receive His grace through the feeble instruments of this least Society.

On Ignatius and prayer, see A. Goodier, SJ, *St Ignatius Loyola and Prayer*, London 1940. On the teaching of the Society of Jesus about prayer see, J.W. O'Malley, *The First Jesuits*, London 1993, pp.162–64.

12 'Another surprise, a shocking one [about the book of Jonah], is Jonah's refusal to shoulder his prophetic burden.' L.C. Allen, *The Books of Joel, Obadiah, Jonah and Micah*, London 1976, p.176.
13 For Jeremiah's call, and his protests, see Jer. 1.4–10. In comparison, how acquiescent was Isaiah when called! – Isa. 6.8!
14 See R.P. Carroll, *Jeremiah* (Old Testament Guides), Sheffield 1989.
15 J. Skinner, *Prophecy and Religion: Studies in the Life of Jeremiah*, Cambridge 1922, p.202.
16 See R.P. Carroll, *Jeremiah* (Old Testament Library), London 1986. For orientation to and approaches in recent books on Jeremiah, see C.S. Rodd, 'Which is the best Commentary? VI. Jeremiah', *ExpT* 98 (1986–87), pp.171–175.
17 Scholars seem unable to come up with a more appropriate term for these passages. They are not confessions of faith, nor are they confessions of sin, rather a confession to God as to how the prophet was feeling.
18 W. Louth, in his *Commentary upon the Prophecy and Lamentations of Jeremiah*, London 1718, quoted by W. McKane, *Jeremiah* (International Critical Commentary), Vol. 1, Edinburgh 1986, p.355.
19 Quoted by F. Heiler, *Prayer: A Study in the History and Psychology of Religion*, tr. S. McComb, Oxford 1932, p.240.
20 R. Davidson, *Jeremiah* (Daily Study Bible), Vol. 1, Edinburgh 1983, p.130.
21 A.S. Peake (*Jeremiah* [Century Bible], Vol. 1, Edinburgh 1910, p.213), observed, 'And the reward of service faithfully rendered is, as in the Parable of the Pounds, more service.'
22 F. Heiler, *Prayer*, pp.259f. See above Ch. 2.
23 F. von Hügel writing to a friend in his last illness offered some advice about prayer in a time of suffering:

> Try more and more *at the moment itself* . . . as spontaneously as possible, to cry out to God . . . in any way that comes most handy, and the more variously the better . . . 'Oh, help me to move on, from finding pain so real, to discovering sin to be far more real' . . . And so on, and so on. You could end such by ejaculations costing your *brains* practically nothing. The all important point is, to make them *at the time with the pain well mixed up into the prayer.*

F. von Hügel, *Selected Letters*, London 1927, pp.231 (his italics). Surely, there is help in some of these Old Testament prayers to pray, 'with the pain mixed up into the prayer'.

24 On the book of Job, see, e.g., J. H. Eaton, *Job* (Old Testament Guides), Sheffield 1985; C. S. Rodd, *The Book of Job* (Epworth Commentaries), London 1990.

25 Gerard Manley Hopkins, 'My prayers must meet a brazen heaven', pp.72f. in *Gerard Manley Hopkins* (The Oxford Poetry Library) ed. C. Phillips, Oxford 1995. See G. S. Wakefield, 'God and some English Poets: 3. Gerard Manley Hopkins', *ExpT* 104 (1992–93), pp.328–332.

26 H. H. Rowley, *Job* (New Century Bible), London 1976, p.265.

27 Quoted by F. Heiler, *Prayer*, p.362.

6 'For him shall endless prayer be made'

1 *King Henry V*, IV, i, 236–243 (Arden edition, London 1954).

2 Gunkel identified the Royal Psalms as Pss. 2; 18; 20; 21; 45; 72; 89; 101; 110; 132; 144.1–11, and today these, making as they do clear reference to the king, would be generally accepted as 'Royal Psalms'. See J. Day, *Psalms* (Old Testament Guides), Sheffield 1990, Ch. 6.

3 Others are Pss. 2; 18; 20; 21; 89; 132; 144.1–11.

4 Some comments of W. Zimmerli are apposite here: 'There is no prayer [in the Old Testament] to the angels of Yahweh, who are mentioned in the Psalms (Ps. 91:11–12), or to the king, such as we find in the so-called monotheism of the period of Akh-en-Aton in Egypt . . . it is Yahweh and Yahweh alone to whom all prayers and supplications are addressed.' W. Zimmerli, *Old Testament Theology in Outline*, tr. D. E. Green, Edinburgh 1978, p.151.

5 Something of the king's responsibilities may be indicated through the expression 'go out or come in', which may refer to leadership in battle.

6 On Deuteronomy and the Deuteronomistic history, see A. H. W. Curtis, *Joshua* (Old Testament Guides), Sheffield 1994, pp.17–21; J.G.McConville, *Grace in the End* (Studies in Old Testament Biblical Theology), Carlisle 1993. See above p.97

7 Examples of these are, v.6: 'righteousness, and in uprightness of heart' (see Deut. 9.5); v.6: 'you have kept for him' (see Deut. 7.9,12); v.8: 'your people whom you have chosen' (see Deut. 7.6).

8 For further details see G. H. Jones, *I & II Chronicles* (Old Testament Guides), Sheffield 1993, Ch. 6.

9 On the Chronicler's sources, see, G. H. Jones, *I & II Chronicles*, Ch. 5.

10 H. W. Wolff has a sermon entitled 'The Essential Prayer', based on the

I Kings 3.6-9 prayer, in his *Old Testament and Christian Preaching*, Philadelphia 1986, pp.39-44.
11 On II Sam. 7 see R. P. Gordon, *I & II Samuel* (Old Testament Guides), Sheffield 1984, pp.71-80.
12 R. E. Clements, *The Prayers of the Bible*, London 1985, p.75.
13 For the Chronicler, David's son Solomon is 'to sit upon the throne of the kingdom of the Lord over Israel' (I Chron. 28.5); even 'Then Solomon sat on the throne of the Lord . . .' (I Chron. 29.23).
14 Quoted by F. Colquhoun, *God of our Fathers*, London 1990, pp.104f.
15 However, it is not always easy to know just what aspects of 'long life' are intended in these prayers: is the thought about eternal life, or long life for the dynasty, or even quite simply preservation in battle?
16 *Ancient Near Eastern Texts Relating to the Old Testament*, ed. J. B. Pritchard, third edition, Princeton 1969, p.397. A similar prayer is found in a building inscription of the Babylonian ruler Nebuchadnezzar II: '. . . give me everlasting life, fullness with a great old age, an established throne, a long reign . . .'. *Near Eastern Religious Texts Relating to the Old Testament*, ed. W. Beyerlin, London 1978, p.115.
17 See p.160 below for the complex matter of the relationship between II Kings 20.2f. and Isa. 38.2f.
18 See Ch. 1 above, pp.34f.
19 On theophany, see the articles 'Theophany', by A. H. W. Curtis in *A Dictionary of Biblical Interpretation*, ed. R. J. Coggins and J. L. Houlden, London 1990, pp.694f.; and S. A. Meier in *The Oxford Companion to the Bible*, ed. B. M. Metzger and M. D. Coogan, Oxford 1993, pp.740f.
20 On prayer in the book of Judges, see Ch. 8 below.
21 See B. S. Childs, *Isaiah and the Assyrian Crisis* (Studies in Biblical Theology, second series), London 1967; R. E. Clements, *Isaiah and the Deliverance of Jerusalem*, Sheffield 1980; G. H. Jones, *I and II Kings* (New Century Bible), Volume 2, London 1984, pp.556ff.; C. R. Seitz, *Zion's Final Destiny: The Development of the Book of Isaiah*, Minneapolis 1991; H. G. M. Williamson, *The Book Called Isaiah*, Oxford 1994, Ch. 8.
22 For the historical details, see, e.g., J. Rogerson and P. Davies, *The Old Testament World*, Cambridge 1989, pp.151ff.; *Israelite and Judaean History*, ed. J. H. Hayes and J. M. Miller, London 1977, pp.446ff.
23 See, e.g., J. Bright, *A History of Israel*, third edition, London 1981, pp.298ff.
24 Another interesting change is effected here by the Chronicler. The Kings account has, 'the angel of the Lord went forth', but the Chronicler lays stress upon *who* sent the angel: 'the Lord sent an

angel'. See S. Japhet *I & II Chronicles* (Old Testament Library), London 1993, p.990.
25. I Chron. 5.20; II Chron. 6.34; 13.14–18; 18.31; 20.5–20; 32.20–22. All these are unique to the Chronicler, or at least are modified from their form in Kings. For details, see R. B. Dillard, *II Chronicles* (Word Biblical Commentary), Waco 1987, pp.118f.
26. Whether or not this incident took place historically has been much discussed. It should be noted that for the reign of Asa, the Chronicler has thoroughly reworked the Kings source. On both these points see, e.g., S. Japhet, *I & II Chronicles*, pp.702–5 and 709f.
27. H. G. M. Williamson, *(I and II Chronicles*, [New Century Bible], London 1982, p.286) says, 'Even in the middle of a battle which he should never have been fighting, Jehoshaphat could find the kind of deliverance which the Chronicler always delights to relate.'
28. Presumably with the intention of reminding the reader of Solomon at the dedication of the temple (II Chron. 6.3–42, on which see pp.179ff. below). Solomon's prayer did indeed envisage just such a crisis as is here described (vv.34f.).
29. S. Japhet, *I & II Chronicles*, pp.793f.
30. See R. P. Gordon, *I & II Samuel* (Old Testament Guides), Sheffield 1984, pp.95ff.
31. R. P. Gordon, *I & II Samuel: A Commentary*, Exeter 1986, p.319.
32. J. Baldwin, *I and II Samuel* (Tyndale Old Testament Commentary), Leicester 1988, p.297.
33. E.g., H. W. Hertzberg, *I & II Samuel* (Old Testament Library), London 1964, p.413. J. Mauchline (*I and II Samuel* [New Century Bible], London 1971, p.325) compares David's situation – of not knowing what is going-on in the counsels of the Lord – with that of Job in Job 1.6–12.
34. H. P. Smith, *The Books of Samuel* (International Critical Commentary), Edinburgh 1912, p.391; W. McKane, *I & II Samuel*, (Torch Commentary), London 1963, p.301.
35. See Williamson, *I and II Chronicles*, pp.388ff.; Dillard, *II Chronicles*, pp.264–66; Japhet, *I & II Chronicles*, pp.1000ff.
36. R. H. Lowery, *The Reforming Kings: Cult and Society in First Temple Judah*, Sheffield 1991, pp.188f., says: 'For the Chronicler, Manasseh . . . is a key symbol of hope, based in trust that Yahweh forgives and blesses beyond imagination those who truly humble themselves and turn from evil. Manasseh . . . becomes the Chronicler's strongest object lesson for restored Israel and their greatest reason to hope for the future.'
37. Japhet, *I & II Chronicles*, p.1001.
38. The Chronicler's prayer of Manasseh, clearly, interested others too,

one evidence of this being the fact that it led to either the composition of, or the assigning of the name of this king to, that prayer which has been transmitted as the Prayer of Manasseh and found in the Deutero-canonical literature (Apocrypha). This is an elaborate prayer, rather in the style of post-exilic Jewish prayer, containing an invocation to God (vv.1–7), a confession of sins (vv.8–10), and a petition for forgiveness (vv.11–15). It is very difficult to date this prayer.

39 On such aspects of kingship see the articles, 'Kingship and Monarchy' by B. Halpern in *The Oxford Companion to the Bible*, ed. B. M. Metzger and M. D. Coogan, Oxford 1993, pp.413–16, and, 'Kingship' by J. H. Eaton in *A Dictionary of Biblical Interpretation*, ed. R. J. Coggins and J. L. Houlden, London 1990, pp.379–82.
40 *Methodist Service Book*, Peterborough 1975, p.B8.
41 Quoted in F. Colquhoun, *God of our Fathers*, London 1990, p.103.
42 A prayer of Basil Naylor, quoted in *The SPCK Book of Christian Prayer*, London 1995, p.173.
43 A prayer of Charles Gore (1853–1932), quoted in F. Colquhoun, *God of our Fathers*, p.183.

7 'My house shall be called a house of prayer'

1 'Four Quartets is a superb achievement, the masterpiece of modern English poetry.' L. G. Salingar, p.457 in *The New Pelican Guide to English Literature*, 7. From James to Eliot, ed. B. Ford, London, 1983. See, G. S. Wakefield, 'God and Some English Poets: 6. T. S. Eliot', *ExpT* 105 (1993–94), pp.167–171.
2 See A. L. Maycock, *Nicholas Ferrar of Little Gidding*, London 1938.
3 T. S. Eliot, 'Little Gidding', *Four Quartets*, Faber & Faber 1944, reproduced by permission.
4 On Tabernacle and Tent, see M. Barker, *The Gate of Heaven: The History and Symbolism of the Temple in Jerusalem*, London 1991, pp.136–38; article 'Tabernacle' in *The Oxford Companion to the Bible*, ed. B. M. Metzger and M. D. Coogan, Oxford 1993, pp.729f.
5 'The human family cannot look upon Yahweh and survive: the gap between the finite and the infinite is too great; it is an experience of which man is incapable.' (J. I. Durham, *Exodus* [Word Biblical Commentary], Waco 1987, p.452). Compare Newman, *The Dream of Gerontius*, where the angel says to the soul of Gerontius:

> Then sight, or that which to the soul is sight,
> As by a lightning-flash, will come to thee,
> And thou shalt see, amid the dark profound,
> Whom thy soul loveth, and would fain approach,–

One moment; but thou knowest not, my child,
What thou dost ask: that sight of the Most Fair
Will gladden thee, but it will pierce thee too.

J. H. Newman, *The Dream of Gerontius*, (Mowbrays Popular Christian Paperbacks), London 1986, pp.33f.

6 'For it is necessary to affirm both that God can be known as intimately present and that he is beyond human reach and knowledge. This problem, that is immanence and transcendence, is inherent in language about God and cannot, as such, be resolved. Indeed what matters is not to dissolve the tension but to recognise it as paradox and to describe it correctly. It is precisely such a theological reflection on the problem of immanance and transcendence that [Ex.] 33.11 points to.' (R. W. L. Moberly, *At the Mountain of God: Story and Theology in Exodus 32–34*, Sheffield 1983, pp.65f.)

7 The issue partly hangs on whether one regards the arrangement of Ex. 33.7–11 + 33.12–23 as logical and purposeful or not. B. S. Childs thinks it is ('. . . although vv.7–11 had once an independent role in early tradition, they have now assumed a new and most appropriate role within the writer's story of Moses' intercession for sinful Israel': *Exodus* [Old Testament Library], London 1974, p.593), whereas J. I. Durham does not ('The five verses of Ex. 33.7–11, therefore, as important as they are, are nonetheless completely out of place in the taut narrative of Ex. 32:1–34:9': *Exodus* [Word Biblical Commentary], p.443)!

8 For further details about the Ark, the Tent of Meeting and the Shiloh sanctuary, see, R. E. Clements, *God and Temple*, Oxford 1965, pp.28–39.

9 For Saul, see, e.g., the article by D. M. Gunn in *The Oxford Companion to the Bible*, ed. B. M. Metzger and M. D. Coogan, Oxford 1993, pp.679–81.

10 On this belief in the divine election of Zion and David, see, e.g., R. E. Clements, *God and Temple*, pp.40–55.

11 See M. Barker, *The Gate of Heaven*, pp.20–22.

12 See Barker, *The Gate of Heaven*, pp.65–68.

13 The matter is complex, and various accounts give different details. See Barker, *The Gate of Heaven*, pp.30–34.

14 Not all would agree with me in this assessment of the book of Ruth. Some would regard the section 4.18–22 as having been added at a later stage. See, M. E. W. Thompson, 'New Life Amid the Alien Corn: The Book of Ruth', *EQ* 65 (1993), pp.197–210, esp.pp.201f.

15 A major technical work that studies this prayer both *synchronically* and *diachronically* is E. Talstra, *Solomon's Prayer: Synchrony and Diachrony in the Composition of 1 Kings 8.14–61*, Kampen 1993.

16 See further D. M. Gunn and D. N. Fewell, *Narrative in the Hebrew Bible*, Oxford 1993, pp.7–12.
17 See Introduction above, pp.6–8
18 A number of scholars suggest that this prayer reflects in some measure the usage of prayer in the temple or the synagogue of the Chronicler's own day – that is, between 500 and 400 BC. (On the date of the Chronicler's work, see above, p.150.) See, e.g., R. Braun, *I Chronicles* (Word Biblical Commentary), Waco 1986, p.283; R. P. Ackroyd, *I & II Chronicles, Ezra, Nehemiah* (Torch Bible Commentaries), London 1973, pp.93f.
19 On this 'distance' between God and his people, and yet their 'closeness', compare the Puritan John Owen (1616–83) in his *Sacramental Discourses*, 'Nothing brings God and man together as a due sense of our infinite distance.' Quoted by G. S. Wakefield, *Puritan Devotion*, London 1957, p.73.
20 In these verses are brought together a range of the Hebrew vocabulary for prayer, words that are discussed in Ch. 2 above:

> [28] Regard your servant's prayer (*t^epillah*) and his plea (*t^eḥinnāh*), O Lord my God, heeding the cry (*rinnah*) and the prayer (*t^epillah*) which your servant prays (*pll*) before you today [29] . . . that you may heed the prayer (*t^eḥinnāh*) which your servant prays (*pll*) to this place. [30] Hear the plea (*t^eḥinnāh*) of your servant and of your people Israel when they pray (*pll*) toward this place.

21 On Deuteronomy's 'name theology', see E. W. Nicholson, *Deuteronomy and Tradition*, Oxford 1967, pp.55f.; J. G. McConville, *Grace in the End: A Study in Deuteronomic Theology*, Carlisle 1993, pp.126–28.
22 See M. Barker, *The Gate of Heaven*, London 1991, pp.32–38.
23 See, e.g., G. Ashby, *Sacrifice: Its Nature and Purpose*, London 1988, pp.26–48.
24 It is widely thought that one of the texts that the Chronicler had before him was the books of Samuel and Kings. See G. H. Jones, *I & II Chronicles* (Old Testament Guides), Sheffield 1993, pp.65ff. A. G. Auld (*Kings Without Privilege*, Edinburgh 1994), has argued that the Deuteronomistic historian and the Chronicler both worked from a common source, not now known to us, but this is a minority view. Apart from the big difference at the end of the prayer, there are some minor variations. In the Chronicles text, God tends to be more exalted than in the Kings text. Thus in II Chron. 6.21 God hears 'from heaven', but in I Kings 8.30 'in heaven' (compare II Chron. 6.23 and 25 with I Kings 8.32 and 34 etc.). Further, whereas in Kings God speaks 'direct', in Chronicles we have 'reported speech' –

compare II Chron. 6.20 with I Kings 8.29. Again, 'Your sons are to *walk in my law*' is found in II Chron. 6.16 in place of *before me* in I Kings 8.25.

25 This phrase can be translated 'remember the faithfulness of David your servant'. The matter continues to be debated as to whether the Chronicler is referring to the on-going mercies of God to the line of David, or whether he wishes to stress the faithful deeds of the king. I think it is the first of these, as my translation indicates.

26 II Chron. 36.22–23 have most likely been added subsequently to the Chronicler's own work, both to give emphasis to hopeful aspects of that work, and also to direct the reader to the books of Ezra (II Chron. 36.22–23 are repeated in Ezra 1.1–3) and Nehemiah, where the continuation of the story of Israel is to be found. See H.G.M. Williamson, *I and II Chronicles* (New Century Bible), London 1982, p.419.

27 For further details, see G.H. Jones, *I & II Chronicles* (Old Testament Guides), Sheffield 1993, Ch. 6.

28 For full details, see E.P. Sanders, *Judaism: Practice and Belief 63BCE–66CE*, London 1992, pp.51–76.

29 Acts 9.20 (Damascus); 13.5 (Salamis); 13.14 (Pisidian Antioch); 14.1 (Iconium); 16.13 (Philippi); 17.1 (Thessalonica); 17.10 (Beroea); 17.17 (Athens); 18.4 (Corinth); 18.19 and 19.8 (Ephesus).

30 Full details are given in H.H. Rowley's *Worship in Ancient Israel: Its Forms and Meaning*, London 1967, pp.213ff. See also, S.C. Reif, *Judaism and Hebrew Prayer*, Cambridge 1993, pp.72–75; L.L. Grabbe, 'Synagogues in Pre-70 Palestine. A Re-assessment', *JTS* NS 39 (1988), pp.401–10; E.P. Sanders, *Judaism: Practice and Belief 63BCE–66CE*, p.198; C.M. Pilkington, *Judaism* (Teach Yourself Books), London 1995, pp.135–37. On synagogue prayer and its theology, see Sanders, *Judaism*, pp.199–207, 260–62. Compare H.A. McKay, *Sabbath and Synagogue*, Leiden 1994.

31 We also read in the New Testament and elsewhere (e.g., in Josephus's writings, [*Antiquities*, XIV.x.23]) of a 'place of prayer' (e.g., Acts 16.1). Probably this is an alternative term for synagogue. See Sanders, *Judaism*, p.199.

32 An elaborate series of prayers that included those for understanding, penitence, forgiveness, redemption, healing, and much else. For a text of this prayer see C.W. Dugmore, *The Influence of the Synagogue upon the Divine Office*, London 1944, pp.114–125. See also P. Bradshaw, *The Search for the Origins of Christian Worship*, London 1992, pp.19f.; Pilkington, *Judaism*, pp.125–27; Sanders, *Judaism*, pp.204–206.

33 Reif, *Judaism and Hebrew Prayer*; Pilkington, *Judaism*, p.128.

34 On this theme see J.D. Levenson, 'From Temple to Synagogue: I Kings 8', pp.143–66 in *Traditions in Transformation: Turning Points in Biblical Faith*, ed. B. Halpern and J.D. Levenson, Winona Lake, Indiana 1981.
35 C.K. Barrett, *The Gospel According to St John*, London 1962, p.168.

8 'I have heard your prayer'

1 F. Trochu (tr. R. Matthews), *The Curé d'Ars*, London 1955, p.63.
2 For details about the Deuteronomistic history, see above, p.97.
3 A.D.H. Mayes, *Deuteronomy* (New Century Bible), London 1979, pp.41f.
4 On 'Contemplation' and 'Meditation', see *A Dictionary of Christian Spirituality*, ed. G.S. Wakefield, London 1983, pp.95f., 261f.
5 Some moderns have suggested that prayer be defined in these sorts of terms. Thus James Borst says prayer is 'awakening to God's presence within', and Simone Weil, 'full attentiveness', (quoted by A. Wierzbicka in L.B. Brown, *The Human Side of Prayer*, Birmingham, Alabama 1994, p.27). But perhaps we need prayer *in order to* awaken us to God's presence within, and to bring us to full attentiveness to God, both matters that Deuteronomy takes as normally existing, and thus does not need to emphasize the element of prayer – apart from occasions when God's forgiveness or continued blessing is being sought in a particular way.
6 On the book of Joshua, see A.H.W. Curtis, *Joshua* (Old Testament Guides), Sheffield 1994.
7 On this theme of the 'ban', see article 'Ban' in *The Oxford Companion to the Bible*, ed. B.M. Metzger and M.D. Coogan, Oxford 1993, p.73.
8 On the subject of war, particularly 'holy war', in the Old Testament, see S. Niditch, *War in the Hebrew Bible*, Oxford 1993.
9 See J.A. Soggin, *Joshua* (Old Testament Library), London 1972, p.122.
10 See A.D.H. Mayes, *Judges* (Old Testament Guides), Sheffield 1985.
11 For details see, e.g., J. Rogerson and P. Davies, *The Old Testament World*, Cambridge 1989, pp.123-132; J.H. Hayes and J.M. Miller, *Israelite and Judaean History*, London 1977, pp.332-363.
12 For literature on the Succession Narrative see R.P. Gordon, *I & II Samuel* (Old Testament Guides), Sheffield 1984, pp.90–94. Gordon (p.90) says pride of place must go to L. Rost, *The Succession to the Throne of David* (Historic Texts and Interpreters in Biblical Scholarship), Sheffield 1982.
13 Rost, *Succession*, p.68.
14 It may be questioned whether this is a prayer, but rather a statement

to Nathan on the part of David. In so far as it is portrayed as a statement from the heart, an expression of penitence, I regard it as a prayer. M. Greenberg, *Biblical Prose Prayer: As a Window to the Popular Religion of Ancient Israel*, Berkeley and Los Angeles 1983, p.59, note 1, regards it as a prayer.

15 As W. Brueggemann ('On Trust and Freedom', *Interpretation* 26 [1972], pp.3–19, see p.13) expresses it : 'David and the other actors in this narrative have enormous power and freedom to act, but they are not free to act as though Yahweh were not there.'

16 Rost, *Succession*, Ch. 1. On the 'Ark Narrative', see R.P. Gordon, *I & II Samuel* (Old Testament Guides), Sheffield 1984, Ch. 3.

17 G. von Rad ('Historical Writing in Ancient Israel', see his *The Problem of the Hexateuch and Other Essays*, Edinburgh and London 1966, pp.166–204) placed great emphasis on this incident being the turning point in Absalom's rebellion and in David regaining his throne: 'We now understand why the historian should pause at this juncture, when the fate of Absalom is sealed, to point out to the reader the theological significance of the events. This was the turning point in the rebellion, and the change in the situation was the work of God himself, who had heard the prayer of the King in his profound humiliation' (p.200).

18 Though it is no part of the Deuteronomistic history, we noted above how the Chronicler (II Chron. 32.1–21) in his account of these events has a further variation in the matter of these prayers: he has both king and prophet praying, and stresses the military provisions that take place alongside the praying. See Ch. 6 above.

19 John Wilkinson, *Egeria's Travels*, London, 1971, p.123 (24.2). Egeria was a Christian traveller who made a pilgrimage to the east between AD 381 and 384, and recorded much that she witnessed, especially in Jerusalem. See P. Bradshaw, *The Search for the Origins of Christian Worship*, London 1992, pp.128f.; Wilkinson, op.cit..

20 W. Sanday and A.C. Headlam (*The Epistle to the Romans* [International Critical Commentary], Edinburgh, fifth edition, 1902, p.221), observe: 'It is not a dead Christ on whom we depend, but a living. It is not only a living Christ, but a Christ enthroned, a Christ in power. It is not only a Christ in power, but a Christ of ever-active sympathy, constantly (if we may so speak) at the Father's ear, and constantly pouring in intercession for His struggling people on earth.' They add, 'A great text for the value and significance of the Ascension.'

21 On this theme of the relationship of our intercessions to those of Christ, see, e.g., J.N. Ward, *The Use of Praying*, London 1967, pp.94f.: 'If our prayer is part of the intercession of the great High Priest, whose love spans the universe, we can play our part in it with

gladness and seriousness ... It is good to bring into our intercessions the thought of the infinity of the divine care. It is beautifully expressed in the Liturgy of Basil the Great: "And those whom we, through ignorance or forgetfulness or the number of names, have not remembered, do Thou, O God, remember them, who knowest the age and the name of each one, who knowest each from his mother's womb. For Thou, O God, art the help of the helpless, the hope of the hopeless, the saviour of the tempest-tossed, the harbour of the mariners, the physician of the sick. Be Thou thyself all things to all men, who knowest each and his petition and his dwelling and his need."'

22 M. Luther, original first published in Klug's *Geistliche Lieder*, Wittenberg 1535, *Vom Himmel hoch da komm ich her*.

23 J. Bunyan, *I will pray with the Spirit* (or *A Discourse Touching Prayer*), pp.227ff. in *The Miscellaneous Works of John Bunyan*, Vol. II, ed. R.L. Greaves, Oxford, 1976, p.264. See also pp.263f.: 'There are some who out of custome and formality, go and pray; there are others, who go in the bitterness of their spirit: The one he prays out of bare notion and naked knowledge; the other hath his words forced from him by the anguish of his soul. Surely, that is the man that God will look at ...'

24 G. Wainwright, *Doxology: The Praise of God in Worship, Doctrine and Life*, London 1980, p.43f., speaks of 'human wrestling with God in prayer', and says, 'Depth psychology has hinted how close love and hate are to one another. A fight may signify not only conflict but also affection between people. There is a powerful literary example of this in the naked wrestling of Rupert and Gerald before the open fire in D.H. Lawrence's *Women in Love*, but the phenomenon is as widespread as lovers' quarrels ... Jacob's night-long wrestling with the unnamed adversary at Penuel (*The Face of God*) and his own acquisition of the new name of Israel (*He who strives with God*, or *God strives*) has continued to haunt the imagination and to provide the language for describing many a personal experience in prayer (Genesis 32.22–32).'

25 G.W. Coats, *The Moses Tradition*, Sheffield 1993, p.60.

26 G.M. Hopkins, 'I wake and feel', and 'No worst'. See *Gerard Manley Hopkins*, ed. C. Phillips (The Oxford Poetry Library), Oxford 1995, pp.151–152.

27 F. Heiler, *Prayer: A Study in the History and Psychology of Religion*, tr. S.McComb, Oxford 1932.

28 J.L. Crenshaw, *Ecclesiastes* (Old Testament Library), London 1988, p.116, thinks it is human speech, but R.N. Whybray, *Ecclesiastes* (New Century Bible), London 1989, p.93, thinks it is a prayer.

29 On this subject of the pessimistic/hopeful natures of the Deutero-

nomistic historian's and the Chronicler's presentations see M. E. W. Thompson, *Situation and Theology: Old Testament Interpretations of the Syro-Ephraimite War*, Sheffield 1982, pp.89f., 100ff.

30. From the letter of 16 July 1944 to Eberhard Bethge: D. Bonhoeffer, *Letters and Papers from Prison*, revised and enlarged edition, 1967, p.360.
31. See above, p.1
32. 'The test of sincere intercession is the commitment to corresponding action', G. Wainwright, *Doxology*, London 1980, p.355.
33. An example of prayer without action from modern times that may be cited is that of George Müller of Bristol, who died in 1898. He had led a very active and successful life devoted to Christian projects and enterprises, and for those things he needed he prayed to the Lord, believing that such prayers would always be answered if there were sufficient trust. We may recall W. James's comment (*The Varieties of Religious Experience*, second edition, London 1929, pp.470f.), 'His God was, as he often said, his business partner. He seems to have been for Müller little more than a sort of supernatural clergyman interested in the congregation of tradesmen and others in Bristol who were his saints, and in the orphanages and other enterprises, but unpossessed of any of those vaster and wilder and more ideal attributes with which the human imagination has invested him. Müller, in short, was absolutely unphilosophical. His intensely private and practical conceptions of his relations with the Deity continued the traditions of the most primitive human thought.'
34. See C. Westermann, *The Living Psalms*, tr. J. R. Porter, Edinburgh 1989, pp.13f. for three possible stages in the history of prayer in the Old Testament. The three stages are: (1) The brief appeals to God, arising directly out of the situation being experienced. (2) The biblical Psalms, which are poetic compositions modelled on the earlier brief appeals to God, and fashioned so as to be used in worship. (3) The evolution of the prose prayer, which is often of an extensive nature. See also C. Westermann, *Elements of Old Testament Theology*, Atlanta 1982, pp.154-6.
35. On New Testament prayer, see O. Cullmann, *Prayer in the New Testament*, London 1995.
36. See J. Jeremias, *The Prayers of Jesus*, (Studies in Biblical Theology, second series), London 1967, pp.54ff.
37. *Theological Dictionary of the Bible*, G. Kittel and G. Friedrich, abridged edition, tr. G. W. Bromiley, p.2.
38. See O. Cullman, *Prayer in the New Testament*, pp.41f.
39. R. E. Clements, *The Prayers of the Bible*, London 1985, p.110.
40. R. Otto, *The Idea of the Holy*, Oxford 1923.

41 Quoted by G.S. Wakefield, *Puritan Devotion*, London 1957, p.78.
42 On the continuation and also the development of the Old Testament tradition of prayer in the New, see P.D. Miller, *They Cried to the Lord*, Minneapolis 1994, pp.304–35. On prayer in the New Testament see, O. Cullmann, *Prayer in the New Testament*.
43 See S.C. Reif, *Judaism and Hebrew Prayer*, Cambridge 1993.
44 J. Baillie, *A Diary of Private Prayer*, Oxford 1936.
45 T.F. Torrance, 'John Baillie at Prayer', *Christ, Church and Society: Essays on John Baillie and Donald Baillie*, ed. D. Fergusson, Edinburgh 1993, pp.253–261, esp.p.259.

For Further Reading

This is a very select Bibliography, listing just ten books that treat aspects of prayer in the Bible. For those who are interested in pursuing the subject of Old Testament prayer further, there are plenty of references to other works in the books of Balantine and Miller listed below.

S. E. Balantine	*Prayer in the Hebrew Bible: The Drama of Divine-Human Dialogue* (Overtures to Biblical Theology), Minneapolis 1993.
	A detailed study of prayer in the Old Testament, with emphasis on complaints (laments); also that prayer brings about new possibilities. He stresses that he writes as a scholar and a Christian believer.
R. E. Clements	*The Prayers of the Bible*, London 1985.
	A study of twenty-five biblical prayers, seventeen from the Old Testament, and eight from the New.
O. Cullmann	*Prayer in the New Testament*, London 1995.
	The main part of this book discusses the prayers in the Synoptic Gospels, especially the Lord's Prayer, and in the other parts of the New Testament.
M. Greenberg	*Biblical Prose Prayer: As a Window to the Popular Religion of Ancient Israel*, Berkeley, Los Angeles, London 1983.
	A gem of a book about the prose prayers found in the narrative sections of the Old Testament.
W. Harrington	*The Bible's Ways of Prayer*, Dublin 1980.
	Seven chapters about Old Testament prayers, and

five about those in the New, with the emphases of 'companionship' and 'faith'.

J. Jeremias	*The Prayers of Jesus* (Studies in Biblical Theology), London 1967.
	A famous study of daily prayer in the life of Jesus and the earliest church, and of the Lord's Prayer.
P. D. Miller	*They Cried to the Lord: The Form and Theology of Biblical Prayer*, Minneapolis 1994.
	A full-scale treatment of Old Testament prayers, and of the developing tradition of prayer in the New.
H. G. Reventlow	*Gebet im Alten Testament*, Stuttgart 1986.
	For those who read German and who want to delve further into Old Testament prayer.
S. C. Reif	*Judaism and Hebrew Prayer*, Cambridge 1993.
	A detailed study of prayer in the synagogue and in the worship of Judaism.
W. Zimmerli	*Old Testament Theology in Outline*, Edinburgh 1978.
	Not a book only about prayer, but with a useful section about it on pp.150–55.

Indexes

Index of Biblical References

Old Testament

Genesis					
1.26f.	3	37–50	21–23	32.30–34	109f., 114
4.1f.	12	43.14	21	32.31f.	99,
4.3–5	13	45.8	21		230 n.19,
4.10	101	48.15f.	22		233 n.21
4.10–12	13	48.20	22	33.7–23	173–75,
4.13f.	13, 38,	50.20	21		241 n.7
	173, 216			33.11	197,
4.15	13	*Exodus*			241 n.6
4.16	14	2.23f.	53, 203,	33.12ff.	233 n.21
12.11, 13	55		210	33.18	55
13.13	100	3.1–12	204	33.20	174
17.18	4	3.7	53	34.6f.	74
18.4, 30	55	3.7, 9	203	36–40	173
18.17–21	102	3.9	53		
18.23–33	55,	5.22f.	4, 55	*Leviticus*	
	100–103	8.8, 9	54	5.1ff.	73
19	100	8.28–30	54	16.21	73
19.29	102	9.28	54	26.40	73
20.7	111,	10.16f.	230 n.19		
	233 n.21	10.17f.	54	*Numbers*	
21.16f.	44	15.2–27	211	11.15	33
23.12	4	16.1–8	211	11.16–30	173
24	14–17	17.1–7	211	12.1–16	173,
24.10–27	17	22.15	137		225 n.15
24.11–14	15f., 69	23.31	157	12.12	55
24.12	55	25–31	173	14.13–19	199
24.26f.	16, 55	32.11ff.	54,	21.7	230 n.19
25.21	54		233 n.21	22.34	230 n.19
32.9–12	18–20,	32.11–14	103–108	23.19	106
	224 n.5	32.11–14,			
		30–34	173		

Deuteronomy

1.11	198, 200
1.34	199f.
2.30, 33, 36, 37	200
3.2, 3, 18, 22	200
3.23–26	198–201
4.1–40	200
4.4	200
4.44–28.68	108
5.1	200
5.8	187
5.22–27, 31–33	200
6.1, 4, 6	200
7.6, 9, 12	237 n.7
9.10, 12–14	200
9.20	201
9.20–26	199f.
9.25–29	108f., 202
10.1, 20	200
11.22	200
12.5, 11	187
12.7	200
13.1ff.	200
13.5	200
18.15–18	99, 111
21.8	199f.
26.1–11	199
26.7	44, 53, 203, 210
26.7, 15	200
26.12–15	200
29.23	232 n.11
30.20	200
31.2, 16	200
31.9	175
32.48	200
34.6	200
34.10	201

Joshua

7.6–9	201f., 232 n.4
7.1–8.29	201
7.7	55
8.1	175
10.1–15	201
10.12–14	201–203, 232 n.4

Judges

2.11–16.31	203
2.15	44
3.9, 15, 30	53, 203
4.3, 23	203
6.6	203
6.36–40	16, 203f.
9.38	55
10.10	203
10.10–16	83, 230 n.19
13–16	204
13.8f.	54, 204
15.8f.	204
15.18	44
16.28	204
17.6	203
19–21	204
20.26	87
21.2–4	204
21.25	203

Ruth

1–4	89–93
1.8–9	4
4.18–22	241 n.14

I Samuel

1ff.	204
1–11	97
1.3, 9, 10, 12–16	175
1.10, 12–18	23–25
1.13	231 n.33
1.15	4
1.26–28	25f.
2.1–10	26–28, 176
3.3, 21	175f.
4–6	206, 215
4.11, 21f.	94
7.2–4	94
7.5–9	94–96
7.6	56, 86
7.7–12	202
7.8	53, 99
8.6–8	96f.
10.8	177
11–15	157
12	97f.
12.10	53, 230 n.19
12.19, 23	111, 233 n.21
13.12	54
14	202
14.33–35	177
15.24f.	230 n.19
15.29	106
31.13	87

II Samuel

1.12	87
2.1–11	177
3–6	177
3.1	177
5.17–25	202
6.18	206
7	152, 168, 178, 238 n.11
7.18–29	152–54
9–20	205–207
12.1ff.	206

12.6, 21–23	87	13.6	54, 156	5.25	70
12.13, 16	205, 207, 232 n.4	17–19, 21	207f.	12.17	70
14.17	205	17.20f.	29f., 34, 232 n.4	14.11	163
15.13–32	206	18.36f.	31f.	15.1– 16.43	192
15.31	205f.	19.4	32	16.35	151
18.25	207	20	156	17.16–27	151–54
18.28	205	22.32	164	21.8	151
21–24	165			21.15–17, 26	151, 166
21.14	54	II Kings		23.30	67f.
22	26	1.1– 10.36	207f.	28.5	238 n.13
24.10–17	71, 165f., 169	4.32–37	225 n.15	29.10–12	185f.
24.25	54	4.33	34, 232 n.4	29.10–19	151
		5.1–14	225 n.15	29.23	238 n.13
I Kings		6.17–20	34f., 232 n.4	II Chronicles	
1–2	205–207	6.23–28	179	1.8–10	150–52
1.20	205	13.4	54, 159	2.17f.	179
1.36	232 n.4	13.14–21	207f., 225 n.15	6.3–42	68, 151, 179ff., 217, 239 n.28
1.47, 48	205, 207, 232 n.4	17	97	6.16, 20	243
3.3	177	18–20	159–62, 208, 215	6.21, 23, 25	242 n.24
3.6–9	148–52, 238 n.10	19.4	232 n.4	6.34	239 n.25
5.10f.	179	20.1–11	155f., 225 n.15	7.12–18	151, 156, 168
8	195	20.2f.	238 n.17	8.7–10	179
8.5	189f., 175	20.3, 5	2	13.14	151
8.14–61	68, 73, 179ff., 216f.	21	170	13.14–18	239 n.25
8.22	37, 51, 68	21.1–18	166–68	14.11	151
8.25	243	22f.	166	17.2, 12–19	88
8.27f.	218f.	24.1, 4	123	18.31	151, 164, 216, 239 n.25
8.29	243	25.9, 13–17	193		
8.30, 32, 34	242 n.24			20.3ff.	56
8.35, 38, 42	51	I Chronicles		20.5–12	88, 151
8.54	37, 51, 68	1.1	193	20.5–20	239 n.25
8.62ff.	189f.	4.10	151	30.6–9	192
8.62–64	179	5.20	53f., 151, 239 n.25	30.18f.	232 n.4
9.10f.	179			30.27	151

32.1–21	151, 160–62, 215, 245 n.18	*Job*		60.6–8	48
		1–14	119	61.6f.	155
		1.21	84	64.1f.	3
32.20–22	53, 151, 239 n.25	6f.	141f.	65.1–2a	221
		7.11–21	142f.	65.2, 5–8	3
32.24	151, 155f.	11.19	54	66.18	225 n.21
33	166–70	14.1	120	69.11	87
33.12, 13, 19	54, 70	15.4	36, 141	72	147
		16.1– 17.16	143	72.1–4	83, 148, 170
36.11–21	193	17.1–5	144	72.5–7	154f.
36.22f.	193, 243 n.26	21.15	36, 54	72.8–11	157
		22.27	36, 54, 141	73	139
		30.20–23	144	77.8	115
Ezra		33.26	54, 141	78.60f.	176
1–3	243 n.26	38.1– 40.2	145	84.9	158
1.1–4	193	40.3–5	145	88.6	157
6.4	232 n.4	42.1–6	145	99.6	93
6.10	82	42.8	145f.	102	73
6.15	193			106.23	103, 111
8.23	54, 86f.	*Psalms*		106.45f.	107
9	80	5.7	51	107.13	53
9.5	37, 51, 67f.	6	73	109.24	87
9.5–15	72–74	11.6	232 n.11	110.4	106
10.1	72	17	41–49	116.1	44
		18.3, 6	158	119.58	54
Nehemiah		20.5, 9	158	119.164	67
1	80	21.4	155	130	44, 57–59, 73
1.4–11	72, 75f.	22.1	44	132.8–10	155, 192f.
1.5	74	22.5	53	132.11–14	178
2.4	83f.	23.4	84	134.2	51
4.4f.	84f.	24.2	157	136.6	157
4.9	87f.	28	49–53	141.2	190f.
5.19	85f.	28.1	46	143	73
6.14	85	28.2	37	144.5–8, 11–15	158
9	68, 80	31.6	39		
9.1	87	32	73	*Proverbs*	
9.6–37	72, 76–79, 230 n.21	35.13	87	15.8	36, 191
		38	73	15.29	37
9.32	74	51	73	28.9	37
13.14, 22b, 29, 31b	85	51.3, 5	43		
		55.17	67		

Index of Biblical References

Ecclesiastes
5.2	213
12.13	213

Isaiah
1.9f.	232 n.11
1.15	37, 217
6	204
6.1–5	218f.
13.19	232 n.11
19.22	54
36–39	159–62
37.4	232 n.4
38.1–22	225 n.15
38.2f.	155, 238 n.17
38.3	2
38.5	221
40–55	117
40.2	117
40.29	169
42.1–4	234 n.25
49.1–6	234 n.25
50.4–9	234 n.25
52.13–53.12	116–18, 234 n.25f.
56.6f.	190
58.3–9	87
63.7–64.12	56, 230 n.19

Jeremiah
1	204
1.6	130
7.12	176
7.16	54, 114f.
11.14	99, 114f.
11.18–20	130–33
11.21–23	131
14	56
14.2–9	56
14.11	99, 114f.
14.12	87
14.13	114f.
14.19–22	56
14.21	114f.
15.1	93, 99, 114f., 233 n.21
15.15–21	133–36
18.20	114
20.7–13	136–40
22.13–19	123
25.8–14	79
26.1–23	123
26.19	54
27.18	54
29.7	82
30–31	116
31.33b–34	116
36.6, 9	87
37.3	114, 233 n.21
37.20	51
42	114
49.18	232 n.11
50.40	232 n.11

Lamentations
2.19	51
3.14	51
4.6	232 n.11
5	56

Ezekiel
16.46–50, 53–55	232 n.11

Daniel
2.20–23	69
6	66–68
6.10	195, 216
7.25	70
9.3	86f.
9.3–9	72
9.3–19	79–82
9.13	54
9.21	67

Hosea
1.2–6, 8f.	112
2.2–5, 8–13, 21–23	112
4.1–19	112
6.1–3	112f., 213
11.1–9, 11	112
12.2–10	112
14.1–3, 5–8	113
14.5–8	112

Joel
1–2	56
1.14	71
2.17	232 n.4

Amos
3.11	111
4.11	232 n.11
5.2–3	111
6.9, 14	111
7.1–3	111f.
7.2b–3a, 4–6, 5b–6a	112
7.1–8.3	111
7.17	111
8.3	111
9.1–4, 10	111

Jonah
1.1–3	1, 126–30
1.5f., 12, 15	1
1.14	5
2.1	5f.
2.2	51

2.2–9	5	5.44	47, 85, 139	7.60	68
2.7–9	191			9.20	243 n.29
3.9f.	106	6.5	68	9.40	68
4.2	106	6.9–13	217	10.3, 30	67
		10.15	232 n.11	12.5	209
Micah		11.23f.	232 n.11	13.1–3	129
3.4	53, 213	11.25f.	217	13.5, 14	243 n.29
7.7	213	13.54	194	14.1	243 n.29
		17.21	87	14.23	87
Habakkuk				16.1	243 n.31
1–3	81, 120–26	*Mark*		16.13	243 n.29
1.2	51, 59	1.39	194	17.1, 10, 17	243 n.29
2.1	59	6.2	194	18.4, 19	243 n.29
3.1, 2–15	5	6.4	131	19.8	243 n.29
3.2	103	11.25	68	20.36	68
		14.32–42	129	21.5	68
Zephaniah		14.36	217		
2.9	232 n.11	15.34	44	*Romans*	
3.10	213	*Luke*		6.1	114
Zechariah		2.37	87	8.15	217
7.2	54	4.16	194	8.31	71
7.2–7	87	6.29	133	8.34	118, 210
7.3, 5	56	10.12	232 n.11	9.29	232 n.11
8.19	56	11.1–4	217	12.5	196
8.21f.	54	17.29	232 n.11		
		18.11, 13	68	*II Corinthians*	
Malachi		22.32	209	2.16	152
1.9	54, 213	22.41	68	12.9f.	129
3.6f.	106f.	23.34	209, 217		
		23.43	14	*Galatians*	
		23.46	217	4.6	217
The Apocrypha		*John*		*Ephesians*	
Judith		2.19–21	195f.	1.16	209
9.1	67	4.20–24	196		
		11.41	217	*Philippians*	
Prayer of Manasseh	239 n.38	12.27f.	217	1.9	99
		17	209	4.13	169
		17.1, 5, 11, 21, 24f.	217	*Colossians*	
New Testament				1.18	196
Matthew		*Acts*		*James*	
5.39	133	3.1	67	5.13–17	209

I Peter		II Peter		Jude	
1.7	44	2.6	232 n.11	7	232 n.11
4.12–19	44			Revelation	
				11.8	232 n.11

Index of Authors

Ackroyd, P.R., 232 n.7, 242 n.18
Allen, L.C., 236 n.12
Alter, R., 225 n.12
Anderson, A.A., 227 n.24, 229 n.5
Ap–Thomas, D.R., 223 n.6, 229 n.6
Ars, Curé d', 197, 244 n.1
Ashby, G., 242 n.23
Auld, G., 242 n.24

Baillie, J., 220f., 233 n.15, 248 n.44
Balantine, S.E., 223 n.6, 224 n.5, 226 n.10, 229 n.12f., 234 n.22, 235 n.6, 249
Baldwin, J., 239 n.32
Barker, M., 240 n.4, 241 n.11–13, 242 n.22
Barrett, C.K., 244 n.35
Barth, K., 233 n.16
Basil the Great, 246 n.21
Baxter, R., 99, 232 n.10
Begrich, J., 40, 226 n.3
Benedict, St, 62f., 228 n.41
Bethge, E., 247 n.30
Bigger, S., 224 n.9
Blenkinsopp, J., 86, 231 n.38, 41f.
Bonhoeffer, D., 78, 216, 230 n.22, 247 n.30
Borst, J., 244 n.5
Boyce, R.N., 228 n.27
Bradshaw, P., 229 n.8, 243 n.32, 245 n.19

Braun, R., 242 n.18
Bright, J., 238 n.23
Brown, L.B., 223 n.2, 244 n.5
Brueggemann, W., 227 n.12, 245 n.15
Bunyan, J., 211, 225 n.21, 230 n.25, 231 n.34, 246 n.23

Calvin, J., 48, 52, 226 n.9, 227 n.18, 228 n.25
Campbell, E.F. Jr, 233 n.1
Carroll, R.P., 236 n.14, 16
Childs, B.S., 8, 224 n.8, 233 n.20, 238 n.21, 241 n.7
Clement of Alexandria, 67
Clements, R.E., 153, 218, 225 n.14, 238 n.12, 21, 241 n.10, 242 n.8, 247 n.39, 249
Clines, D.J.A., 230 n.18, 231 n.33, 37, 41f.
Coats, G.W., 211, 225 n.9, 234 n.27, 246 n.25
Coggins, R.J., 224 n.7, 238 n.19, 240 n.39
Colquhoun, F., 231 n.39, 240 n.41, 43
Coogan, M.D., 232 n.5, 238 n.19, 240 n.4, 39, 241 n.9, 244 n.7
Cosin, J., 230 n.25
Craigie, P.C., 47, 226 n.5, 227 n.17
Cranmer, T., 74
Crenshaw, J.L., 246 n.28
Cromwell, O., 170

Index of Authors

Cullmann, O., 223 n.1, 247 n.35, 38, 248 n.42, 249
Curé d'Ars, 197, 244 n.1
Curtis, A. H. W., 232 n.8, 237 n.6, 238 n.19, 244 n.6

Davidson, R., 236 n.20
Davies, P. R., 229 n.1, 238 n.22, 244 n.11
Day, J., 237 n.2
Dillard, R. B., 239 n.25, 35
Dugmore, C. W., 243 n.32
Durham, J. I., 229 n.14, 233 n.8, 240 n.5, 241 n.7

Eaton, J. H., 237 n.24, 240 n.39
Egeria, 209f., 245 n.19
Eslinger, L., 225 n.13

Fergusson, D., 248 n.45
Fewell, D. N., 224 n.7, 242 n.16
Forster, P., 229 n.15
Friedrich, G., 247 n.37

Gehman, H. S., 225 n.17
Goldingay, J., 230 n.26
Goodier, A., 236 n.11
Gordon, R. P., 232 n.6, 238 n.11, 239 n.30f., 244 n.12, 245 n.16
Gore, C., 171, 240 n.43
Grabbe, L. L., 243 n.30
Gray, J., 232 n.1
Greaves, R. L., 225 n.21, 230 n.25, 246 n.23
Greenberg, M., 78, 230 n.23f., 245 n.14, 249
Gunkel, H., 40, 147, 226 n.3
Gunn, D. M., 224 n.7, 241 n.9, 242 n.16

Halpern, B., 240 n.39, 244 n.34
Harrington, W., 249
Hasel, G. F., 53, 228 n.28f.
Hayes, J. H., 223 n.7, 238 n.22, 244 n.11

Headlam, A. C., 245 n.20
Heiler, F., 1f., 48, 56, 136, 223 n.5, 227 n.19, 231 n.35, 236 n.19, 22, 237 n.27, 246 n.27
Herbert, G., 75
Hertzberg, H. W., 239 n.33
Hippolytus, 67
Holladay, C. R., 223 n.7
Hollings, M., 234 n.28
Hopkins, G. M., 143, 212, 237 n.25, 246 n.26
Houlden, J. L., 238 n.19, 239 n.39
Hubbard, R. L. Jr, 232 n.1
Hügel, F. von, 119, 234 n.1, 236 n.23

Ignatius, St, of Loyola, 235 n.11

James, W., 247 n.33
Japhet, S., 167, 239 n.24, 26, 29, 35, 37
Jay, E. G., 229 n.8–10
Jeremias, J., 229 n.5, 247 n.36, 250
Johnson, Dr Samuel, 86
Jones, B. W., 231 n.29
Jones, G. H., 225 n.16, 18, 229 n.3, 237 n.8f., 238 n.21, 242 n.24, 243 n.27
Josephus 243 n.31

Kittel, G., 247 n.37
Knight, G. A. F., 232 n.5
Kraus, H. J., 228 n.38
Kuyper, L. J., 233 n.16

Lacocque, A., 229 n.4, 231 n.29
Levenson, J. D., 244 n.34
Liebreich, L. J., 230 n.21
Louth, W., 236 n.18
Lowery, R. H., 239 n.36
Lowth, W., 134
Luther, M., 57f., 146, 210f., 246 n.22

Index of Authors

McConville, J. G., 232 n.8, 237 n.6, 242 n.21
McKane, W., 236 n.18, 239 n.34
McKay, H. A., 243 n.30
Macquarrie, J., 2, 223 n.4, 225 n.20
Mason, R., 234 n.2
Mauchline, J., 239 n.33
Mayes, A. D. H., 244 n.3, 10
Meier, S. A., 238 n.19
Metzger, B. M., 232 n.5, 238 n.19, 240 n.4, 39, 241 n.9, 244 n.7
Miller, J. M., 238 n.22, 244 n.11
Miller, P. D., 107, 229 n.12, 232 n.9, 233 n.13f., 17, 248 n.42, 250
Moberly, R. W. L., 225 n.9, 233 n.19, 241 n.6
Montgomery, J. A., 225 n.17, 231 n.27f.
Müller, G., 247 n.33
Murray, R., 41, 226 n.4

Naylor, B., 171, 240 n.42
Newman, J. H., 240 n.5, 241 n.5
Nicholson, E. W., 242 n.21
Niditch, S., 244 n.8

O'Malley, J. W., 236 n.11
Origen, 20f., 67f., 225 n.8
Otto, R., 218, 247 n.40
Owen, J., 242 n.19

Payne, R., 235 n.8
Peake, A. S., 236 n.21
Phillips, D. Z., 2, 223 n.3
Pilkington, C. M., 243 n.30, 32, 33
Porteous, N. W., 81f., 231 n.31
Porter, J. R., 247 n.34
Pritchard, J. B., 238 n.16
Prothero, R. E., 39, 226 n.1, 228 n.35

Rad, G. von, 19, 225 n.6, 11, 235 n.10, 245 n.17
Reif, S. C., 230 n.21, 243 n.30, 243 n.33, 248 n.43, 250
Reventlow, H. G., 223 n.6, 250
Rodd, C. S., 236 n.16, 237 n.24
Rogerson, J., 238 n.21, 244 n.11
Rost, L., 244 n.12f., 245 n.16
Rowley, H. H., 146, 233 n.21, 237 n.26, 243 n.30
Rudolph, W., 231 n.42

Salters, R. B., 235 n.7, 9
Sanday, W., 245 n.20
Sanders, E. P., 243 n.28, 30–32
Sawyer, J. F. A., 226 n.7f., 227 n.20, 228 n.30–32
Seitz, C. R., 238 n.21
Sibbes, R., 219
Skinner, J., 132, 225 n.19, 236 n.15
Smith, H. P., 239 n.34
Soelle, D., 1, 223 n.1
Soggin, J. A., 244 n.9

Talstra, E., 241 n.15
Tertullian, 67
Thomas, D. W., 231 n.32
Thompson, M. E. W., 231 n.30, 232 n.2f., 234 n.23, 235 n.3, 5, 7, 241 n.14, 246 n.29
Torrance, T. F., 220f., 248 n.45
Tripp, D., 231 n.40
Trochu, F., 244 n.1

Underhill, E., 79, 84, 230 n.25

Vianney, J–B–M., 197, 244 n.1

Wainwright, G., 246 n.24, 247 n.32
Wakefield, G. S., 228 n.35, 231 n.40, 234 n.28, 237 n.25, 240 n.1, 242 n.19, 244 n.4, 248 n.41
Ward, J. N., 245 n.21

Weil, S., 244 n.5
Weiser, A., 47, 58, 227 n.17, 228 n.37, 40
Westermann, C., 20, 44, 46, 101, 225 n.7, 10, 226 n.6, 11, 227 n.14, 228 n.36, 232 n.12, 247 n.34
Whybray, R. N., 234 n.25f., 246 n.28
Wierzbicka, A., 223 n.2, 244 n.5

Wilkinson, J., 245 n.19
William III, 154
Williamson, H. G. M., 78, 84f., 229 n.2, 230 n.20, 231 n.33, 36, 41, 238 n.21, 239 n.27, 35, 243 n.26
Wolff, H. W., 235 n.10, 237 n.10

Zimmerli, W., 237 n.4, 250

Index of Names and Subjects

Aaron. 93, 104
Abraham, 4, 100–103, 111
Abraham's servant, 14–17

Book of Common Prayer, 211f.

Cain, 12–14, 37f., 101, 173
Christ, 14, 85, 209f., 218f.
Chronicler, 150
'Confessions' of Jeremiah, 130–40
Cyrus (the Persian), 82f.

David, 152–54, 165–67, 177f.
Deuteronomic 'name' theology, 187
Deuteronomistic History, 97, 149
Diachronic method, 181–85

Eighteen Benedictions, 195
Eli, 24–26
Elijah, 28–34
Elisha, 34f.

Gideon, 16
God, answering prayer, 28, 46, 70, 96, 129
  hearing prayer, 17, 46, 52
  immanence of, 174, 219
  immutability of, 106f.
  repentance of, 106f.
  transcendence of, 174, 218f.

Hannah, 4, 23–28, 175f.
Herod's Temple, 194
Hezekiah, 1f., 155f., 159–62, 208, 221

Intercession, definition of, 5
Invocation, 19, 42, 186f.
Isaac, 15–17

Jacob, 18–23
Jehoshaphat, 164
Jeremiah, 114–16, 130–40
Jerusalem Temple, 177ff.
Jewish prayer books, 195
Job, 140–46
Jonah, 1, 126–30
Joseph, 21–23

Lord's Prayer, 217

Kyrie Eleison, 80

Manasseh, 166–68
Mishnah, 67f., 229 n.7, 11
Moses, 4, 93, 103–10, 173–75, 209

Naomi, 4, 89–93
Nehemiah, 83–88

Petition, definition of, 5

Index of Names and Subjects

Prayer, address to God in, 217f.
and cult, 77
and fasting, 86f., 95, 129
and healing, 29f., 34f., 225 n.15
and human action, 20, 87f., 92–93, 207, 215f., 224 n.5
and kingship, 147–71
and magic, 215, 220
and manipulation, 35f., 103, 105f., 220
and mission, 126–40
and offering of life, 109f.
and purity of life, 61–63
and sacrifice, 95, 189–91
and suffering, 140–46
and synagogue, 194f.
and theodicy, 125f.
contribution of Old Testament, 220f.
definition of, 2–4
ground of, 20, 102, 105
Hebrew vocabulary of, 42f., 46, 50f., 53–55, 203f., 242 n.20
in Judaism, 220
in New Testament, 220
in synagogue, 217
language of, 32, 77–79
'mystical', 213
natural religious activity, 66
of Hittite King, 155
place of, 172ff., 216f.
prevalence in religions, 2f.
'prophetic', 213
posture for, 37, 51f., 68
silent, 24f.
spirit of, 60f.
spoken, 24f.
spontaneous, 78f., 84
teaching about, 217
theological approaches to, 215f.
times of, 67f.
towards Jerusalem, 68, 189–92, 217
unacceptable to God, 37f.
without human action, 16, 215f., 247 n.33
Prayerful blessing, 21f.
Prayers, composed, 55f.
for forgiveness, 57–59
for long life, 154–56
for vengeance, 47, 52, 85, 133
formal, 65, 78f.
forms of, 216
in Amos, 111f.; see also Index of Biblical References
in Ark Narrative, 206, 215f.
in battles, 34f.
in Chronicles, Ch.6, 192–94, 214
in Daniel, Ch.3
in Deuteronomistic History, 198–209, 215
in Deuteronomy, 198–201
in Ecclesiastes, 82
in Elijah, Elisha cycles, 28–35, 207f.
in Esther, 213
in Exodus, see Index of Biblical References
in Ezra, Ch.3
in Genesis, see Index of Biblical References
in Habakkuk, 120–12; see also Index of Biblical References
in Haggai, 82, 213f.
in Hosea, 112–14; see also Index of Biblical References
in Isaiah, see Index of Biblical References
in Jeremiah, Ch.5; see also Index of Biblical References
in Joel, see Index of Biblical References
in Jonah, 126–30; see also

Index of Biblical References
in Joseph Story, 21–23
in Joshua, 201–203
in Job, 36, 140–46
in Judges, 203f.
in Kings, see 'prayers in Deuteronomistic History'; Index of Biblical References
in Lamentations, see Index of Biblical References
in Leviticus, see Index of Biblical References
in Malachi, see Index of Biblical References
in Micah, see Index of Biblical References
in Nahum, 82, 213
in Nehemiah, Ch.3
in Numbers, see Index of Biblical References
in Obadiah, 82, 213
in Proverbs, see Index of Biblical References
in Psalms, Ch.2; see also Index of Biblical References
in Royal Psalms, Ch.6
in Ruth, 89–93, 215f.
in Samuel, see 'prayers in Deuteronomistic History'; Index of Biblical References
in Song of Songs, 82, 213
in Succession Narrative, 205–207, 214–16
in Zechariah, see Index of Biblical References
in Zephaniah, see Index of Biblical References
of adoration, 27f.
of complaint (lament), 41–56, 210–12
of confession, 57–59, 71–82, 165–68, 188f.
of contemplation and meditation, 201, 244 n.4
of distress, 32f., 119ff., 210–12
of intercession, 29f., 52f., 76, 82, 89–118, 188, 209f.
of lament (complaint), 41–56, 210–12
of petition, 19, 31f., 76, 83–86, 188
of praise, 69f.
of praise and thanksgiving, 16f.
of thanksgiving, 27f., 52, 59–63, 69f.
Private devotions in ancient Israel, 25
Prophets as intercessors, 98f., 111–16

Rebekah, 15–17
Royal Psalms, 147, 237 n.2
Ruth, 89–93, 215f.

Sacrifice, 189f.
Samuel, 26–28, 93–99, 111, 175–77
Saul, 177
Sennacherib, 159–62
Servant (in Isa.40ff.), as Intercessor, 116–18
Servant (in Isa.40ff.), as Moses–like figure, 118
Servant Songs (in Isa.40ff.) 116–18
Shiloh, 175–77
Society of Jesus, 129f.
Solomon, 148–52
Solomon's Temple, 178–93
Synagogue, 194–96
Synchronic method, 181–85

Tabernacle, 173, 240 n.4
Tent, 173–75, 240 n.4,

Zerubbabel's (or 'Second') Temple, 193ff.